Southeast Asia

Crossroads of the World

Southeast Asia

Crossroads of the World

2ND EDITION

Clark D. Neher

Foreword by Sean Dolan and James Collins

NORTHERN

ILLINOIS

UNIVERSITY

PRESS

DeKalb

© 2004, 2010 by Northern Illinois University Press

Published by the Northern Illinois University Press in conjunction with the Center for Southeast Asian Studies, DeKalb, Illinois 60115

Manufactured in the United States using postconsumer-recycled, acid-free paper.

All Rights Reserved

Maps: *The Central Intelligence Agency World Factbook*

Photographs: Clark Neher, Arlene Neher

Cover Design: Julia Fauci

Library of Congress Cataloging-in-Publication Data

Neher, Clark D.

Southeast Asia : crossroads of the world / Clark D. Neher ; foreword by Sean Dolan and James Collins.—2nd ed.

p. cm.

Originally published: 2004. With new foreword.

Includes bibliographical references and index.

ISBN 978-0-87580-641-9 (pbk. : acid-free paper)

1. Southeast Asia. I. Title.

DS521.N45 2010

959—dc22

2010033326

CONTENTS

FIGURES

FOREWORD

Sean Dolan and James Collins

Southeast Asia is a region of overwhelming diversity. It is home both to hip, technically sophisticated urbanites living in some of the world's premiere cities and to rural farmers and fisher folk living in villages that are struggling to establish basic utilities along with Internet and cellular phone access. In terms of religion, both indigenous and world religions (alongside their regionally unique variants) thrive in Southeast Asia. The large number of Southeast Asians who speak not only a local language or dialect but also a national language, such as Indonesian or Thai, and a global language, such Chinese or English, attest to the region's linguistic diversity.

The primary purpose of this text is to provide an introduction, however preliminary, to the diversity encountered in Southeast Asia. However, before exploring the histories, political systems, and cultures of the region, it is necessary to first address a very basic theoretical issue: in what ways does "Southeast Asia" constitute a subject appropriate for academic study? The issue here is that while we often think of global regions as naturally occurring—Western Europe, for example, is an obviously distinct region from the Middle East—as we become more familiar with the histories and cultures of any such region, it becomes evident that its identity is as much dependent on the contingencies of history and international politics as on any sort of natural necessity or logic. As a result of these two competing intuitions there are, perhaps predictably, two extreme positions regarding global regions. The first claims that such regions are mere constructions reflecting the interests of international business, militaries, and politicians who ultimately fund academics who, in turn, codify these interests in maps and a variety of other kinds of area studies–based scholarship. Advocates of the second position argue that global regions really do reflect geological and cultural realities. That is, existing geological and cultural realities are reflected in global regional divisions.

Southeast Asia's status as a region is perhaps even more susceptible to this sort of debate than other regions; the term "Southeast Asia" itself is relatively recent, becoming popular only around the time of the Second World War. From a cultural or historical perspective the greatest impediment to treating Southeast Asia as an integral region is the diversity within it.

The eleven nations composing Southeast Asia are often divided into two regions. Mainland Southeast Asia includes Burma (also called Myanmar), Cambodia, Laos, Thailand, and Vietnam. Island or Insular Southeast Asia includes Brunei, East Timor, Indonesia, Malaysia, Singapore, and the Philippines. These two regions exhibit significantly different characteristics. The most commonly spoken languages of Island Southeast Asia, for example, are members of the Austronesian family of languages (Chapter 2 includes information about languages); while the common languages of Mainland Southeast Asia are from a number of different language families including Tai-Kadai, Austroasiatic, and Sino-Tibetan. Similarly, while the predominant religion in mainland Southeast Asia is Buddhism, the majority of people in Island Southeast Asia are Muslims (religion is discussed in Chapter 4). Even in geography the two differ: Island Southeast Asia is characterized by heavily forested (at least at one time) islands separated by seas, while Mainland Southeast Asia is home to some of the world's greatest rivers—the Irrawaddy in Burma and the Mekong in Burma, Laos, Thailand, Cambodia and Vietnam—and a number of mountain ranges.

Even within these two regions there is considerable variation. While the majority of Buddhists in Mainland Southeast Asia are adherents to the Theravada school, the Mahayana school of Buddhism is common in Vietnam. More generally, Vietnam has borrowed more extensively from China than other Southeast Asian countries. For example, clans play an important role in many Vietnamese kinship systems similar to their role in Chinese kinship systems. Vietnamese political systems have also tended to be more influenced by Chinese political systems than other parts of Southeast Asia. While Islam is the most widely practiced religion in Island Southeast Asia, it is a minority religion in the majority-Catholic Philippines and East Timor as well as in Singapore, which is dominated by a number of religious practices from China. Even in Indonesia, the country with the world's largest population of Muslims, Islam is not the national religion; rather there are six recognized religions in Indonesia: Buddhism, Catholicism, Confucianism, Hinduism, Islam, and Protestantism.

The above is, of course, only a selection of differences between and within the Mainland and Island regions of Southeast Asia. There are an uncountable number of other such differences in an array of categories beyond what has been considered above. Frustrating even further the claim that Southeast Asia should be studied as a cohesive region is the fact that many of the characteristics of the region are not limited to the eleven nations that constitute the region. The Theravada Buddhism practiced by most Mainland Southeast Asian Buddhists, for example, shares a history with and is similar to Theravada Buddhism in Sri Lanka. Similarly, Islam in Indonesia and Bangladesh share a number of unique characteristics. Or returning to the above example of the Austronesian languages predominant in Island Southeast Asia: the languages of Micronesia, Polynesia, and Madagascar also belong to the Austronesian family. And the connections between Chinese and Vietnamese kinship and political systems have already been mentioned.

Together these examples provide some reason to reject the notion of a Southeast Asian region. On the one hand, the internal cohesiveness of the region is undermined by its diversity; on the other, similarities between Southeast Asian populations and populations outside the region chip away at its external boundaries. Thus, it is not clear what unifies the region or what distinguishes it from other regions.

While neither the internal diversity of the region nor its connections to populations outside the region can be denied, these may not be sufficient to deny that Southeast Asia is a region. It is important, for example, not to exaggerate the separateness of Mainland and Island Southeast Asia. While it is true that Mainland Southeast Asia is predominantly Buddhist and Island Southeast Asia is majority Muslim, there are, of course, a variety of religions practiced in both subregions. Buddhism is an important religion particularly among the flourishing Chinese minority in Indonesia, just as Islam is followed by the Malay minority in Southern Thailand. The ethnic Cham communities of Vietnam and Cambodia provide further evidence of the inadequacy of a simple distinction between Mainland and Island Southeast Asia. Despite living in Mainland Southeast Asia, the Cham speak an Austronesian language and the majority are Muslim—both characteristics more commonly associated with Island Southeast Asia. The point here is that while general distinctions between Mainland and Southeast Asia are possible, they should not obscure the shared features of the regions that become evident from a less macro-perspective.

Scholars of Southeast Asia have replied to the argument that, because of its prolific borrowing from other regions, Southeast Asia lacks definite borders by turning the argument on its head. This heavy borrowing from other regions may be a defining characteristic of Southeast Asia as a region. Historically India and China, Southeast Asia's immediate neighbors to the northwest and northeast respectively, have been the world's largest centers of both population and commercial production and trade. Because of its location between these two economic behemoths, Southeast Asian communities were drawn into trade from the very earliest times. It is through these early trade routes that Hinduism and then Buddhism arrived in Southeast Asia.

As sailing technology advanced, it became evident that more goods could be shipped more quickly and safely by sea than by established land routes through Central Asia (the Silk Road). This preference for maritime shipping resulted in Southeast Asia becoming one of the most strategic locations along a trade network that first connected China and India and then continued west to include the Middle East and ultimately Europe. Goods moving in either direction passed through Southeast Asian ports.

Maritime traffic passing through Southeast Asia was regulated by the monsoons. These seasonal winds predictably begin blowing across Southeast Asia from the southeast to the northwest in May and June and reverse course about six months later. Because of the predictability of the monsoon, Southeast Asian ports were convenient spots to undertake trading while merchants waited for the winds to change directions so they could complete their journey. In addition to the shipped goods, Southeast Asian goods were also traded at these ports. While such goods included a variety of jungle products, the most valuable and sought after Southeast Asian goods were spices such as nutmeg and cloves from the Molucca Islands (located south of the Philippines in eastern Indonesia). The availability of these valuable goods increased the attraction of the Southeast Asian ports.

In addition to benefitting maritime trade, the predictability of the monsoons contributed to the development of agriculture in Southeast Asia. While the winds blowing from the southeast were dry, the winds from the northwest absorbed moisture over the Bay of Bengal and reliably brought rain. Thus the monsoon became the basis for many Southeast Asian agricultural cycles. As you will read in Chapter 3, while some early Southeast Asian civilizations were based on maritime trade, others were based on rice agriculture, and both benefitted from the predictability of the monsoon winds.

While dependence on the monsoons is one of the most common characteristics shared by Southeast Asian societies, there are a number of others. Many scholars have noted a common disposition among Southeast Asian systems of social organization to trace kinship bilaterally (or cognatically)—that is, kinship is traced equally through paternal and maternal lines, which allows people the option of affiliating with the father's or mother's kin, or both. This is important because bilateral kinship is often associated with relative gender equality (the topic of gender is discussed in Chapter 4). Although the precise meaning of "relative gender equality" is debated among researchers, women in Southeast Asia often do play active roles in agriculture, trade, and making decisions concerning family finances. Similarly, gender is not an important factor in determining inheritance in most Southeast Asian societies. While it would be overly simplistic to claim that women and men are equal in Southeast Asia, women's status in the region tends to be markedly higher than those of women in either India or China.

Another feature widely dispersed throughout Southeast Asia is a style of leadership centered around people of prowess (Southeast Asian political systems are discussed in Chapters 6 and 7). Prowess is achieved through the demonstration of spiritual power, oratory skills, military might, and diplomacy. People willingly affiliate themselves with people of prowess and become clients of these more powerful patrons. However, this also means that if a person appears to lose prowess, clients may seek a different patron. In other words, people of prowess must constantly cultivate their relationships with their clients or they risk losing them. So leadership is not fixed; rather, it is open to anyone able to demonstrate prowess and so is quite flexible.

The above examples are again only a brief selection of some of the features widely dispersed throughout Southeast Asia. If we return now to the question initially posed concerning the degree to which Southeast Asia may be rightly regarded as a discrete global region, how should we respond to the two positions already suggested: that it is clearly and unproblematically a region or that it is only a pseudo-region? Clearly arguments can be constructed supporting either conclusion. Some of the characteristics discussed above, particularly Southeast Asian communities' connections with those outside Southeast Asia, can be pressed to support either of the conclusions depending on the perspective adopted. The ability of either of these positions to capture certain realities about Southeast Asia suggests a moderate position ought to be adopted. We can accept that Southeast Asia is a region of incredible diversity—that there are exceptions to even the most widely dispersed common characteristics—but still see Southeast Asia as a region enmeshed in mutually similar historical, political, and economic processes.

In fact, it seems that researchers are interested in Southeast Asia as a region just for this reason—it is a fascinating arena for comparative research. While historically the entire region was heavily influenced by its more populous and powerful neighbors, India and China, the effects of these interactions are uneven throughout the region. Similarly, while the whole of Southeast Asia had to contend with European colonialism, a variety of strategies, ranging from armed resistance to compliance and negotiation, were adopted to do so. In the post-colonial period, each of the countries making up Southeast Asia have pursued their own notions of nationalism, resulting in governments ranging from burgeoning democracies to monarchies and to military or communist authoritarian regimes. Southeast Asian countries continue to exhibit considerable diversity in coping with current trends in globalization and the demands of international markets and political systems. (For example, Malaysia has an advanced economy integrated into the global financial world, while Burma is economically and politically isolated.) So it is through this generally shared trajectory that Southeast Asia can be seen as a region, and it is the variation within this trajectory that makes it a fascinating region to study.

With the establishment of ASEAN (Association of Southeast Asian Nations) in 1967 it appears that there is general recognition among Southeast Asians as well that they are part of a global region larger than their individual countries. However, it must be noted that the membership of ASEAN has changed several times since its founding and does not include East Timor (East Timor participates as an ASEAN observer rather than as a member). So, the region generally regarded by researchers as comprising Southeast Asia is not perfectly reflected in ASEAN's membership.

Southeast Asia is a complex region and continues to change very rapidly. Over the past three decades it has become increasingly urbanized; education has been expanded; and the population tends to be literate and technologically savvy. A brief introductory text such as this one can provide only an overview of the complex processes through which Southeast Asia has been and continues to be constructed, as well as some sense of the ways in which researchers have approached the region. Ultimately, the aim of this book is to pique interest in this fascinatingly diverse region and point toward resources through which particularly interesting aspects can be more fully investigated.

In the chapters that follow you will read more extensive accounts of the diversity of Southeast Asia hinted at in this foreword. Chapter 2 explicitly discusses regional diversity in terms of ethnicity, geography, and religion. Chapter 3 lays out the early history of the region by examining a number of its early civilizations. Southeast Asian culture—particularly religion, gender, family relations, art, and ritual—is discussed in Chapter 4. Chapter 5 provides a comparative discussion of village life in several different cultural settings. The recent history and current political issues of the region as well as several of its most influential leaders are discussed in Chapters 6 and 7. Finally, Chapter 8 reflects some of the current problems, including security threats and terrorism, faced by the region as well as its future prospects.

DISCUSSION QUESTIONS

1. What objections can be raised against the claim that Southeast Asia is a discrete global region? What reasons support the claim that Southeast Asia should be treated as a global region? In your opinion, should Southeast Asia be regarded as a global region?

2. What are the two subregions that comprise Southeast Asia? What features distinguish these regions, and what characteristics do they share?

3. Why do you think Southeast Asia is referred to as a "crossroads"?

SUGGESTED READINGS

Clark D. Neher's *Southeast Asia in the New International Era* (Westview Press, Boulder, 1999) is an outstanding overview of the region, particularly from the perspective of political science. Another general overview can be found in Ross Marlay and Clark Neher's *Democracy and Development in Southeast Asia* (Westview Press, Boulder, 1995). This book defines Asian-style democracy and demonstrates the connection between nations' levels of economic development and levels of democratization.

Victor T. King and William D. Wilder's *The Modern Anthropology of South-East Asia* (Routledge Curzon, London, 2003) is a particularly strong introduction to the region from an anthropological perspective.

The two-volume work *Southeast Asia in the Age of Commerce* (Yale University Press, New Haven, 1988 and 1993) by Anthony Reid established Southeast Asia's role and importance in early trade networks.

Finally, numerous region and country maps are available online from Central Intelligence Agency's *The World Factbook* (https://www.cia.gov/library/publications/the-world-factbook/) and *The Website of the National Geographic Society* (www.nationalgeographic.com).

ACKNOWLEDGMENTS

In this second edition, I remain surrounded by colleagues and students who share my passion for the study of Southeast Asia. This passion has led to the present book, *Southeast Asia: Crossroads of the World,* which is designed specifically as an introduction for students who have little or no background in the region. I acknowledge the Associates of the Center for Southeast Asian Studies at Northern Illinois University who have graciously shared their knowledge about Southeast Asia and their excitement about an introductory textbook. Both undergraduate and graduate students at Northern Illinois University have provided numerous ideas about the kind of information students need to understand this fascinating area of the world. The Center staff, led by Nancy Schuneman, have contributed in myriad ways to the completion of the book. Some paragraphs have been adapted from my previous book *Politics in Southeast Asia* (Schenkman Publishing Company, Cambridge, Massachusetts, 1979). I am especially indebted to former Editors of the Center's Southeast Asia Publications program, Edwin Zehner and Peter Ross, and to Julia Lamb, the Center's Outreach Coordinator, for their help with research and editing. Edwin has contributed substantially to this textbook by means of his conscientious editing and fact checking.

I am grateful to the United States Department of Education for naming Northern Illinois University a National Resource Center and for partially funding the publication of this volume. I cannot imagine more vibrant faculty and students than those affiliated with the University's Center for Southeast Asian Studies.

This book is dedicated to the new generation of students who want to understand Southeast Asia more fully, whether they be in secondary schools, community colleges, liberal arts colleges, or universities. *Southeast Asia: Crossroads of the World* is a prelude to a complex region, a jumping off text designed to entice students into learning more from the abundant literature written by scholars from around the world.

Asia

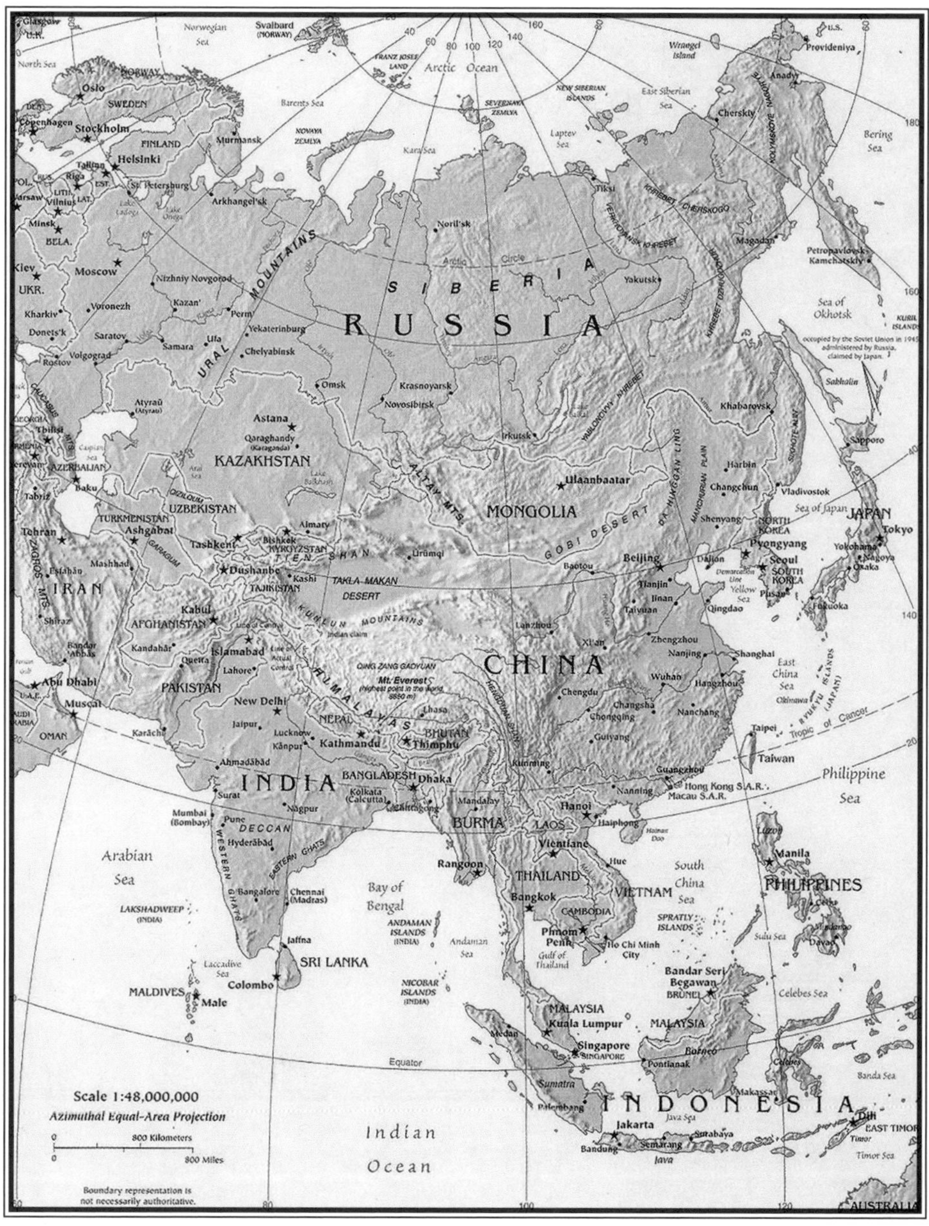

Arctic Ocean
RUSSIA
SIBERIA
URAL MOUNTAINS
KAZAKHSTAN
UZBEKISTAN
TURKMENISTAN
MONGOLIA
CHINA
INDIA
PAKISTAN
AFGHANISTAN
IRAN
NEPAL
BHUTAN
BANGLADESH
BURMA
LAOS
THAILAND
VIETNAM
CAMBODIA
MALAYSIA
INDONESIA
PHILIPPINES
JAPAN
NORTH KOREA
SOUTH KOREA
SRI LANKA
MALDIVES
OMAN
Taiwan
GOBI DESERT
TAKLA MAKAN DESERT
KUNLUN MOUNTAINS
HIMALAYAS
TIEN SHAN
ALTAY MTS.
DECCAN
Mt. Everest (highest point in the world 8850 m)
Moscow
Beijing
Tokyo
Seoul
Pyongyang
Ulaanbaatar
Astana
Tashkent
Ashgabat
Dushanbe
Bishkek
Kabul
Islamabad
New Delhi
Kathmandu
Thimphu
Dhaka
Colombo
Male
Rangoon
Bangkok
Vientiane
Hanoi
Phnom Penh
Kuala Lumpur
Singapore
Jakarta
Manila
Bandar Seri Begawan
Dili
Taipei
Tehran
Muscat
Abu Dhabi
Arabian Sea
Bay of Bengal
Indian Ocean
South China Sea
East China Sea
Philippine Sea
Sea of Japan
Sea of Okhotsk
Bering Sea
Yellow Sea
Andaman Sea
Celebes Sea
Java Sea
Tropic of Cancer
Equator
AUSTRALIA
EAST TIMOR
Scale 1:48,000,000
Azimuthal Equal-Area Projection
800 Kilometers
800 Miles
Boundary representation is not necessarily authoritative.

Southeast Asia

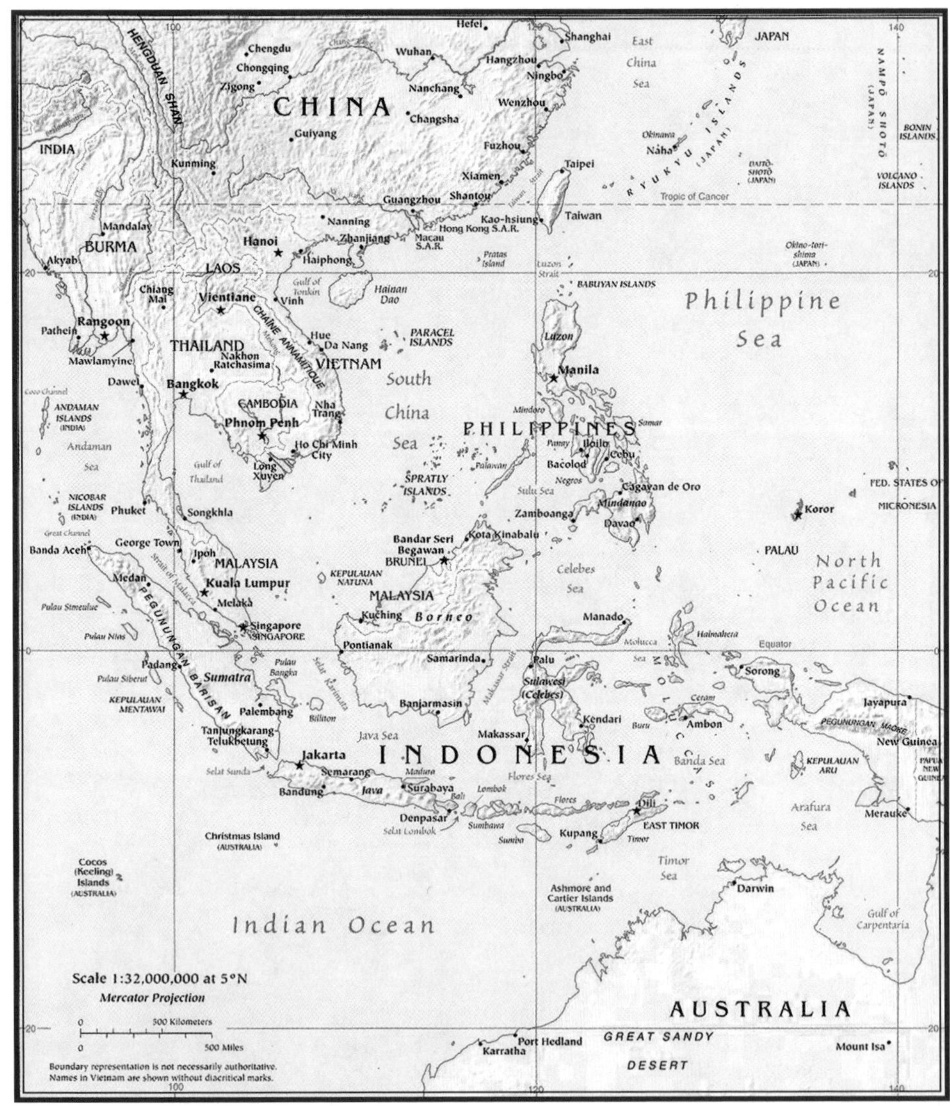

1

INTRODUCTION

The term "Southeast Asia" originated during World War II to describe the area south of China and east of India. No area in the world is as diverse as this region, which is composed of the eleven nations of Brunei, Burma (Myanmar), Cambodia, East Timor, Indonesia, Laos, Malaysia, Philippines, Singapore, Thailand, and Vietnam. Each of the eleven nations contains highly varying ethnic groups, languages, religions, and traditions. It is impossible to generalize about life in Southeast Asia without specifying whether the generalization encompasses urban or rural settings; Islamic, Buddhist (Theravada or Mahayana), or Catholic religionists; or Malay, Khmer, Siamese, Vietnamese, Lao, Burmese, Shan, or Chinese (the list is endless) peoples. It is safe to remember that diversity is a more salient attribute of Southeast Asia than is homogeneity.

Southeast Asia has something for everyone open to new adventures. Imagine yourself in a village Buddhist temple, surrounded by saffron-robed monks chanting in Pali and meditating to purify their minds. The serene environment is a striking contrast to the nearby vegetable market where hundreds of villagers animatedly talk about the day amidst loudspeakers blaring Asian and Western music. Or imagine you are climbing a volcano in Indonesia, surrounded by the lushest landscape you have ever seen. Through the jungle, you see the Borobudur complex, a famous eighth-century Buddhist monument that now seems out of place in this overwhelmingly Islamic land. From below you can hear the *bedug* drum from the mosques calling the people to one of five daily prayers.

You might find yourself in the middle of a Southeast Asian city, breathing in carbon monoxide and noticing that your white shirt has turned gray from the pollution. You wonder how anyone lives with such noise, squalor, and stress. What a contrast with the customary serenity of the villages, which are still islands of peace except when city relatives arrive on their loud motorcycles. In one of the major cities, you may be invited to dine at the home of a wealthy acquaintance, where you will be astounded by the luxurious gardens and fountains, the several Mercedes Benz automobiles in the garage, and the many servants who serve you with great deference, bowing deeply as they present you with plates of exotic fruits and curries. You have just seen an example of the huge gap between rich and poor that exists throughout all of Southeast Asia.

In Vietnam you will look in vain for evidence of the destruction brought about by America's longest war. Instead you will find a vibrant society and you will be surprised at how graciously you are received by the Vietnamese, who will exclaim: "You number one!" the moment they learn you are American. You will meet a heroic people moving in new directions now that the government has opened up the economy and reduced the degree of oppression. But in neighboring Cambodia your conversations will be poignant as you realize that virtually everyone has close relatives who were executed or starved by the genocidal Khmer Rouge regime that ruled from 1975 to 1979. Fully one in four Cambodians were killed during that horrific time.

Southeast Asia is also rapidly changing. Just twenty years ago, the region's societies were overwhelmingly rural, impoverished, and isolated. But levels of income, rates of literacy, and levels of college education have all risen rapidly, and new technologies have been adopted quickly. Change is so great and so rapid that last year's statistics are already outdated. In the year 2003 the great capital cities of Southeast Asia—such as Bangkok (Thailand), Manila (Philippines), Jakarta (Indonesia), Hanoi (Vietnam), and Kuala Lumpur (Malaysia)—look more and more like Western cities, with huge skyscrapers (the tallest building in the world, Petronas Tower, is in Kuala Lumpur), traffic jams, luxury hotels and restaurants, and a vibrant capitalist economy. Soon, the majority of the region's inhabitants will be city rather than village people. During the 1980s and 90s Southeast Asians enjoyed the world's most rapid increase in standard of living. The region has less poverty each year (except for the financial crisis that began in 1997 and affected Thailand, Indonesia, and Malaysia most severely). Isolation is also a thing of the past. Few Southeast Asians are far from roads, trains, telephones, and televisions, while trade and investment have made the people increasingly participants in the global economy. The quiet, poor, and isolated Southeast Asia of the 1960s can now be found only in a few far-away villages.

Subregions

Southeast Asia is commonly divided into two subregions. Mainland Southeast Asia borders China on the north and India on the west. It consists of Burma, Cambodia, Laos, Thailand, and Vietnam. From earliest recorded times its strategic location along the trade routes from India to China has made Mainland Southeast Asia a crossroads for the movement of people, goods, ideologies, crafts, and religions. The great rivers of the mainland, such as the Irrawaddy in Burma and the Mekong in Laos, Thailand, Cambodia, and Vietnam, have brought immigrants from China to help populate the land, which is famous for its remarkable fertility. Meanwhile, sea trade routes brought ideas and religions from India. Hinduism was the first religion to arrive, but it was later replaced by Buddhism. Today, Theravada Buddhism predominates in Burma, Thailand, Laos, and Cambodia, while Mahayana Buddhism prevails in Vietnam.

Insular, or "Island," Southeast Asia consists of Brunei, East Timor, eastern Malaysia (on Borneo's northwest shore), the Malay peninsula, Indonesia, the Philippines, and Singapore. Like the mainland, Insular Southeast Asia has been a crossroads of peoples and traditions. Southeast Asia's geographical position as a link between the great Indian, Chinese, and Australian civilizations has contributed to a succession of migrations, immigrations, and invasions that have brought new ideas and a dynamic quality that is lacking in more homogeneous societies. From India to Indonesia and Malaysia came Hinduism and Buddhism, but these religions were replaced by Islam, likewise coming via India, which in the 1400s and 1500s became the principal religion. Meanwhile, in the 1500s, the Catholic religion was introduced to the Philippines when the Spanish colonized the country.

The religions Buddhism and Islam are as diverse as Southeast Asia itself. As they were assimilated and adapted to the numerous local traditions, they produced many unique practices and belief systems. It is therefore more proper to speak of "Javanese religions" and "Acehnese Islam" than a national Indonesian "Muslim" religion. These local forms of the world religions have assimilated earlier animistic beliefs into their more formal religious doctrines. As a result, the worship of magico-religious spirits remains a part of the daily religious life of most Southeast Asians.

People

Some 440 million people live in Southeast Asia. Indonesia's 220 million account for half of that total, while only 300,000 live in Brunei. Much of the population is under the age of thirty, because life expectancy is lower than in the West and because until recently Southeast Asians had large families. As recently as the 1970s, high population growth rates were the norm throughout the region, and in some places they still continue. The Philippines, for example, has a 2.4 percent yearly increase in population, which means that the population doubles every generation. However, countries such as Thailand, Singapore, and Malaysia have cut their population growth rates in half as a result of government campaigns to promote contraceptives and smaller families. The outcome has been a massive change of behavior and values among Southeast Asians. Large families used to be preferred so that children could help in the fields. Increasingly, families with two children are becoming the norm so that the young can be fully educated and given the best chance for a higher standard of living.

Almost all young Southeast Asians are literate, because most of the countries offer free, mandatory schooling for about eight years. However, some young people still must leave school to work in the agricultural fields or to tend domesticated animals such as water buffalo, oxen, cattle, and chickens. Boys were traditionally given the first opportunity for schooling, but the pro-male bias has faded and girls now constitute the majority of the children going to school. Everywhere you go you can see urban and rural children in their school uniforms, usually bright, clean, ironed white shirts and blouses worn with dark pants or skirts. But only a small minority of the people, about 5 percent, ever attend universities.

In the early 1960s, 80 percent of all Southeast Asian adults were rural farmers. Today, only half of the population is employed in the fields. (Singapore is an exception because 100 percent of its population is urban.) The migration to the cities has come about because agriculture has mechanized, because many parents have subdivided their farms among their children (eventually leading to "postage-size" farms), and because rural people believe that they will have better income in the cities. During the past three decades, rural to urban migration has created huge slum areas and rising urban unemployment while increasing the incidence of psychoses among people who were once surrounded by village supporters but now suffer alienation in the impersonal cities.

For much of modern history, the best positions for educated or prominent family members were in the civil service, which provided security, access to important contacts, and opportunities for corruption. But as free-enterprise economies prospered in most Southeast Asian nations, domestic and multi-national corporations became the employers of choice. In the past two decades, a fantastically wealthy minority (less than 10 percent) of the population has amassed enormous amounts of money and property, leading to a profusion of luxury homes, restaurants, and resorts catering to the new elite classes. Many visiting tourists, seeing only these wealthy westernized people, return home without realizing that the overwhelming majority of Southeast Asians live simply, often poorly, and retain traditional values.

Welcome to Southeast Asia. This crossroads of history and cultures has remarkable beauty and as considerate and cultivated a people as you will ever meet. This book is designed to provide you with just enough knowledge to make you want to know even more and to entice you to travel and see the region for yourself.

The following chapters continue the theme of diversity in Southeast Asia. Each provides a different perspective for looking at the region. In the next chapter you will learn about the geographic, ethnic, linguistic, and religious diversity of Southeast Asia. You will then read about the historical origins of and influences on Southeast Asians as you look at the great civilizations of Angkor, Majapahit, and Pagan. The chapters on history seek to explain how external forces from China, India, the Middle East, and the West (through colonialism) influenced the direction and character of the various nations. Southeast Asia has been the home of magnificent historical epics, and to understand them is to understand more fully the daily lives of the people today. It is also impossible to grasp modern Southeast Asia without studying some of the significant cultural traditions that have pervaded the area for hundreds of years. Accordingly, the chapters on culture and village life explore the area's richly diverse cultural and social patterns, with special emphasis on the lives of the villagers who constitute the majority of Southeast Asia's citizens. By contrast, the chapters on recent history and politics feature discussions of the area's elites, the people who dominate the region's politics, economies, and social life. Separate sections on each of the eleven nations will provide you with an overview of the significant events in each country's history and the most significant issues facing Southeast Asians today. You will read about the nations' governments, economies, significant leaders, and you will also learn about their place in the international sphere and their processes of democratization. Finally, you will read personal histories of some of the region's most influential and controversial leaders. Welcome to Southeast Asia! The journey has begun.

DISCUSSION QUESTIONS

1. How can we view Southeast Asia as a meaningful entity? In what ways is the region homogeneous and worthy of being studied as a unit?

2. Describe Southeast Asia geographically. What is the best way of dividing the region?

3. Why is Southeast Asia known as a "crossroads"?

SUGGESTED READINGS

For general overviews of Southeast Asia see Clark D. Neher, *Southeast Asia in the New International Era* (Westview Press, Boulder, 1999). A chapter is devoted to each of the Southeast Asian nations, focusing on their political culture, institutions, economy, and international relations. Another general overview is Ross Marlay and Clark Neher, *Democracy and Development in Southeast Asia* (Westview Press, Boulder, 1995). That book seeks to define Asian-style democracy and then shows the relationship between level of economic development and level of democratization in each of the Southeast Asian nations.

Although authored some thity-five years ago, Robbins Burling's *Hill Tribes and Padi Fields: Life in Mainland Southeast Asia* (Prentice-Hall, Englewood Cliffs, New Jersey, 1965; reprinted in 1992 by the Program for Southeast Asian Studies, Arizona State University, Tempe, Arizona) remains a solid overview of the region.

Detailed regional and individual country maps are available online from the Central Intelligence Agency's *The World Factbook 2004* (www.odci.gov/cia/publications/factbook/index.html) and *The Website of the National Geographic Society* (www.nationalgeographic.com).

2

REGION OF DIVERSITY

No comparable area of the world has such a range of geographic, ethnic, linguistic, and religious diversity as does Southeast Asia. For that reason, it is difficult for Westerners to absorb the tremendous amount of information available about the region. Many nations of Southeast Asia have hundreds of minority groups, some with fundamentally different customs, traditions, religions, and languages. For people who live in homogeneous cultures, the presence of multiple ethnic groups is confusing. For people accustomed to a predominant religion, the close proximity of many belief systems is bewildering. For people who hear and read the same language from newspapers, television, radio, and neighbors, the cacophony of numerous languages is disconcerting. And for people used to a moderate climate, tropical weather all year round is incomprehensible. (Southeast Asians often facetiously refer to their seasons as "hot," "hotter," and "hottest"). It is precisely these differences from the West, as well as the complexity of the area, that makes Southeast Asia such an exciting place to study. This great diversity has resulted from thousands of years of trade, invasion, and migration as peoples from outside nations came to Southeast Asia to find fortune or peace. These sojourners interbred with indigenous inhabitants to produce the rich ethnic and cultural variety that characterizes the crossroads of Southeast Asia.

Southeast Asian diversity can be seen in Table 1, which presents demographic, economic, and political data that help us recognize the area's similarities and differences. It is interesting to compare the data in the table with data from just two and a half decades earlier when Southeast Asia was fundamentally different from the present. Populations have increased rapidly, as has life expectancy, which has lengthened more than a decade in every Southeast Asian nation. In addition, Southeast Asia has enjoyed rapid economic development and rising standards of living. For example, in Malaysia, Singapore, Indonesia, Thailand, and Vietnam the annual per capita GDP has grown more than tenfold in just thirty years. These astonishing improvements are indicative of a region that is more satisfactorily meeting the needs of the people.

Note also that there is a trend toward democratic governments and away from authoritarian governments in Cambodia (still in transition), Indonesia, the Philippines, and Thailand. Authoritarian governments have retained power in Brunei, Burma (Myanmar), Vietnam, and Laos, while the governments in Malaysia and Singapore have remained "semi-democracies" in that they hold free elections for a representative parliament but place significant restrictions on the people's freedoms.

Table 1. Southeast Asia in 2001

Country	Political System	Per Capita GDP (PPP)*	Population (million)	Life Expectancy (years)	Internet per 1,000
Brunei	Absolute monarchy	n/a	0.3 (0.2 in 1975)	76.1	102.3
Burma (Myanmar)	Military authoritarian	n/a	48.2 (30.2)	57	0.2
Cambodia	Transition to democracy	$1,860	13.5 (7.1)	57.4	0.7
Indonesia	Semi-democracy	$2,940	214.4 (134.4)	65	19.1
Laos	Communist authoritarian	$1,620	5.4 (3.0)	53.9	1.9
Malaysia	Semi-democracy	$8,750	23.5 (12.3)	72.8	273.1
Philippines	Semi-democracy	$3,840	77.2 (42)	69.5	25.6
Singapore	Semi-democracy	$22,680	4.1 (2.3)	77.8	411.5
Thailand	Semi-democracy	$6,400	61.6 (41.3)	68.9	57.7
Vietnam	Communist authoritarian	$2,070	79.2 (48)	68.9	12.4
Japan	Democracy	$25,130	127.3 (111.5)	81.3	384.2
USA	Democracy	$34,320	288 (220.2)	76.9	501.5

Data from United Nations Development Programme, Human Development Report 2003, Oxford University Press, New York, 2003. Gross Domestic Product (GDP) is the value of all goods and services produced in one year. Purchasing Power Parity (PPP) takes into account price differences between countries for a more accurate measure of national wealth. Official statistics are not yet available for East Timor, but informal data suggest a per capita GDP (PPP) of $500, the lowest in Southeast Asia.

- PPP = Purchasing Power Parity

Geographic Features

Mainland Southeast Asia includes Burma, Thailand, Laos, Cambodia, and Vietnam. The mainland's most prominent geographic feature is the rivers flowing from Tibet and China, which were the principal means of dispersion for migrants from the north. The longest of the rivers is the Mekong, which begins in the Tibetan mountains, runs past the Burma border, meanders through Laos, bends around Thailand, cuts through the heart of Cambodia, and ends at the great Mekong Delta in southern Vietnam. The Irrawaddy also flows from the Tibetan mountains, but it moves more directly southward as it cuts through Burma to the Indian Ocean. The Chao Phraya in Thailand and the Hong (Red River) in Vietnam also played a significant part in distributing the peoples of southern China throughout the mainland. These migrants intermarried with indigenous peoples to become the forerunners of modern Burmese, Thai, Khmers (Cambodians), and Vietnamese. Most of their great kingdoms no longer exist, but there is still evidence of their once flourishing civilizations.

Some migrants were forced to the mountains, where they became isolated from the majority lowlanders. These hill peoples often practice shifting, or *swidden*, agriculture, in which farmers move to new fields every few years while they allow the old fields to regenerate.

Swidden Agriculture

Until recently, many of Southeast Asia's hill peoples practiced shifting, or *swidden*, agriculture in which they moved to new fields every few years. When farmers cleared new fields, they burned the cleared material, partly as a means of fertilizing the soil. After a few years they moved to new fields so that the old farms could regenerate with new vegetation. By this means the hill peoples avoided overfarming the nutrient-poor highlands. Some people refer to *swidden* agriculture as "slash-and-burn" agriculture, a term implying that *swidden* agriculture is a major cause of environmental destruction. This notion is misleading, because until recently *swidden* agriculture was an ecologically appropriate adaptation to environmental conditions. In recent years the criticism has become more valid, because as upland areas became increasingly overpopulated, many highlanders no longer had new fields to which they could move. As a result the old fields were not being allowed to lie fallow. Today many highlanders have abandoned *swidden* farming for more stationary kinds of agriculture that are oriented to outside markets.

As a result of their constant movement from place to place, these highland peoples developed political forms that were fundamentally different from those of the plains people, who practiced an irrigated agriculture that tied people more firmly to particular places by requiring longer-term labor-intensive investments in canals, dikes, and water gates. The great rivers of Southeast Asia remain important for transportation. Alongside them have sprung up most of the mainland's most populous cities.

Mainland Southeast Asia is also characterized by great plains where rice, an irrigated crop perhaps native to Southeast Asia, became the dietary staple that supported the great majority of people. Historically, villages were established where rice was plentiful, and time, food, religion, family structure, seasons, and dress were defined in terms of the growing of rice. In Thailand, for example, the verb "to eat" is "to eat rice." Today rice is still the dominant crop in the plains, but modern agricultural techniques such as tractors, fertilizer, and water pumps have contributed to the diversification of crops. Fruits, vegetables, and even dairy products are now produced in many agricultural areas.

Although most mainland Southeast Asians lived near rice paddy fields, just thirty years ago forests covered almost 70 percent of the mainland. Today, less than 20 percent of the mainland is forested, because rampant and illegal logging has devastated the mountainous regions. Wood is used for building homes and furniture, for cooking, and for export to first-world nations that have few forests. "Hill tribe" people living in the mountains of Burma, Thailand, Laos, Cambodia, and Vietnam have also cut down forests to plant their crops. The resulting deforestation has changed climatic conditions, contributing to an increase in droughts and floods throughout the region.

Insular Southeast Asia includes the Malay peninsula (technically an extension of the mainland), the island of Singapore, and the great stretch of islands that includes Indonesia, Brunei, East Timor, and the Philippines. East Timor is the area's newest nation. Though East Timor declared its independence from Portugal in 1975, it was immediately occupied by Indonesia and was not recognized as an independent state until 2002 when Indonesia agreed to grant sovereignty. The new nation is located on the eastern half of the island of Timor, in the southeast portion of the Indonesian archipelago and northwest of Australia. As for Indonesia itself, the most significant islands include Sumatra, Java, Borneo (shared with Malaysia and Brunei), Sulawesi, Bali, and the Moluccas (the Spice Islands). Java is one of the most densely populated areas in the world. In the Philippines, significant islands include Luzon, Mindanao, the Visayas, and the Sulu archipelago. In Island Southeast Asia the sea is the crucial geographic entity, because it has served as the link among the nations for trade, invasion, war, tourism, migration, and cultural diffusion. Hindu and Islamic influences arrived by sea from the India and the Arab world, and they remain salient throughout the area (except in the Philippines, where Spanish colonialists brought Catholicism). The seas made cultural borrowing very easy, and they are largely responsible for the distinctively eclectic character of the region's civilizations. The various external forces coming by sea did not displace the indigenous cultures, but rather added to them in ways that have made Southeast Asia's traditions unique.

Both mainland and insular Southeast Asia are a part of "monsoon Asia," an area where great rains emanating from the sea bring water for agriculture. There is no snow anywhere in Southeast Asia, except on the highest peaks of northern Burma. The temperature is always hot, again except for the highest elevations. The need for water is an important variable. Droughts occur when the monsoon rains do not arrive on time, and floods ensue when they stay too long. Southeast Asia has prospered because of the rains and because of the rich plains, valleys, and deltas that have made agricultural pursuits rewarding. Agricultural surpluses have given rise to cities, towns, villages, and great civilizations.

The Environment

For centuries, Southeast Asia was underpopulated. Wars were fought for control of human labor rather than control of land, and enemy troops were rarely killed in great numbers. Land was abundant. There was little conflict over expanding farms, because people who wanted more land could simply move to a new area. Much of the unfarmed land was forested. For example, until the 1970s, fully 70 percent of Thailand's land was covered by forest, so there was plenty of bamboo and teak wood for building materials. Watersheds in the forests collected monsoon rainwater for gradual release later, and the rivers were clean and filled with fish.

The remarkable growth of population and economic activity over the past four decades has fundamentally changed Southeast Asia's ecology and environment. As the population increased, land became scarce for the first time ever. Previously, the region's states had fought for control of manpower, but now conflicts arose over control of land, the scarcity of which was affecting the lives of ordinary people. Farms were forced to become smaller because there was no place to expand. Building needs caused forests to be depleted of their wood. The formerly abundant teak trees have nearly disappeared, the percentage of forested area in Thailand has dropped from 70 percent to 17 percent, and rivers have silted because the forest can no longer hold the rain water. Economic development has also fouled the environment. Few rivers can be fished because of the pollution in the water, and not one Southeast Asian city is free from air pollution. Indeed, the level of smog is so high that city inhabitants are said to live a full decade less than their rural neighbors, who live in areas where pollution is less pervasive.

Ethnic Diversity

Most Southeast Asian countries have significant ethnic and linguistic minorities.

Table 2. Ethnic Groups as of 1999

Country	Ethnic Groups	Country	Ethnic Groups
Brunei 0.3 million people	Malay 64% Chinese 20% Other 16%	Malaysia 21.3 million	Malay and Other indigenous 58% Chinese 26% Indian 7% Other 9%
Burma (Myanmar) 48.4 million	Burman 68% Chinese 3% Shan 9% Mon 2 % Karen 7% Indian 2% Rakhine 4% Other 5%	Philippines 79.3 million	Christian Malay 91.5% Muslim Malay 4% Chinese 1.5% Other 3%
Cambodia 11.6 million	Khmer 90% Vietnamese 5% Chinese 1% Other 4%	Singapore 3.5 million	Chinese 76.4% Malay 14.9% Indian 6.4% Other 2.3%
Indonesia 216.1 million	Javanese 45% Sundanese 14% Madurese 7.5% Coastal Malays 7.5 % Other 26%	Thailand 60.6 million	Thai 75% Chinese 14% Other 11%
Laos 5.4 million	Lao Loum (lowland) 68% Lao Theung (upland) 22% Lao Soung (highland, including Hmong and Yao) 9% Vietnamese and Chinese 1%	Vietnam 77.3 million	Vietnamese 85–90% Chinese 3% Other (including Muong, Tai, Meo, Khmer, Man, and Cham) 15–10%

Ethnic heterogeneity has been a source of both strength and weakness. The varied sources of ethnic, cultural, and linguistic patterns have infused the area with new ideas and a dynamic quality that is lacking in more homogeneous societies. At the same time, the ethnic diversity has resulted in crises of integration as ethnic divisions threaten the area's stability.

Mainland Southeast Asians

A particular problem arose when Western nations colonized the area without taking its ethnic makeup into consideration. The Western colonialists arbitrarily drew boundary lines that had not previously existed and that often divided a particular minority group among two or more nations. For example, many Shan and Karen live in the mountainous areas of northern Thailand, while the bulk of these peoples live in Burma. Similarly, northeast Thailand is inhabited predominantly by Lao, Hmong, and other ethnic groups that originate in Laos.

Northeast Thailand is also home to many ethnic Cambodians. Thailand's southernmost provinces are populated not by Buddhist Thai but by Muslim Malays.

Karen

The Karen are an ethnic minority originally living in the highlands of southeastern Burma (though many also live in the Irrawaddy Delta and some live across the border in Thailand). They differ from the Buddhist Burman majority by being mostly Christians. They have long sought autonomy from the Burmese government in Rangoon. Ever since independence, the Karen have been involved in armed insurgencies against the government, with the separatist movement being led most recently by the Karen National Union. Thus far, the Burmese government has refused to grant autonomy and has dealt harshly with the insurgents.

Burma's geographic conditions have influenced its ethnic divisions. Much of the country is cut off from the rest of the world by mountains or heavy forest. Rural Burma is populated primarily by Burmans (68 percent) and by numerous minority groups such as the Shan (9 percent), Karen (7 percent), Rakhine (4 percent), Chinese (3 percent), Mon (2 percent), and Indians (2 percent). The Karen people live along the border with Thailand, and so the number of Karen actually living within Burma is difficult to know. Chinese migrants live primarily in cities. They have become merchants and traders, and they dominate rice trade, milling, and mining. Indians are most often laborers, money lenders, and traders.

Hmong

The Hmong are a minority ethnic group who migrated from southern China to the mountains of Laos in the nineteenth century. During the war in Vietnam and Laos, the Hmong worked closely with the Americans, in particular with the Central Intelligence Agency. Thousands of Hmong were forced to flee after the communist victory in 1975. Many of them eventually came to the United States.

In Cambodia, Vietnamese and Chinese immigrants have settled in and near the urban centers. In Laos, ethnic groups of great variety have migrated southward from the mountains in the north. As in most of mainland Southeast Asia, the most important ethnic divisions in Laos are between highland and lowland people, the latter constituting the majority. Even this distinction involves a great deal of complexity, because the different peoples have traditionally stratified themselves at different altitudes.

Island Southeast Asians

In Indonesia there are an estimated one hundred ethnic groups, and more than two hundred distinct languages are spoken. Indonesia's national motto, "Unity in Diversity," reflects a theme found throughout Southeast Asia: the need to bring unity and to promote nationalism among minority groups. Indonesia's diversity is explained partially by its archipelagic geography. Ethnic groups lived on individual islands, surrounded by seas that kept them isolated from others. Only in recent years have these islanders been assimilated into the larger nation-state by means of the mass media and the increased ease of communication and transportation. The Indonesian government's establishment of mandatory instruction in a single national language, *Bahasa Indonesia,* has been successful in ameliorating the differences and encouraging more homogeneity of culture.

Indonesia's ethnic groups practice many different customs. The Acehnese, who live on the northern tip of Sumatra, are a patrilineal people famous for their strong adherence to Islam and their defiance of colonial rule. The Minangkabau of western Sumatra are also Muslim, but they are more matrilineal than the Acehnese. The Batak live in the highlands of northern Sumatra. Over the past one hundred years they have become overwhelmingly Christian as a result of missionary proselytizing.

Bali is considered one of the world's premier paradises because of its geographic beauty, five-star resort beaches, stunning terraced rice fields, and beautifully decorated temples. The island is inhabited by the Balinese, who are famous for their Hindu rituals. They were the only major group in all of Southeast Asia to remain Hindu. Balinese society is highly stratified, almost like a caste system, and every person instantly and automatically can tell a person's caste by learning the person's name.

By far the largest and most influential ethnic group in Indonesia is the Javanese, who live mostly in the central and eastern parts of the island of Java, the country's governmental and cultural center. Nearly half of all Indonesians are Javanese. Famous for their refinement *(halus)*, their pleasant appearance, and their high respect for authority, the Javanese have for centuries dominated every aspect of Indonesia. The Javanese perform the *wayang,* the traditional shadow puppetry, and they have deep knowledge of the country's mythology. Islam is their principal religion, although believers vary in their degree of orthodoxy. For example, the *santri* strictly follow Islamic teachings, while the *abangan* are more concerned with ceremonies.

East Timor's population is about one million people (the number is an estimate as no formal census has been taken) who are mostly Austronesian (Malayo-Polynesian) and Papuan, with a small Chinese minority. The nation's official language is Tetum, but Indonesian, Portuguese, English, and about sixteen indigenous languages are also spoken. The major religion, to which about 90 percent adhere is Roman Catholic, and the other 10 percent are mostly Muslim, Protestant, Hindu, and Buddhist. Animism pervades all of the religions.

Ethnicity is of particular importance in Malaysia. The most important minority is the Chinese, who were brought to Malaysia by the British colonialists as laborers and wholesalers. They now constitute about one-third of Malaysia's population. The other important ethnic group is the Indians, who became laborers on plantations and entered the textile business. The Chinese and Indians are not Muslims and therefore have experienced little assimilation into the majority Malay culture. The Ibans, Bidayuhs, Kadazans, and Muruts of eastern Malaysia (Sarawak and Sabah) constitute important ethnic groups in the upper half of the island of Borneo. For political reasons they are grouped with Malays, but in fact they are culturally distinct.

The great majority of the Philippine population are Malayo-Polynesian peoples. The country's population is collectively called Filipino, but there are in fact numerous ethnic and linguistic groups. The primary languages are Tagalog (spoken on the portion of Luzon that includes the capital, Manila), Ilocano (northern Luzon), Cebuano (island of Cebu), and Ilongo (spoken in the Visayan islands of the central Philippines). Each of these languages corresponds to one of the country's major ethnic groups, which include Tagalog, Ilocano, Cebuano, Ilongo, Bicolano, Waray, Pampango, and perhaps seventy others.

Chinese and Indians

The Chinese and Indian minorities are the most economically powerful ethnic groups in the region. Initially, they were brought to Southeast Asia primarily by Western colonialists in order to work as manual laborers. The Chinese and Indians worked in the tin mines and rubber estates, and they helped to build the infrastructure of the major cities, often doing the work that the indigenous peoples refused to do. Eventually, they moved from labor to management. Today the Chinese and Indians are usually urban and are owners of small shops, large corporations, banks, and lending agencies. They have amassed fortunes that have given the Chinese, in particular, an economic clout disproportionate to their numbers.

In most Southeast Asian countries, the Chinese represent a small percentage of the population, being only about 10 percent of the populations of Thailand, the Philippines, Vietnam, Burma, Laos, Cambodia, and Indonesia, but about 35 percent of the population of Malaysia. The Chinese have traded in Southeast Asia for hundreds of years, but in the nineteenth and twentieth centuries thousands of them also came to live permanently. The Chinese are mostly urban and are disproportionately involved in business pursuits. Some estimate that the Chinese control over 50 percent of the Indonesian economy. This situation has led to tensions and even pogroms against the Chinese. After the overthrow of President Sukarno in Indonesia in 1965, about half a million Chinese were executed, ostensibly for alleged communist ties. Similarly, following the resignation of President Suharto in 1998, there were anti-Chinese demonstrations throughout the archipelago.

Thailand and the Philippines have assimilated the Chinese minorities with far fewer problems than have Indonesia and Malaysia. Assimilation has been most pronounced in Thailand, where, partly because the Chinese and Thai are both Buddhist, there have been no strictures against interaction and intermarriage. Assimilation has been least in Malaysia and Indonesia, owing to Islamic restrictions. In Malaysia, where the Chinese constitute one-third of the population, the government has set forth numerous laws and policies that have limited the group's economic and political roles.

Hill Peoples

Perhaps the most salient division in Southeast Asia is between the plains people and those who live in the hills and mountains. The hill groups remain economically impoverished and politically powerless. They have historically been more nomadic than the lowlanders, and (except for the Karen in Burma) have had weaker, less integrated political structures. The lowlanders, by contrast, developed tightly structured village communities often ruled by feudal or bureaucratic chiefs.

Ethnic Conflict

Throughout the region, the many different ethnic groups live side-by-side with their diverse languages, religions, customs, occupations, and educational and social statuses. As in much of the rest of the world, these differences give rise to prejudices and stereotypes. Throughout the region the people in the plains view hill tribes as uncivilized. Meanwhile, rural Malay farmers view the urban Chinese and Indians as arrogant, pagan, exploitative, and clannish, and in return the Chinese and Indians view Malays as lazy and fatalistic. Negative stereotypes such as these can be found everywhere. They belie the myth that there is no discrimination or prejudice in Southeast Asia.

Linguistic Diversity

The many languages spoken in Southeast Asia exemplify the region's diversity. They represent a variety of language families, and in many places the dominant language has changed over the years. Linguists disagree on the grouping of some of the major languages, but the general consensus is as follows: The Sino-Tibetan language family includes Chinese, Burmese, Karen, and a host of lesser-known languages. The Austro-Asiatic family includes Mon, Khmer (Cambodian), and probably Vietnamese. The Austronesian family includes Cham, Malay, Indonesian, and Tagalog (and other languages of Indonesia and the Philippines). The Tai-Kadai group includes Thai, Lao, and Shan; some linguists have related this family to Sino-Tibetan, while others relate it to Austronesian. The Hmong-Mien family (also known as Miao-Yao) includes Hmong and several other highland languages; its deeper connections are controversial. In addition to the various indigenous languages, there are some recent arrivals. Chinese has become the major language of Singapore, and various Chinese dialects are spoken in urban areas throughout Southeast Asia. Indian languages are also spoken in some communities in Malaysia and Singapore. English has become the principal international language among the educated.

Thai (Siamese) is the dominant language of Thailand. It is closely related to the Lao spoken in Laos and to minority languages spoken in Burma (for example Shan) and in parts of Vietnam (for example Black Tai). Burmese is spoken in much of Burma, and related languages are found in minority mountain areas of the country.

Burmese Names

The Burmese use honorifics when addressing others. For example, the term for "mister" is "U," as in U Thant or U Nu. The word "U" connotes respect. The most respectful honorific for women is "Daw" as in "Daw Aung San Suu Kyi." The word "Daw" means "aunt" but does not necessarily mean a family relative.

At birth Burmese are given names based on the day of the week they are born. Children born on a Monday are given names beginning with a letter appropriate only for that day. Differing from the practice in Western nations, Burmese can change their names as they go through life. Burmese do not inherit family names, and married women do not adopt the name of their husband.

Vietnamese is the dominant language of Vietnam, and related languages are spoken among many hill peoples in Vietnam, Laos, and Thailand. A thousand years ago Khmer dominated much of mainland Southeast Asia, but that language became less widely used as a result of Burmese and Thai incursions into the area once controlled by the Khmer. Today Khmer is the national language of Cambodia and is spoken in portions of Vietnam, Laos, and Thailand. Mon-Khmer languages are also spoken among numerous minority ethnic groups.

Malay is spoken in Brunei, Malaysia, parts of Indonesia, and the four southern provinces of Thailand. Malay is also the foundation for numerous minority languages throughout the region and is the basis for *Bahasa Indonesia,* also known as Indonesian. Indonesian is the official language of Indonesia and is also understood by Malaysians. Many closely related local languages are spoken throughout the Indonesian archipelago, including Acehnese and Minangkabau in Sumatra, Javanese and Sundanese in Java, and Balinese on the island of Bali.

Pilipino (a variant of Tagalog, the major dialect in the northern island of Luzon) is the designated national language of the Philippines. Cebuano is the major language in the southern islands of the Philippines, and virtually every major island in the archipelago has its own indigenous language. Since the American colonization English has been the *lingua franca* of the Philippines. However, in the past decade the government has made an effort to have Pilipino become the national language. Laws have been passed to make it the required language of teaching in schools and universities, but it has not succeeded as the national language to the degree that *Bahasa Indonesia* or Malay have succeeded in Indonesia and Malaysia respectively.

Cham

The Cham were once the majority ethnic group in present-day Vietnam, which their Champa kingdom dominated up to the fifteenth century. Today they are almost extinct. The remaining Cham are mostly Muslim and can be found in highland areas of Vietnam and Cambodia. In Cambodia they were targeted for death during the genocidal regime of the Khmer Rouge in 1975–79.

The Cham language used to be dominant in the central part of present-day Vietnam, but the Chams were pushed out by the Vietnamese and the language is now spoken only by a few highlanders.

Within the urban areas of all the Southeast Asian nations, Chinese language dialects such as Yunnanese, Hokkien, Cantonese, Hakka, and Tiechiu are spoken by Chinese involved in business pursuits. In the past two decades English has become another *lingua franca,* especially among the educated and those who deal in international affairs.

The characteristics of Southeast Asian languages vary greatly. In Thai, the meaning of a word often depends on the tone shape of the syllable. The standard Thai taught in schools has five tones: high, mid, low, rising, and falling. Burmese, Lao, Chinese, and Vietnamese are also tonal, though each has a different tone system. In yet other Southeast Asian languages tones are no more important than they are in English. Another contrast among the languages is that much of the Malay and

Indonesian vocabulary is constructed by means of prefixes and suffixes, while the Thai and Vietnamese languages tend not to do this. *Bahasa Indonesia* is relatively easy to speak and write; there are no tenses, and verbs are not conjugated. As with the Thai language, regional Indonesian languages use special vocabularies depending on the status of the person to whom one is speaking.

The languages' written versions also differ. Many of the scripts were adopted or adapted from foreign sources such as India, Arabia, China, and Europe. Indian scripts have been modified into Burmese, Thai, Lao, Khmer, and Javanese. These languages have no spaces between words except at the ends of sentences or clauses. The Indic-derived scripts have all evolved differently. The letters have different shapes, unneeded characters have been removed from the Indic originals, and tone marks and other symbols have been added where needed. Roman scripts are used by Vietnamese, Indonesian, Malay, and Tagalog and other Filipino languages. Vietnamese was originally written in a Chinese-style script, but French missionaries developed the Roman-based alphabet used today. This new system, known as *quoc ngu*, uses diacritical marks above and below letters to mark tones and to indicate variant pronunciations of certain vowels and consonants.

Southeast Asian languages reflect the importance placed on status in these societies. For example, there are many words meaning "I" and "you." The word to be used depends on the relative status of the persons conversing. If a peasant speaks to his landlord, he uses a word for "I" that reflects his perceived lowly status. In return, the landlord uses personal pronouns that reflect his superior status. In contrast, the English language has only one word for "I," no matter what the status of the persons communicating. A person says "I" whether talking with a child or with the president of the United States. In Southeast Asia, that would be unthinkable. Hierarchy and deference are also shown by verb choice, as in the different words used for the verb "to eat." In Thai, depending on the status of the people to whom one is speaking, one chooses from among elegant (*raprathaan)*, polite (*thaan)*, informal (*kin*), or rude (*daek)* words meaning "to eat." In Javanese, a language spoken (in addition to *Bahasa*) by almost half of all Indonesians, the word choices are even more complex and even more hierarchically oriented. Javanese is a rich language, full of nuance and considered elegant when spoken well.

Religious Diversity

Southeast Asians adhere to a wide variety of religions. In some countries, such as Burma, Cambodia, and Indonesia, a single religion is dominant. In others, such as Malaysia and Singapore, the people follow a wide variety of religions.

In most areas the dominant religion has changed over the centuries. For example, Indonesia and Cambodia were once primarily Hindu, but today Indonesia is predominantly Muslim and Cambodia is Theravada Buddhist.

Hinduism

At one time, Hinduism was the major religion of Southeast Asia. Perhaps no outside culture has played as important a role as that of India in the shaping of Southeast Asia. Its impact has been especially strong in the realm of government and the arts. Late in the first century A.D., Indian culture (especially Hinduism and Mahayana Buddhism) was disseminated throughout Southeast Asia by Indian traders who established marketing centers that eventually evolved into important towns. Brahman priests also instructed people in Hindu beliefs. Hinduism spread rapidly and influenced languages, religious beliefs, literature, the arts, and styles of government and social organization.

Historians say that Southeast Asia was "Hinduized" or "Indianized" in this period, referring to the influence of the Hindu and Mahayana Buddhist religions, which coexisted in much of the area. Indic influences gave rise to major political and religious centers, the most famous being the great civilization based at the Angkor complex located in Cambodia, which flourished from the ninth to thirteenth centuries. Hinduism would have been particularly attractive to the ruling classes. At Angkor, in accordance with Hindu beliefs, the leaders were god-kings, or *devarajas*, a notion that fits the elitist nature of the religion. The political order was (and still is in the minds of some Southeast Asians) seen as a microcosm of the cosmic order. The king was to his kingdom as God is to the cosmos. Great monuments were built to the glory of the rulers, as at the complexes of Angkor and the Borobudur (in present-day Java, Indonesia), which sought to replicate the structure of the cosmos.

Hinduism lost its dominance in a period running roughly from the 1200s through the 1400s, and the region's early Mahayana Buddhism faded away with it. (The Mahayana Buddhism found in Southeast Asia today came later from China.) Hinduism's elitist doctrine was a cause of its decline. The Theravada Buddhism, Islam, and (in the Philippines) Christianity that replaced early Indic religions were more egalitarian traditions that put salvation in the hands of individuals and made them responsible for their own behavior and fortunes. Today, there are almost no Hindus except on the island of Bali located east of Java in Indonesia. It is difficult to find Hindu temples in Southeast Asia except in Bali, in cities with Indian communities, and at ancient sites such as Angkor in Cambodia. However, influences of the Hindu tradition can still be found in the great literary epics such as the *Mahabharata* and *Ramayana*, while the principles of absolutism and hierarchy introduced by Indianization remain essential aspects of Southeast Asian politics today.

Table 3. Religious Adherence in the Late 1990s

Country	Religions	Country	Religions
Brunei 0.3 million people	Muslim (official) 63% Buddhist (Mahayana) 14% Christian 8% Indigenous Beliefs and Other 15%	Malaysia* 21.3 million	Muslim Buddhist (mostly Mahayana) Taoist Hindu Christian Sikh Shamanism (in E. Malaysia)
Burma (Myanmar) 48.4 million	Buddhist (Theravada) 89% Christian 4% Baptist 3% Roman Catholic 1% Muslim 4 % Animist 1% Other 2 %	Philippines 79.3 million	Roman Catholic 83% Protestant 9% Muslim 5% Buddhist (Mahayana) and Other 3%
Cambodia 11.6 million	Buddhist (Theravada) 95% Other 5%	Singapore 3.5 million	Buddhist (Chinese Mahayana) 28% Muslim (Malays) 16% Christian 19% Hindu 5% Taoist 13% Other (including Sikh and Confucianist) 19%
Indonesia 216.1 million	Muslim 88% Christian 8% Protestant 5% Roman Catholic 3% Hindu 2% Buddhist (Mahayana) 1% Other 1%	Thailand 60.6 million	Buddhist (Theravada) 95% Muslim 4% Other 1%
Laos 5.4 million	Buddhist (Theravada) 60% Animist and Other 40%	Vietnam* 77.3 million	Buddhist, Taoist Roman Catholic indigenous beliefs Muslim Protestant Cao Dai Hoa Hao

*Accurate percentage of population data for religious adherents in Malaysia and Vietnam were not available at the time of publication.

Animism

The one religion that can be found throughout Southeast Asia is animism, a belief in spirits that exist everywhere, including rice fields, homes, buildings, roads, and trees. The spirits can be found in both animate and inanimate objects, and some may be related to one's own ancestors. All of these spirits must be propitiated. Throughout the history of Southeast Asia the life of the peasant has been one of great risk, with constant threats to the maintenance of life itself. The spirits inhabiting the rice fields, homes, forests, and communities are believed to determine the quality and quantity of the harvest, the health of oneself and one's loved ones, the safety of travel, and the general well-being of the realm. Spirit worship provides a satisfying explanation for the vicissitudes of life by placing the blame for suffering on malicious spirits rather than on the sufferers themselves.

In earlier centuries, animism was an important counterweight to Hinduism and Mahayana Buddhism. Both of these Indic religions were aristocratic, whereas animism appealed more to ordinary people. Animism is still the primary religion of many indigenous ethnic groups. It has also been assimilated into more formal religions such as Buddhism and Islam, resulting in new syncretic traditions that are unique to each locality. For example, much of the Islam practiced on the island of Java is more appropriately referred to as Javanese Religion, because it unites elements of Islam and animism in a combination uniquely characteristic of Javanese culture.

Confucianism

While the rest of Southeast Asia was being Indianized, Chinese influence was spreading in Vietnam. China ruled Vietnam for about one thousand years, from 111 B.C. to 939 A.D. The Chinese brought Confucianism, a belief system begun by the moral philosopher Confucius (551 B.C. to 479 B.C.). In contrast to the Indianized area of Southeast Asia, where "god-kings" ruled, the Chinese Confucian administrative system was a hierarchical, structured bureaucracy administered by a mandarinate schooled in a classical education.

Confucianism is a complex set of beliefs emphasizing harmony, stability, consensus, hierarchy, and authority. Confucius postulated a universal moral order that remains in harmony as long as everyone from the emperor on down carries out his or her duty by fulfilling obligations to inferiors and superiors. Confucianism emphasized five relationships: subject to ruler, son to father, wife to husband, younger brother to elder brother, and mutual respect among friends. Except for the fifth, these hierarchical relationships were tightly structured with clear expectations about the correct way to behave. At the pinnacle of Confucianist societies was the emperor, who ruled with the "mandate of heaven." Below him came the mandarinate scholar-officials, the educated, the landholders, and, at the bottom, the peasants and laborers. Floods and other calamities were interpreted as signs that the Confucian leaders were not properly ruling their kingdoms and had lost the "mandate of heaven." The natural world was a model of the human world, and when nature was out of control, the leaders could be overthrown.

Confucianism did not establish a formal ritual nor was there a priesthood similar to that of Hinduism, Buddhism, or Islam. Hence, many scholars have viewed Confucianism not as a religion but rather as a secular philosophy about how best to lead one's life. Whether as a philosophy or a religion, the teachings of Confucius ("Do not do to others what you yourself would not like") have become an influential creed. Confucianism has had a profound effect on life in Southeast Asia, especially in Vietnam, in Singapore, and among the Chinese in cities throughout the region. Some commentators believe that the Confucian emphasis on order, hard work, and merit is responsible for the region's rapid economic development. Confucian influence has persisted even in communist Vietnam. Communist party officials in North Vietnam became the new ruling class, even though many were not highly educated or particularly scholarly. Their devotion to the cause of nationalism explained their high standing.

Buddhism

Buddhism is the major religion of mainland Southeast Asia. Before the 1500s, Buddhism could be found even in present-day Indonesia, where the great Buddhist Borobudur complex, built in the eighth century, still stands as one of the greatest marvels of the world. Today, Buddhism is the state religion in Burma, Laos, Cambodia, and Thailand. It is the dominant religion in Vietnam, and it is also practiced in the Chinese communities of Malaysia and Insular Southeast Asia. The Buddhism in Vietnam and Singapore is of the Mahayana ("greater vehicle") variant, while in Burma, Laos, Cambodia, and Thailand the dominant form is Theravada Buddhism ("wisdom of the elders"), which is also known as Hinayana ("lesser vehicle").

Like Hinduism, Buddhism was imported from India. It came in several separate streams. Theravada Buddhism penetrated mainland Southeast Asia from India by way of Sri Lanka (formerly Ceylon). By about 500 A.D., this form of Buddhism had been established in Burma and was moving eastward across the mainland. In contrast to Hinduism, Theravada Buddhism was introduced directly to the people rather than indirectly through the ruling classes. It was attractive for several reasons. Buddhism created a more egalitarian religious community (even the monarchs had obligations as laypeople), and the religion was more easily assimilated to local cultures than was Hinduism. Also in contrast to Hinduism, the Theravada Buddhist monkhood practiced the principles of otherworldly simplicity and frugality. Mahayana Buddhism also reappeared, traveling from India through China to become the dominant religion of Vietnam. Nineteenth-century Chinese immigrants also brought Mahayana Buddhism to Singapore and other urban areas.

The Emerald Buddha

The most revered Buddha image in Thailand is the Emerald Buddha residing in the main temple of the Grand Palace in Bangkok. Thousands of Thai people and foreign tourists pay homage to this small Buddha every day. Despite its name, the 30-inch-tall image is actually made of jade. According to legend, it first appeared in northern Thailand in 1434 when lightning hit a temple, revealing a stucco image that appeared to be translucent. The brilliant color was viewed as a positive omen. The image found its way somehow to Vientiane, Laos, and in 1780 the future king of Thailand, Rama I, captured the image and brought it to Bangkok, where he installed it at the site of his new capital. The Emerald Buddha has been in the royal Grand Palace temple ever since.

Theravada Buddhist practice is normally not mystical. Theravada monks are revered as teachers and are taught to stay out of politics. Mahayana Buddhism is more mystical and involves the belief in *bodhisattvas* (Buddhas-to-be, usually local deities that are considered to have nearly become Buddhas). Many modern Buddhists of both traditions practice meditation so that they can eventually enter *nirvana,* the absence of suffering. Yet, local Buddhist traditions have also been syncretic, absorbing elements of animism and Hinduism.

The founder of Buddhism was Siddhartha Gautama, who is believed to have been a prince in southern Nepal. Disturbed by his growing awareness of life's sufferings and by the impermanence of existence, he devoted himself to a lengthy religious quest to find the meaning of life. Buddhists do not consider Prince Siddhartha a god. Instead, he is viewed as a great teacher who achieved enlightenment and then shared his knowledge with the public. During his religious quest he tried numerous experiments, such as starvation, gluttony, and self-denial. He eventually rejected these ways for the "middle path," teaching moderation in all things.

As he shared his teaching, the Buddha established the order of Buddhist monks, the *sangha,* a still-thriving society of men who have chosen to devote themselves full-time to study and practice. The *sangha,* or monkhood, was for centuries the most important institution of the Buddhist nations. Its role is to enable men to devote themselves exclusively to the Buddhist way, but as an institution it has also functioned to spread and interpret the Buddha's teachings, thereby helping the lay people develop a Buddhist orientation to life. As an institution of men who have devoted themselves to a pure lifestyle, the monkhood functions as a field of merit, so that laypeople may accumulate good *karma* through their support and donations. Monks are not allowed personal belongings. They must shave their heads, be celibate, and fast after noon every day. In traditional Thai society, all males from Buddhist families would become monks, most of them for just three months. By becoming a monk the man provided merit and assured good *karma* for himself and for his family. In contemporary times, the *sangha* plays a less significant role than it once did, because the citizenry has become more concerned with materialist matters and fewer males are choosing to enter the *sangha*.

Sangha

In mainland Southeast Asia, the Buddhist monkhood is known as the *sangha*. In Thailand, virtually all males used to enter the monkhood at some time in their lives, thereby providing merit to their parents. The monk's head is shaven, he wears yellow robes, and he follows monastic rules including celibacy, sleeping on mats, and fasting after noon. Most men stay in the monkhood for three months or less, but some remain in the robes much longer.

The *sangha* is highly respected in mainland Southeast Asia. Experienced monks are teachers, spiritual counselors, and leaders in community development. The monks integrate Buddhist societies and act as symbols of the people's best values. At present, fewer boys are joining the *sangha* because this style of Buddhist practice is not as central to modern life as it was in more traditional societies.

Buddhism is not a God-oriented system of faith and worship. Beliefs such as the notion of a supreme being must not be taken on faith. Rather, all teachings must be evaluated in light of one's experience and reason. The Buddha guided his followers by pointing out the path on which they can proceed, but each person must tread the path himself. The religion's most distinctive doctrine is *karma*, the notion of cause and effect. Good deeds will eventually benefit the doer of the deed, either in this life or a later life. Merit can be made by giving food to monks, refurbishing temples, leading the life of the middle path (moderateness in thought and action), becoming a monk, and following the Buddhist precepts. The accumulated merit can help lead to a better existence, but the ultimate goal is *nirvana*, the complete cessation of suffering. To achieve *nirvana*, one must be freed from the cycle of karmic rebirth and must live by the Four Noble Truths. The first Noble Truth holds that all existence is suffering (because even pleasures are impermanent); the second teaches that suffering results from desire; the third teaches that suffering will cease when desire and greed cease; and the fourth indicates the Noble (Eightfold) Path that one must follow to bring suffering to an end. Buddhism emphasizes the need to withdraw from society in order to meditate and to perfect the discipline that is necessary for achieving *nirvana*.

Figure 1. Shwedagon Pagoda, Rangoon, Burma

Shwedagon Pagoda

Perhaps the most famous Buddhist temple in the world is the Shwedagon Pagoda in Rangoon, the capital of Burma. Venerated by all Burmese for its status as a great spiritual shrine, the Pagoda is said to house relics of the Buddha. Many centuries old, the Pagoda is indescribably spectacular. The building sits on top of a hill and is covered with gold leaf and with gems such as diamonds, sapphires, and rubies. Each day thousands of pilgrims climb the hill and circle the pagoda clockwise. By refurbishing the pagoda, Buddhists make merit to help assure that their next existence will be positive.

For most Southeast Asian Buddhists, especially those in Thailand, this rather formalistic account of Buddhism is no longer an accurate picture of religious life. Modern Buddhism is more worldly and practical. Traditionally, in Buddhist Southeast Asia the temples were the educational centers and the monks served as teachers. But in contemporary times, secular schools have been constructed and the monks rarely perform as teachers except in the most rural areas. Consumer capitalism has also made inroads, and the people are increasingly attracted to a variety of spirit cults. Today, the temples continue to be centers for "making merit," an important part of Buddhist life in which people invest in a better future by means of their donations. Southeast Asians make offerings to increase their wealth, to ensure success on an exam, to acquire a job, and to obtain the many other benefits that are a part of modern life. Few still seek redemption through asceticism or a search for *nirvana*. Those who do are likely to focus on Buddhist teachings as a type of philosophy or a form of psychology, with *nirvana* as a metaphor for the state of inner peace. Hence, throughout Southeast Asia there is tension between modernity and the formal teachings of Buddhism.

Islam

Islam is the state religion of Malaysia and Brunei and the formal religion of 90 percent of all Indonesians (Indonesia is the most populous Islamic country in the world). Before the twentieth century, Muslims also predominated in Mindanao, the southernmost island of the Philippines, but large-scale migrations of Christian Filipinos have displaced them on most of the island. Muslims are also the majority in the four southern provinces of Thailand, and Muslim minorities can be found throughout Southeast Asia in the cities and among the hill peoples.

Muslims believe in a single, all-powerful God known as Allah. Islam is an ethical religion based on the teachings of the Koran, a book which contains the words of Allah as spoken to the prophet Mohammed during the years 610–622 A.D. The word "Islam" means surrender, and the religion has an austere tone emphasizing submission to Allah. Islam does not have a complex or even formal church organization. Instead, the focus is on individuals and their relationship to the almighty and judgmental Allah. The bedrock act which all Muslims share is the confession of faith: "There is no God but Allah and Mohammed is his Prophet." Repeating that phrase, and believing it, makes a person a Muslim. Islam is actually a way of life, and it includes prescriptions for all areas of daily behavior. Islamic laws establish rules on how and what to eat, when to wash, how to pray, and what to wear. There are Islamic laws relating to marriage, business operations, and almost all other aspects of life.

Islam arrived in Southeast Asia long after Animism, Hinduism, and Buddhism. Islam spread to the islands sometime in the thirteenth century, having been brought by Muslim traders and religious leaders. Islam has changed over centuries, assimilating elements of Hinduism, Buddhism, and animism to meet the needs of its adherents. The Islamic variants that can be found throughout Southeast Asia display diverse rituals, beliefs, and values. For example, the rituals of urban Muslims differ from those of rural Muslims.

In Indonesia there are three subtraditions of Islam. Adherents of the *Santri* variant stress the Islamic aspects of the religion, emphasizing the five ritual acts that they see as the heart of the religion. The first act is the confession of faith. Prayers constitute the second act; their recitation five times each day provides comfort and helps resign the worshiper to Allah. Fasting, the third act, is prescribed for Ramadan, the ninth lunar month. The pilgrimage to Mecca once in a lifetime is the fourth ritual act. The fifth is the payment of a religious tax, the *zakah*, for the purpose of aiding the poor. The *Abangan* variant stresses the animistic aspects of Indonesian syncretism and is principally practiced by the peasant element of the population. The *Prijaji* variant shows the lingering influence of Hinduism and is most common among the bureaucratic element of society. The adherents of this third variant tend to emphasize hierarchy and status in social relationships.

Because Islam has no formal ecclesiastical hierarchy, Islamic laws are an especially important aspect of the religion. For example, gambling, money-lending, drinking of alcohol, and the eating of pork are forbidden. Women must cover their bodies and faces and are subject to the dictates of their male family members. In Indonesia these requirements are often not followed, because of the fusion of beliefs adopted by the variant Islamic sects. But in Malaysia, there is little intermarriage between Malays and Chinese precisely because of the Islamic requirement that all Muslims must marry within their religion and must follow the ritual requirements.

The September 11, 2001 terrorist attack on the United States brought Islam into American consciousness. Many Americans assumed that terrorism was intrinsic to Islam, and that the religion was a force that Americans would be combating forever. Part of the weakness of this assumption is that Islam is neither homogeneous nor monolithic. The heterogeneity is especially clear in Southeast Asia where many Muslims view themselves as distinct ethnic minorities rather than as part of a unified religious group. In many places, Muslim ethnic groups are disadvantaged. In Burma, for example, the Rohingyas are an ethnic Islamic minority who have been marginalized and exploited by the Burmese military. In the southern Philippines, about four million Muslims have supported rebellion against the Catholic-dominated government in Manila. In Malaysia, about eight million Muslim Malays live in a nation economically dominated by the indigenous non-Muslim Chinese. Though Malaysia's Muslims are a majority religious group, and though the Malays are politically dominant, they have a lower standard of living than do the Chinese. In Thailand, the four southern provinces are populated mostly by Muslims, but they play only a minor role in central Thai politics and have been discriminated against for decades.

Only in Indonesia (and in tiny Brunei) are Muslims the great majority (about 90 percent) who dominate every facet of life. (The minority Chinese in Indonesia are disproportionately involved in the economic sector.) Nearly 200 million Muslims live in Indonesia making it the most populous Muslim country in the world. As noted previously, there are several long-standing subtraditions of Islam in Indonesia, as well as a growing number of "fundamentalist" groups. Some of the latter, demonstrating a radical strain, have incorporated terrorist efforts into their activities.

Fundamentalism has increased in all religions, including Christianity and Hinduism, and has altered the political forces in many of the world's countries. The rise of a more radical Islam in Indonesia stems from many sources, the most important being a notion that modernity (mostly viewed as Westernism) had vanquished the traditional Islamic beliefs and left Muslims behind. The Iranian revolution of 1979, which brought the Ayatollahs to power and humiliated the United States, strengthened the radical movement in Indonesia. However, until 1998, the oppression by the Suharto regime had kept the movement controlled. But the downfall of his regime opened new opportunities for younger Muslim leaders who desired an Islamic state, an end to the "decadent" bourgeois values of the Indonesian elites, and renewed respect for Islam by the "unfaithful."

Muslims, both traditional and radical, feel a strong sense of brotherhood with other Muslims. That feeling comes from the notion of the *ummah,* or community of believers. Like other religions, Islam has a diversity of sects. Yet this potential for division is balanced by commonalities such as the *Haj* (the pilgrimage to Mecca) and the common prayers. Local Muslim schools, called *pesantren* in Indonesia, add to the sense of unity. This concept of the community helps explain why Muslims of virtually every society disagree with American policy in the Middle East (which is viewed as anti-Islam and pro-Israel), why Muslims feel victimized by Western colonialism, and why Muslims in Southeast Asia overwhelmingly disagree with American policy in Iraq.

Christianity

Christianity, or more accurately Catholicism, came to the Philippines with the Spaniards in the sixteenth century. The Filipinos, who practiced animism, were open to a more structured belief system that presented a satisfying explanation for the travails of the poor. In the early years, local Christian religious leaders encouraged the masses to act against the established exploitative order, suggesting that Jesus Christ glorified the poor. Catholic priests in the villages became strong proponents of the poor while many leaders higher in the church hierarchy supported the elites who, in return, gave the church significant tax benefits. Catholicism meshed easily with the hierarchical patterns of society and strengthened the forces of the elites. Today, 80 percent of Filipinos are

Catholic, while another 10 to 15 percent practice other forms of Christianity, primarily Protestantism. East Timor is the region's only other Catholic nation, with 90 percent of its population following the religion, which in this case was brought by the Portuguese in the sixteenth century.

Figure 2. Notre Dame Cathedral, Saigon, Vietnam

In Vietnam, a small but significant minority of the people (between 5 and 10 percent) worship in the Roman Catholic Church as a result of the work of French missionaries who arrived in Vietnam in the eighteenth and nineteenth centuries, well before the country's colonization by the French. Many northern Catholics migrated south when the country was divided in 1954. From 1954 to 1963, South Vietnam's President Ngo Dinh Diem, himself a Catholic, favored that religion, which he considered a bulwark against the communism of the north. The majority of the people in South Vietnam, being Buddhist, resented the special privileges, including high level positions in the government, that Diem gave his fellow Catholics. This popular resentment contributed to Diem's downfall in 1963 (see Chapter 6). After the communist takeover of 1975, Catholics were told not to worship in their churches, and many of their religious edifices became museums. However, the churches began to fill again when Vietnam started liberalizing in the late 1980s.

Protestant missionaries began coming to Southeast Asia in the nineteenth century. In order to reduce competition, the Presbyterians,

Methodists, Baptists, Lutherans, Dutch Reformed, Salvation Army, and other missions divided the region for purposes of proselytizing. The missionaries were most successful in converting animist hill tribe peoples, and they were less successful among the formally Buddhist and Muslim religionists of the lowlands. In the late twentieth century, newer missions from more fundamentalist and pentecostal Christian churches have also had success in converting hill tribe people and lowlanders living in remote areas. Protestant churches can now be found throughout the region, usually in rural areas and in the mountains.

DISCUSSION QUESTIONS

1. What are the principal reasons for Southeast Asia's diversity?
2. What are the major elements of Southeast Asian diversity?
3. Show how rice has been central to Southeast Asian societies.
4. Has ethnic diversity in Southeast Asia had a positive or negative impact on the stability of the region?
5. How has the Chinese ethnic group influenced urban Southeast Asia?
6. Is it necessary to speak a Southeast Asian language in order to understand the culture of the region?
7. Discuss the similarities and differences among Buddhism, Islam, Christianity, Animism, and the other religions of Southeast Asia.

SUGGESTED READINGS

The most up-to-date coverage of diversity in Southeast Asia is Thomas R. Leinbach and Richard Ulack, eds., *Southeast Asia: Diversity and Development* (Prentice Hall, New Jersey, 2000). The editors have brought together fifteen outstanding scholars, who contribute essays covering Southeast Asia's physical environment, cultural patterns, demography, urbanization, rural development, tourism, transportation, and gender relations. The essays deal both with the region as a whole and with individual nations.

3

HISTORICAL HIGHLIGHTS

Prehistoric humans have lived in Southeast Asia for at least a million years, and probably for two million. Little is known about the lives of the original inhabitants. There is no consensus among archaeologists about the early years or about the evolution of the various lines of hominids, which include *Homo erectus,* a close relative of our species whose fossils can be found in central Java. The movements of the various prehistoric groups are also unclear, because no one is sure when and how the seas rose to separate the once huge land masses into the islands of Indonesia. As scholars learn more about the origins of Southeast Asia, a coherent history will emerge, but thus far the information is too sparse to achieve anything more than speculations.

For years, scholars assumed that the original inhabitants of Southeast Asia remained extremely primitive until influenced by higher civilizations in China and India. However, recent scholarship has revised this view. It now seems clear that the original inhabitants of Southeast Asia developed autonomous civilizations long before the first contacts with outsiders from China and India. The movement of technologies may have been from Southeast Asia to China as much as the other way around. Basketry, pottery, clothing, and tools may all have an origin in Southeast Asia rather than outside the region. Southeast Asian food producers most likely farmed several thousand years before the peoples of nearby regions. Rice cultivation, once thought to have started in China, may actually have begun in Southeast Asia.

Following are snapshots of some of the most important kingdoms, monuments, and events in the history of Southeast Asia. The purpose is to provide basic insights rather than lists of details. The account is not meant to be comprehensive, and readers wishing to learn more should consult the books listed at the end of the chapter.

China and the Vietnamese State

In 111 B.C., when Vietnam was not yet a nation-state, Chinese armies invaded the northern delta region and incorporated "Nam Viet" into the Han empire. The Chinese were eager to control the rich, fertile area of the Red River Delta, and their occupation lasted some one thousand years. Vietnamese nationalists mounted periodic revolts against the Chinese. The most famous of the revolts was led by the Trung sisters, who achieved a few years of freedom from Chinese rule. However, the sisters were eventually defeated, and they drowned themselves to avoid capture. They are celebrated in Vietnam as exemplars of the Vietnamese nationalist spirit.

Trung Sisters

In 39 A.D., when the Chinese occupied Vietnamese territory, the Trung sisters began an uprising, united the people, and overthrew the Chinese rulers. Three years later, the Chinese retaliated and defeated the sisters. In honor of their courageous stand against the foreign occupiers, the Trung sisters have been made national heroines. Statues in their honor can be found throughout Vietnam.

The Chinese rulers did all they could to assimilate the Vietnamese into China. They created Confucian bureaucratic and family structures and co-opted the Vietnamese aristocracy. The Chinese built roads and harbors, Sinicized rural agriculture, and organized the area in accordance with Chinese customs. Not until 939 A.D. did the Vietnamese regain their independence. The tenacious struggle of the early Vietnamese became a symbol inspiring later struggles against invaders from France, Japan, and the United States. The thousand-year rule by the Chinese also provides a symbolic basis for Vietnam's traditional distrust of its northern neighbor.

Ironically, Vietnam's search for national identity received its greatest impetus during the thousand-year period of Chinese domination. The ability of the Vietnamese to emerge from that period with many of their traditions intact epitomizes the nationalist urge that has pervaded Vietnam's history. Subsequent Chinese interventions were defeated by the Vietnamese despite the overwhelming military superiority of the Chinese. Similarly, the struggles against French colonialism, Japanese occupation, and, more recently, American intervention reflect the importance of Vietnamese nationalism.

For the next nine centuries a series of dynasties ruled Vietnam. The most famous was the Ly dynasty. Hanoi was established as the capital and the Vietnamese declared war on the Champa kingdom located in what is now central Vietnam. The Cham capital was sacked in the eleventh century and the kingdom destroyed by the fifteenth century. Today, only a few Chams survive in the highlands. The Vietnamese continued moving southward, destroying any peoples that barred their path, until they had advanced to the Mekong Delta.

The French colonial period began with the occupation of Saigon in the 1860s and culminated in French control of all of Vietnam by 1884. The French kept the Vietnamese emperor on the throne but allowed him no real authority. The French extracted Vietnam's natural resources, attempted to convert the Vietnamese to Christianity, created a new class of elite bureaucrats, built roads, and cleared jungles, but they did almost nothing to educate the masses.

During the era of French colonialism, Vietnam was divided into three areas: Tonkin was in the north, with Hanoi as the capital; Annam was the middle region, with Hue as the capital; and the south was known as Cochin China, with Saigon serving as the capital. This division was congruent with the geographic regionalism that had existed in the tenth century A.D., when the Vietnamese began their southern movement from the region the French would later call Tonkin.

Traditionally, the northerners have seen themselves as modern, progressive, and efficient, while they have seen the southerners as lazy. The people of the central region consider themselves highly cultured, the northerners grasping, and the southerners rustic. Meanwhile, southerners regard themselves as pacifistic and their northern neighbors as aggressive and violent.

In addition to these regional stereotypes, national unification has had to overcome the cultural and political dichotomy between the rural areas and the cities. Communication between the cities and villages scarcely existed, and such interaction as there was consisted largely of the exploitation of the peasantry by the mandarin class. Despite this divisiveness there has remained a nationalist continuity in the form of anticolonialism and anti-neoimperialism.

Angkor

Angkor was a great empire, based in Cambodia, that from the ninth to fifteenth centuries dominated most of mainland Southeast Asia. Angkor was led by great kings such as the famous ninth-century monarch Jayavarman II. Its capital was inhabited by a million people. It is difficult to imagine a more magnificent civilization. The culture of Angkor's rulers was heavily influenced by India and the Hindu religion. The kings were *devarajas*—god-kings—who were viewed as incarnations of the great gods Siva and Vishnu. The city they ruled mirrored the celestial realms, and its great stone monuments represented the mountains of the gods. Angkor's stone ruins can still be seen in present-day Cambodia, although all of the wooden and thatch houses that encircled the monuments have been lost.

There are many interpretations of how this great civilization was built, how it was sustained, and how it eventually fell. Angkor's location was an obvious site for a Khmer capital because it was close to the Tonle

Sap, a great lake feeding into the Mekong River that provided Angkor with communications to the outside world. The Tonle Sap is a rare geographical phenomenon. During the rainy season the rivers swell so much that water from the Mekong backs up into the Tonle Sap, increasing the lake's size some ten times. In the dry season, when the river levels drop, the water flows out of the lake. The constant back-and-forth movement of water brings fresh deposits of soil to the adjoining lands, making the area one of the most fertile in the world.

Figure 3. At Angkor, a god-king gazes over his realm

Life at Angkor is vividly portrayed on the bas-reliefs of the Angkor temples. There are pictures of rabbits, buffalo, rhinoceroses, and elephants. Chamber orchestras play music. There are carvings of land battles, market scenes, cockfights, prayers, the washing of clothes, and the brushing of teeth. All the Hindu gods are portrayed. Explicit sexual practices are shown. The reliefs portray daily dress, housing, furniture, and recreational pursuits. From the reliefs it is possible to gain a full sense of the lives of the people, even though the empire's zenith occurred almost a thousand years ago.

The Angkor area contained an intricate hydraulic network of canals, dams, reservoirs, and dikes that were used for irrigation, flood control, and transportation. The irrigation system allowed the growing of two rice crops per year. The building and management of the great moats and reservoirs required structure and organization. The kings made the

Figure 4. Carving of apsaras (celestial dancers) at Angkor

Figure 5. Ruins of the Bayon Temple complex at Angkor

reservoirs a part of the ritual apparatus of kingship, a manifestation of the spiritual power concentrated in the ruler. The combined focus on ritual and on economic management resulted in a labor-intensive society led by divine power.

Angkor declined in the thirteenth and fourteenth centuries, and its temples later became overgrown by jungle. The kingdom's exhaustion was brought about by extravagant building projects, debilitating wars against the Siamese, conflicts among rival dynasties, the deterioration of the elaborate hydraulic network, debilitating epidemics of diseases such as malaria, and the increasing importance of overseas trade (meaning that capitals needed to be closer to the sea). Also contributing was the rise of Theravada Buddhism with its more egalitarian message. Buddhism undermined the rigid and elitist hierarchy because it did not support the belief in god-kings.

Amazingly, the stone monuments of Angkor were not known to the western world until a Frenchman, Henri Mouhot, came across the site in 1860. He was thunderstruck by the magnificent temples, which had not been used for some four hundred years. The temples' grandeur subsequently made them famous tourist attractions.

Early Indonesian Kingdoms and Monuments

The great early Indonesian kingdoms were built by Hindu and Buddhist rulers. In the seventh century, Hinduism was already the dominant religion of Java, Sumatra, and neighboring islands. The states that developed in this area are known as "Indianized" states because of their cultural ties to India. The best known of these early Indianized kingdoms are the Srivijayan Empire based in Sumatra and the Shailendra and Majapahit kingdoms of Java.

In the seventh century the Srivijaya kingdom rose on the island of Sumatra, basing its capital at Palembang near the Strait of Malacca. For some six hundred years, Srivijaya controlled much of Sumatra, peninsular Malaya, and Borneo. Its power lasted through the fourteenth century. Srivijaya was a kingdom of great wealth. It was an intermediary trade center, or *entrepôt*, that linked the Middle East, India, and China. Almost all shipping from China to points west (and vice-versa) passed through straits controlled by this kingdom. Ships from the Middle East, India, and China brought their treasures of tea, silk, silver, iron, cotton, sugar, and salt to Srivijaya. Srivijaya collected tolls and harbor taxes, protected merchants from pirates, and assured continued trade among kingdoms around the world. To ensure its strong position, the Srivijayan rulers sent tribute to the Chinese in return for Chinese agreement to use Srivijaya as a preferred port of call.

It is interesting to compare Srivijaya with modern-day Singapore. Like Srivijaya, Singapore is an *entrepôt* in the Strait of Malacca. Also like

Srivijaya, it is a nation of huge wealth, much of it coming from trade and from ships that call at the port. On the other hand, Singapore has never exercised control over the straits the way that Srivijaya did.

The kings of Srivijaya did not oppress their subjects. The Hindu-Buddhist governing system was hierarchical, but villages were mostly autonomous. That is, they were free from effective central control. The rulers adopted an indigenous code of conduct on how rulers and subjects should treat each other. The code became the foundation of *adat,* a term referring to Indonesian-Malay custom that in many areas still has the force of law. *Adat* assured that the rulers did not mistreat the citizenry, and that the citizenry, in turn, gave deference to the rulers.

Mandala

Throughout Southeast Asia one can find examples of the mandala, a cosmologically potent figure that is thought to replicate the universal order of the cosmos. Mandalas have been used in the organization of political systems, in urban planning, and in religious architecture. In a mandala polity, a geometric system of subordinate political units is arrayed around a capital. In the center of the mandala is the primary temple and the king's palace. The capital is surrounded by circles of subordinate realms whose capitals are arrayed towards the four or eight points of the compass. The units get larger (and often more autonomous) as the rings of subordinates become increasingly distant from the center, whose organization they also replicate. In Burma, mandalas also appear in urban and religious architecture. The walled city of Pagan was laid out as a mandala. The Hindu temple of Angkor Wat and the Buddhist stupa of the Borobudur were also conceived according to this pattern. The nineteenth-century capital of Burma, Mandalay, was laid out as a perfect mandala, hence the city's name.

While the Srivijaya kingdom was flourishing in Sumatra, the Shailendra dynasty ruled much of Java during the seventh and eighth centuries. The dynasty was powerful, but it lasted only about one hundred years. In central Java the Shailendras built the magnificent Buddhist Borobudur complex, still one of the most stunning religious and tourist sites in the world. The enormous complex, one of the largest religious edifices anywhere, was constructed in the eighth century (the exact dates are unknown). Like Angkor Wat, the Borobudur was a symbolic representation of the sacred Mount Meru, being built in a series of circling terraces. The Borobudur is in the shape of a stupa, and each of its concentric terraces is studded with hundreds of Buddhist statues. In addition, the Buddhist path to salvation is symbolized on the Borobudur's terraces by means of scenes from the life of the Buddha that indicate his progress to *nirvana*. Today, thousands of pilgrims visit the complex each year even though it is situated in Muslim Indonesia.

Java was also the home of rulers who built Majapahit, an influential empire in East Java that was the last of the great Hindu-Buddhist states in island Southeast Asia. This fourteenth-century kingdom remains a source of national pride even in modern-day Muslim Indonesia. Despite its symbolic importance, Majapahit was not a mighty imperial center like Burma's Pagan or Cambodia's Angkor. Even at its height, Majapahit controlled only the central and eastern regions of Java and perhaps the islands of Bali and Madura. Majapahit's most famous leader was Gajah Mada, the ruler of East Java from 1330 to 1364. (Today this king is remembered in the name of Gajah Mada University in Jogyakarta, one of Indonesia's most distinguished universities.) By 1520, Majapahit no longer held sway and power had shifted to new political centers elsewhere in the archipelago.

Malacca

The Srivijayan kingdom fell in the 1300s when rival kingdoms invaded. As Srivijaya was declining, Muslim merchants arrived in Malaysia and Indonesia, bringing the religion of Islam. Muslim missionaries taught the people to read and write and introduced a system of social justice based on Muslim teachings. Throughout Malaysia and the Indonesian archipelago, many people became Muslims. The wave of conversion began on the northern tip of Sumatra and expanded through the area over a period of some two hundred years.

With the decline of Srivijaya, the city of Malacca on the west coast of the Malay peninsula emerged as the major trading post in the straits between present-day Malaysia and Indonesia. The legend of Malacca's founding is that the Srivijayan ruler, Paramesvara, crossed from Sumatra to the Malay peninsula to find a place to escape from the Javanese kings. One day when he was out hunting, his dogs were attacked by a tiny mousedeer they were chasing (a mousedeer is about the size of a big cat). Taking the mousedeer's fortitude as a positive omen, Paramesvara settled at that place, naming the new settlement *Melaka* (Malacca) after the type of palm tree under which he was standing at the time. The new Malacca empire controlled commercial shipping lanes for goods that came from India and China. It soon became the major port for trade in cloth, spices, and tin. By the fifteenth century, Malacca's ruler had become a Muslim and soon thereafter Islam was the national religion.

Malacca's independence ended when the Portuguese, who arrived in Southeast Asia in the early 1500s, forcefully took Malacca as a colony in 1511. The Portuguese were the first Western colonialists to come to Southeast Asia. Since at first they were the only Westerners engaged in the region, they became immensely wealthy for a while. But eventually

Malacca and the spice trade passed from Portuguese to Dutch control, and in 1795 the city passed in turn to the British.

Figure 6. Some of the thousands of temples at Pagan

Pagan

The Kingdom of Pagan in present-day Burma appeared at the same time as Angkor and Majapahit, becoming established in the middle of the ninth century. The capital city, which was also named Pagan, was located on the Irrawaddy River in a fertile region of Upper Burma. The Pagan kingdom was Burma's golden age. Some 13,000 temples were built in and around the capital city. Its most famous ruler was Anawrahta (ruled 1044–1077), who united the kingdom and introduced Theravada Buddhism. King Anawrahta ruled an empire about the same size as present-day Burma. The Pagan kingdom broke up in 1287, when its capital was overrun by soldiers from Kubilai Khan's Mongol empire. The Mongols did not end Pagan's importance as a cultural center, but they did end the region's dynamism and growth.

Today, Pagan is breathtaking. It is one of the most spectacular sights in all Southeast Asia. The multitude of temples is unsurpassed, and about 2,200 of them are still standing. Yet, few Westerners have visited, because Pagan is off the tourist routes and the current military dictatorship does not encourage tourism. Recently, the government has "cleaned" and "refurbished" the monuments. This activity dismays scholars who believe that the restoration is destroying the old temples and erasing important clues for understanding Burma's past. However, the government officials desire to improve their *karma* by making merit, and they know that one of the most expeditious means of doing so is by restoring temples. The sad consequence is that Pagan is in the process of losing its historical authenticity.

Thai Kingdoms

Until the thirteenth century, much of present-day Thailand was at least nominally controlled by the Khmer Empire at Angkor. In the eleventh to thirteenth centuries Angkor was gradually displaced by Thai leaders who established the Kingdom of Sukhothai. The new kingdom was headed by paternalistic kings who were said to be protectors of the people in wartime and "fathers and advisors" of their subjects in peacetime. King Rama Kamhang, the inventor of the Thai alphabet, wrote a now famous inscription:

> During the lifetime of King Rama Kamhang the city of Sukhothai has prospered. There are fish in its waters and rice in its rice fields. The Lord of the country does not tax his subjects, who throng the roads leading cattle to market and ride horses on their way to sell them. Whosoever wishes to trade in elephants or horses does so; whosoever wishes to trade in gold and silver does so. When a commoner, a noble or a chief falls ill and dies, or disappears, his ancestral home, his clothes, his elephants, his family, his rice granaries, his slaves, the plantations of areca and betel inherited from his ancestors, are all transmitted to his children. If commoners, nobles, or chiefs have a dispute, the king makes a proper inquiry and decides the matter with a complete impartiality. He does not enter into agreements with thieves and receivers. If he sees rice belonging to others, he does not covet it, and if he sees the riches of others he is not envious. To whomsoever comes on elephant-back to seek him and put his own country under his protection, he will extend his support and assistance. In the gates of the palace a bell is hung; if anyone in the kingdom has some grievance or some matter that is ulcerating his entrails and troubling his mind, and wishes to lay it before the king, the way is easy: he has only to strike the bell hung there. Every time King Rama Kamhang hears this appeal, he interrogates the plaintiff about the matter and gives an entirely impartial decision.

King Rama Kamhang's inscription has become central to the lore of the "paternalistic kings" who ruled Sukhothai. Whether the inscription is primarily propaganda or an accurate representation of King Rama Kamhang's character, the words have become as legendary for the Thai as the Gettysburg Address is for Americans. The putative accessibility of the Sukhothai kings was in striking contrast to the hierarchical absolutism of the old Khmer empire and of the future Ayuthayan kingdom.

The Sukhothai kingdom declined after King Rama Kamhang died in 1298. In 1350 a competing Thai capital was established some two hundred miles south at Ayuthaya. Over the next century Ayuthaya (also known as Siam) gradually absorbed what was left of Sukhothai. The Kingdom of Ayuthaya lasted over four hundred years and provided much of the political and cultural foundations for contemporary Thailand.

The concept of kingship in Ayuthaya was influenced by contacts with the declining empire of Angkor. Ayuthayan monarchs were less accessible and more autocratic than the patriarchal and earthly Sukhothai kings. In Ayuthaya the citizenry had to shut their windows and face away from the monarch when the king passed by, lest they risk a pellet in the eye from the bow of one of the king's guards. As at Angkor, the Thai Buddhist kings laid out their capitals and palaces in cosmological fashion so as to match the universal order as described in Hindu tradition. The people of the Ayuthayan kingdom were also organized hierarchically by means of an elaborate scheme in which the rank of every citizen, from king to slave, was measured by an intricate system of status marks known as *sakdi na* (power over fields). The *sakdi na* system was abolished in the nineteenth century, but to this day Thailand remains a status-oriented society that shows the system's lingering influence.

The Ayuthayan kingdom fell to the Burmese in 1767. The capital was plundered so heavily that its once magnificent buildings were reduced to rubble and never rebuilt. The Thai martial leaders who restored the Siamese kingdom established new capitals further down the river. King Taksin established the capital in Thonburi. Then, in 1782, the first king of the Chakri dynasty, Rama I, moved the capital across the river to Bangkok, where the Chakri kings continue to reign as the sovereigns of the Thai people.

Sulu Sultanate

Histories of Southeast Asia often ignore the great Malay maritime states that were based on trading, slaving, and raiding. One of the most prominent of these states was the Sulu Sultanate, a Muslim kingdom that arose in the fifteenth century and survived well into the 1800s. The Sulu state was based in a chain of islands in the southwest Philippines just northeast of Borneo. The Sulu civilization was based on a society of boat-dwelling nomadic mariners (a way of life since abandoned). These wandering boatmen used the sea lanes for trade, communications, and wars. After the coming of Islam a centralized government was formed under the leadership of a sultan. The new sultanate was a "segmentary state" composed of sub-units. The leaders of these sub-units were bound to the center primarily through networks of person-to-person relationships similar to patron-client ties.

European writings are the main source of information about the Sulu Sultanate. These writings suggest that from the seventeenth to the nineteenth centuries the sultanate's major activities were piracy and slavery. This claim should not be taken out of context. The Sulu world's complicated patterns of social life and economic activity truly did include a form of slavery. Because power depended on control over persons, land, and trade, the state sanctioned raiding and the recruitment of slaves from dependent communities. However, instead of focusing solely on piracy and slavery, as the contemporary Europeans did, we should also note the Sulu Sultanate's qualities as a sophisticated state that built a huge political infrastructure and a coastal trading network.

Following Spain's colonization of the Philippines in the 1500s, the various peoples living in Sulu fought continuously against the Spanish. The sultanate's power did not collapse until the Spanish colonizers ended all shipping to the Sulu archipelago. Even then, the sultanate remained unsubdued. In 1898 the Philippines passed from the Spanish to the Americans, and in the early 1900s American troops invaded the sultanate and took control of the capital in Jolo town. In 1915, the sultan formally relinquished his administrative power, although he retained a religious role.

Western Colonization

From the earliest civilizations to the present-day Southeast Asians have had continual interaction with external societies. They have shown a remarkable capacity to retain the integrity of their indigenous cultures while choosing which aspects of foreign cultures to assimilate. Southeast Asians have been great borrowers, but they have always adapted outside ways to produce their own unique forms and institutions. By the sixteenth century the forces of Hinduism, Buddhism, and Islam had shaped every aspect of life in Southeast Asia, but their forms were different there than in India. European colonialism had a more direct impact than the Indians did, yet in the larger stream of things, the Europeans were just another cultural influence. Therefore, despite the many changes that it brought, colonialism merely disturbed the overall flow of Southeast Asian history. Colonialism drastically altered the sociopolitical systems of the elites, but continuity and autonomy prevailed among the majority of the people.

In the early 1500s, the map of Southeast Asia bore little if any resemblance to the nation-state system found today. The area consisted of numerous small kingdoms lacking formally delineated boundaries. Instead of working to define stable borders, the rulers focused on enhancing the health and prestige of the realms' cosmological centers. The kingdoms continually clashed as they competed for land, people, and trade. The scope of each polity's sovereignty fluctuated as kingdoms rose and fell in the region's constantly shifting networks of power relations.

Western colonialism began in 1511 when Malacca was captured by Portuguese mariners sailing east from Europe, Africa, and India. For nearly a century, the Portuguese were a dominant power throughout the region. But the Portuguese trading empire was soon displaced by other European powers, until the Portuguese were left with only a few outposts.

The Spanish arrived shortly after the Portuguese. By 1571 the Spanish had taken control of the Philippines, thereby halting the northward spread of Islam. They colonized the islands for nearly four hundred years. The most famous explorer for the Spanish monarchs was Ferdinand Magellan, who had been sent to find a new route to the Spice Islands (eastern Indonesia). Sailing west from Spain and the Americas in an expedition that would be the first to circle the globe, Magellan landed unexpectedly in 1521 on Mactan Island in the central Philippines. There he was killed by Lapulapu, the indigenous leader of Mactan. The Spanish colonialists erected a monument that said:

> to glorify God, Spain, and Ferdinand Magellan.

In the twentieth century the Philippine Republic erected its own monument:

> Here, on 27 April, 1521, Lapulapu and his men repulsed the Spanish invaders, killing their leader, Ferdinand Magellan. Thus, Lapulapu became the first Filipino to have repelled European aggression.

The two divergent statements indicate the vastly different perceptions of Europeans and Southeast Asians regarding the arrival of the Westerners.

English and Dutch adventurers and merchants arrived in Southeast Asia in the late sixteenth century. They initially voyaged to the region as members of chartered companies such as the East India Company. In 1602 the Dutch founded Batavia (now Jakarta), in western Java, which became a major trade center. The Dutch quickly established control over trade in the Indonesian archipelago. Over the centuries they gradually took territorial control as well. The British, on the other hand, moved into Southeast Asia more gradually. At first they were more concerned with expanding control in India, and in Southeast Asia they preoccupied themselves with trade. But in the middle and late 1800s they also established territorial sovereignty in several areas. In step-by-step stages they took over Burma, Malaya, Brunei, and Singapore. The takeover of Burma was particularly significant because it shored up Britain's empire against threats from dissident Indians (who themselves were under British rule) and because it gave the British a powerful presence in the heart of mainland Southeast Asia. The takeover of Malaya and Singapore was important because it gave the British a stronghold at the crossroads of Southeast Asian trade.

By the 1850s, European colonialism was well under way, though much of Southeast Asia remained independent. Few of the classical

Southeast Asian kingdoms still existed. Angkor, Pagan, Srivijaya, Sukhothai, Ayuthaya, and Majapahit had all fallen, although the Sulu Sultanate and the Vietnamese Empire remained. In Burma, new kingdoms and empires had risen in place of Pagan, but by 1850 the country's southern provinces were in the hands of the British. In Thailand the Bangkok-based Siamese kingdom that replaced Ayuthaya was in control of present-day Thailand along with most of present-day Laos, northern Malaysia, and western Cambodia. Siam and Vietnam were sparring over what was left of Cambodia.

In the late nineteenth century the rest of Southeast Asia rapidly fell under European control. The Dutch completed their conquest of the East Indies. The British conquered the rest of Burma and extended their "protection" to the Malay sultanates. The Americans took the Philippines from the Spanish, and the French took Vietnam, Cambodia, and Laos.

French colonialists arrived in the mid-nineteenth century, and they soon took control of the area that became known as French Indochina (Cambodia, Laos, and Vietnam). Religious freedom was the pretext for colonization. French Catholic priests had arrived in the previous century. The Vietnamese government was displeased when the priests began gaining converts, so in the middle 1800s it imprisoned and even killed some of the priests. In 1858 a French naval force was sent to Vietnam to obtain religious liberty for the priests, and the French soon began establishing territorial control. In 1863, Cambodia accepted French protection to avoid being swallowed by Thailand and Vietnam. By 1867 the French had occupied Saigon and the southernmost part of Vietnam (this area became known as Cochin China). In 1884 France took control of the rest of Vietnam, splitting the country into three sections. The French formally colonized Cochin China (Vietnam's southern area), while Annam (the central area) and Tonkin (the northern area) became French protectorates (that is, the emperor stayed on the throne while the French took most of the power). At the end of the century Laos was absorbed into French Indochina to keep it from being dominated by the Thais.

Thailand, then known as Siam, was the only Southeast Asian kingdom to remain independent. In their negotiations with the French and English, the Thai monarchs, principally King Mongkut (ruled 1851 to 1868) and his son King Chulalongkorn (ruled 1868 to 1910), convinced the Europeans that if Siam remained independent it could be a buffer between the French on the east and the British on the west. Both to impress the Europeans and to satisfy their own vision of the country's needs, these kings launched modernization efforts, abolished slavery, provided for effective budgeting, built schools, and rationalized the bureaucracy. The Thai also gave up territory in Laos, Cambodia, and Malaya to appease the western imperialists.

By 1913 the westerners had divided up Southeast Asia with boundaries that have lasted until the present. In the four centuries of colonial expansion, a period lasting from the early 1500s to the post-World War II era, the British had conquered the areas now called Malaysia, Singapore, Brunei, and Burma while the French came to control present-day Laos, Cambodia, and Vietnam. The Indonesian islands were incorporated into the Netherlands Indies, while the Philippines were colonized first by the Spanish and later by the United States. The Portuguese who had begun the colonial era now controlled only East Timor. Siam had escaped formal colonization.

The motivations for imperialism varied. Governments and private corporations were seeking to exploit natural resources and cheap labor for economic gain. Merchants went abroad to make their fortunes. The politicians and militarists who came in their wake sought to consolidate business holdings, "bring civilization" to the natives, and add to the motherland's power and glory. Meanwhile, missionaries tried to convert the people to Christianity.

Colonial rule differed from country to country, but several common elements can be discerned. First, colonial rule eventually resulted in the formation of territorially stable nation-states that had definite boundaries and fostered notions of common nationality. Prior to the coming of the westerners, the Southeast Asians had not been concerned about boundaries, ethnicity, or nationhood. Many of the kingdoms had been ethnically and culturally plural states held together by the center's fluctuating ability to attract followers. The European imperialists established clearly delimited boundaries whose security they guaranteed, thereby introducing a sense of stability and order to the region. But the arbitrary boundaries they established show that the Europeans were more concerned with defining spheres of influence than with reflecting the region's ethnic makeup. The new boundaries often cut through the territory inhabited by particular ethnic groups. For example, the inhabitants of northeast Thailand are ethnically Lao, the southernmost provinces of Thailand are populated by Malay Muslims, and the northern provinces are peopled with Shan, Karen, and other hill groups that have ethnic affinity with groups in Burma. Some Malay groups lived in both Malaysia and Indonesia. The island of Timor was divided between the Dutch and Portuguese.

In addition to establishing modern boundaries, colonialism was also responsible for the growth of modern economics. A money economy was introduced and labor was organized for the production of raw materials. Ports, railways, and roads were built as infrastructure for the movement of goods and resources. The colonialists also built hospitals (which improved health conditions), and schools (which taught Western academic subjects). Ironically, many of the Western-trained students later became anti-Western nationalist leaders.

Economic development changed the region's ethnic makeup. The new plantations and mines required large numbers of skilled and unskilled laborers, but the Southeast Asian peasants found factory labor crude and antithetical to traditional values. Consequently, the colonialists imported Chinese and Indians to work in the factories, the tin mines, and the rubber, sugar, and coffee plantations. The Chinese and Indian immigrants eventually became traders and businessmen, and today they continue to enjoy economic power far beyond their numbers.

Under colonialism a plural economy developed. A minority of the inhabitants got rich by producing on a large scale for world markets while the majority remained dependent on subsistence agriculture and produced for local consumption. This plural economy created a growing gulf between the rich urban-oriented aristocrats and bureaucrats and the poor rural peasants. The former became part of the money economy, while the latter continued producing for their own subsistence needs.

The urban centers were transformed by the colonial economy. Rural areas were less directly affected, but they were also changed in important ways. The peasants were systematically exploited both by the Europeans and by the indigenous aristocrats, and rural land was appropriated for new plantations producing coffee, sugar, and rubber. With the growth of plantation agriculture, a new agricultural proletariat arose whose survival depended on money lenders and urban landowners.

Colonialism in the Philippines

Before the Spaniards arrived in the 1500s, the Philippine islands were home to many diverse, dispersed groups. There was no unified single Philippine civilization. Instead, there were many separate agricultural, hunting, and fishing communities, some of them nomadic, and all of them fiercely independent. Filipinos lived in *barangays,* village communities consisting of about thirty extended families. (In contrast to the nuclear family of parents and children, extended families include parents, children, grandparents, aunts and uncles, and other close relatives.) The religion of the islands was animism. The people propitiated potentially useful (yet potentially harmful) spirits that were believed to dwell in trees, houses, and the fields. Evil spirits were kept at bay by amulets worn on the body.

Many aspects of modern-day Philippine society stem from Spanish rule. Under the Spanish, most Filipinos became Catholic Christians. Today over 90 percent of the population is Christian. Another product of Spanish rule is the feudalistic economic system that concentrates financial power in the hands of a few Spanish-Chinese-Filipino families.

The United States took control of the Philippines in the wake of the brief but important Spanish-American War of 1898. The Filipinos had already been fighting vigorously against the Spanish, and they initially hoped to ally with the American newcomers. The American navy defeated the Spanish fleet, and it also facilitated the return of Aguinaldo, a Philippine revolutionary leader who had been exiled a few years earlier. By the end of the Spanish-American war the Filipino revolutionaries controlled most of the country. But in the peace negotiations the Americans and Spaniards agreed to transfer the Philippines to the United States. The United States landed troops at Manila and fought a sham battle with the Spanish defenders, ostensibly to convince the Filipinos that the Americans had saved them from the Spanish. Fighting soon broke out throughout the islands as the Filipinos rose against the United States in a guerrilla war that lasted almost four years until the Americans gained full control.

The American colonial regime was in some respects the most enlightened in Southeast Asia. The Americans felt a responsibility to "uplift and civilize" the Filipinos. They also desired to reproduce in the Philippines a republic modeled on the American style of democracy, and they partially succeeded in this goal. However, the Americans also exploited the country economically. They went to the Philippines to exploit the nation's natural resources, including sugar and fruit, and to have a base for the lucrative China trade. The legacy of the colonial economy continues to affect the islands.

On the plus side, the American administrators implemented massive programs to build economic infrastructure. They also brought in health care, fostered American-style democracy, and made widely available a level of education that had formerly been enjoyed only by aristocrats. When the United States left the Philippines, fully 65 percent of Filipinos were literate (up from 5 percent at the end of Spanish rule). Filipinos continue to value the democratic government and secularized education brought by the Americans.

On the minus side, under American rule the country's wealth continued to concentrate in the hands of a few top families. In addition, the Americans exploited the country's natural resources. The Philippines became economically and culturally dependent on the United States as the Philippine economy was assimilated into the American economy. American products became status symbols while Filipino products were deemed third-rate.

Over the years, nationalist sentiment continued to grow among the Filipinos. The Americans promised eventual independence, but World War II intervened before the target date. During the Japanese occupation from 1942 to 1945, most of the elite collaborated with the Japanese, but the country's top leaders went into exile with America's General

MacArthur, and the mass of the people supported the Filipino guerrilla resistance. The experience of resisting the Japanese strengthened nationalist sentiments even further. After the war, some of this sentiment and experience was turned against the Americans.

The Philippines proclaimed independence on July 4, 1946, but with a number of arrangements, including free trade agreements, which enabled the United States to maintain economic dominance. The ruling elites who desired to retain their economic power cooperated with the Americans to stay in power. Nevertheless, the postwar Philippines had more freedom of speech and of the press than existed in any other Southeast Asian nation. A two-party system developed with free competition between the parties. The presidency fluctuated from one party to another until 1969, when Ferdinand Marcos became the first president to be re-elected. Three years later, Marcos made arrangements to keep himself in power indefinitely.

Despite the islands' economic development under American administration, many Filipinos were still poor at the time of independence, and the devastation of World War II had made them poorer. During the 1940s and 1950s the low standard of living was responsible for one of the largest and most important peasant rebellions in contemporary Southeast Asia. Known as the Hukbalahap (Huk) rebellion, this peasant movement had roots in smaller uprisings in the past, and it still plays a role in Philippine politics. The Huk rebellion began as an anti-Japanese movement but eventually became a nationalist, anti-American, and anti-Philippine-government guerrilla resistance. The rebel leaders demanded fundamental changes in the feudalistic economic system that exploited farmers and enriched elites. They demanded better conditions, a larger share of the harvest, and fairness. Their struggle had almost universal peasant support. The United States government provided sizable support to the Philippine government's efforts to suppress the Huks, because the rebellion occurred at the height of the cold war, when Americans were concerned about fighting the spread of communism. The Americans feared communist domination of the Huk movement, though in fact the Huks were remarkably free from communist influence. By the late 1950s, the peasantry had been exhausted by the struggle, and the rebellion petered out. But the Huk insurgency remained important in the national consciousness. Filipino presidents proceeded to give lip service to the rebellion's goals, though none of the Philippine governments have ever fundamentally reformed village conditions.

Revolutionary ferment remained important in later decades. The Communist Party of the Philippines (CPP) grew during the 1950s and 60s. The CPP's military arm, the New People's Army (NPA), has now been carrying out insurgency activities for four decades. The NPA's strength has come from disillusioned peasants, especially tenant farmers and day laborers, whose hopes for a better life were lifted in the 1960s by Marcos's announcement of a New Society and then dashed by his unfulfilled promises. In 1986 Corazon Aquino's rise to the presidency weakened the NPA, as she promised meaningful land reform and improvement in the standard of living. Aquino's promises also proved empty. Yet by 1999 the domestic communist threat had ebbed even though rural Filipinos remained poor.

Nationalism

The development of nationalism was perhaps colonialism's most important consequence. Nationalism is a sense of strong identification with and feeling toward the nation. Southeast Asian nationalism arose as a result of the colonialist conception of the nation-state. It also included an anticolonial sentiment and a desire to emphasize traditional indigenous ways. The classical kingdoms had been nonintegrated dynastic principalities, but the new nations created within the colonial boundaries were unified territorial states. In addition, in one of the major ironies of Southeast Asian history, most of the leaders of the nationalist movements were indigenous intellectuals who had been trained in the West or in colonially established schools. These intellectuals were inculcated with Western values only to become the spokesmen for anti-Western nationalist doctrines. Their observations of the colonialists also taught them how to organize.

The anti-colonial nationalists were an organized, effective leadership group that could mobilize the peasantry. Nationalist intellectuals articulated the importance of a broad, nation-wide perspective that transcended narrow clan or village identities. Steeped in appreciation of Western technology, they argued that industrialization was the only path to eventual independence. They expressed contempt for the land-owning aristocracy who had fared so well under colonialism and who now opposed the nationalists.

In Indonesia the nationalist movement began in the early 1900s, responding, ironically, to a period of relatively enlightened rule in which the Dutch were seeking to liberalize the political system. In the Philippines, the nationalists arose against what they considered the patronizing attitudes of the Americans, who considered Filipinos to be their "little brown brothers."

The Vietnamese provide a particularly outstanding example of the anti-colonial dynamic. The nationalist revolt in Vietnam reacted to the French policy of economic exploitation, *corvée* (forced) labor, and control over huge estates at the expense of the impoverished peasantry. Vietnamese nationalist resistance to French rule was initially led by "mandarins" who viewed the French as usurpers of their power. However, as French rule was consolidated and French economic interests increasingly dominated urban life, the mandarins found they could profit from closer ties with the colonialists. Soon the peasantry was forced to toil for both its French and its elite Vietnamese masters. Peasant taxes were increased to pay for the huge colonial budget, and peasant life was worse under the French rule than under the previous feudal regimes. Though the mandarins had begun to collaborate, other groups continued to protest French rule. In the early 1900s communist groups became active, and they eventually took over leadership of the nationalist movement. In 1939, the Vietnamese communist leader Ho Chi Minh united several groups into a nationalist front group known as the Vietminh. At the end of World War II the Vietminh took control from the defeated Japanese occupation forces. They fought the returning French for eight years.

Thailand's nationalism was unique because the country was never colonized. Thai nationalism lacked the visceral anti-western ideology common to the movements in other nations. It focused instead on issues of modernity and ethnicity. In 1932 a group of officials and military officers rid the country of its "anachronistic" system of government by overthrowing the absolute monarchy. The kings became constitutional monarchs and henceforth the government was run by military and civilian rulers. In 1939, Prime Minister Phibun Songkram changed the name of the country from Siam to Thailand, ostensibly to draw attention to the national pride of the ethnic Thai. Phibun Songkram desired to unite all speakers of Thai and related languages, including related peoples such as the Lao in Laos.

World War II

On December 8, 1941 (December 7, American time), World War II came to Southeast Asia. Japanese forces attacked throughout the region. In just a few months the Europeans were expelled everywhere. In most areas the Japanese retained control until their defeat in 1945.

The Japanese conquest strengthened nationalist movements by shattering the myth of Western invincibility. At last, Asians had defeated Europeans. The Europeans would never again be viewed as invincible. The Japanese were viewed as fellow Asians and their accomplishments gave the Southeast Asian nationalists hope of achieving their own independence. The Japanese also placed more Southeast Asians in administrative positions.

However, Japanese occupation policies were harsh, especially in countries that had a significant Chinese population. The Chinese were especially savaged because Japan was already at war with China and they viewed the Southeast Asian Chinese as potential traitors. In many places the heavy-handed Japanese occupation sparked increasing resistance. In 1942 many Southeast Asians had seen a Japanese victory as inevitable, and they joined the Japanese because they wanted to be on the "winning" side. However, Japanese repression was so strong that Southeast Asians gradually moved toward hostility.

The response to Japanese rule differed from country to country. In some places the Japanese had received cooperation from independence movements. In Indonesia, the Japanese gained the good will of the citizenry by releasing imprisoned nationalist dissidents, such as Sukarno, the nation's future president. Sukarno then collaborated with the Japanese as a means of defeating the Dutch and moving toward independence. In Malaya, on the other hand, the Japanese avoided forming an "independent" government, primarily because they did not trust the large Chinese population. In still other countries, such as Burma, the Philippines, and Vietnam, the nation's future leaders were active in the anti-Japanese resistance, even though the Japanese had increased the local people's participation in the countries' administrations.

Japanese Occupation of Malaya

On December 8, 1941, Japanese troops moved into Malaya from the north. They rapidly advanced southward to the fortress of Singapore, which surrendered on February 15, 1942. Japan declared that Western colonialism had ended and that henceforth Asia would be ruled by Asians. However, the Japanese were more ruthless than the British, and wartime conditions were bad. Malaya suffered from economic chaos, food shortages, disease, and an absence of law and order.

When the British returned in 1945, they reinvigorated the economy and rationalized the administration. However, Malayans wanted to be sovereign in their own nation, and they eventually achieved independence in 1957.

Thailand was attacked along with the rest of Southeast Asia, but the country retained its "independence" by capitulating quickly, allowing the Japanese unfettered movement throughout the Kingdom, and declaring war against the allied powers. The Thai were therefore able to emerge from the war with their nation and people intact. After the war, Thailand convinced the Allies, particularly the Americans, that it should not be punished for joining the Japanese. The Thai indicated that "they hadn't really meant it" when they declared war against the United States, and as a result they were treated as a nation that had been occupied rather than as a nation that had fought on the wrong side of the war.

In the Philippines, many people fought valiantly against the Japanese, while others collaborated. Most of the common people opposed the Japanese occupation. The level of distrust increased each year, as Japanese brutality convinced most Filipinos that their lives had been better under the Americans than under their Asian "liberators." On the other hand, many Filipino administrators rallied to the Japanese because they thought that the Japanese would emerge victorious and because the Japanese encouraged local politicians to administer the nation. After the war these elite collaborators were able to continue their careers partly because the returning American general Douglas MacArthur believed that their expertise was needed to rebuild the country.

In Vietnam, resistance against the Japanese was a springboard to independence. By the end of the war the Vietminh forces led by Ho Chi Minh had created "liberated" zones in some parts of the country, and when the Japanese were defeated in August 1945, the Vietminh moved into the remaining areas. On September 2, 1945, Ho Chi Minh declared Vietnam's independence. The French did not respect Ho Chi Minh's declaration, and with financial support from the United States they sent troops to try to reestablish their former power in Indochina. The result was an eight year war between the French and the Vietnamese.

The Struggle for Independence

The Japanese defeat in 1945 opened the floodgates of nationalistic spirit and spurred demands for total independence. The nationalist leaders faced great odds. Southeast Asian nations emerged from World War II with their economic and political structures in shambles. Except for Thailand, each Southeast Asian nation also had to cope with the European nations' attempts to regain their lost colonies. Furthermore, the local leaders were in discord over the best way to secure independence and over the best kind of society to establish.

The road to independence differed from place to place. Indonesia and Vietnam declared independence immediately after Japan's defeat, and both had to fight the returning colonial powers. Indonesia fought for four years until the Dutch granted sovereignty in 1949. Vietnam's war lasted eight years until the French were defeated in 1954. Burma negotiated its independence, gaining sovereignty in 1948 without having to engage in war. Laos's and Cambodia's transitions to independence were smoother than Vietnam's, and the two countries were granted independence in the early 1950s. Malayans gained gradual self-government over a twelve-year period and in 1957 independence was granted to the Federation of Malaya. Singapore gained its independence the same year. Philippine independence had been promised since before the war, and in 1946 the country moved peacefully into its new status. Brunei did not want independence at all, and it remained a British colony until 1984.

The nationalists who initially led post-colonial Southeast Asia attacked Western dominance, but at the same time they adopted Western methods and outlooks as they proclaimed and exhibited their independent status. They also used nationalist ideology to integrate the countries' disparate peoples. Nationalist leaders had to deal with the competing desires of promoting local identity and of copying Western economic and political progress. On the one hand, they desired to retain traditional values and to be independent of the West. But on the other hand, they desired to adopt the nationalism, technology, and secularism of the developed Western societies.

A sense of euphoria accompanied the achievement of independence, but the good feelings did not last long. At first, the nationalist leaders worked primarily to build national unity and pride; day-to-day administrative and economic problems were treated as secondary concerns, although they soon became major issues. The uncertainty of the independence period stimulated expectations among the citizenry which could not possibly be met by governments that were still attempting to establish viable political structures. All of the Southeast Asian nations enjoyed a good measure of territorial integrity and were fairly successful at building national identity. However, there were growing tensions between the different generations of leaders. For example, in Indonesia the older "solidarity makers" such as President Sukarno clashed with younger, more pragmatic "administrators" such as Sukarno's successor Suharto.

Authoritarian regimes soon became the norm in much of Southeast Asia. By the 1970s military regimes ruled in Thailand, Cambodia, Burma, Indonesia, and South Vietnam; North Vietnam was under communist rule; and the Philippines and Laos were ruled by civilian dictatorships. In 1975, Laos and Cambodia passed to communist rule, while South Vietnam was united with the communist North. Only Malaysia and Singapore boasted even quasi-democratic governments.

Not until the 1990s did democracy became an important part of the region's politics. By the year 2000 Thailand, Indonesia, Singapore, Malaysia, and the Philippines were led by elected civilian leaders, and Cambodia was struggling with transition to democracy, while Burma, Laos, and Vietnam continued to be ruled by authoritarian regimes.

DISCUSSION QUESTIONS

1. What are the principal outside influences on Southeast Asian history? Do they affect history more or less than do indigenous leaders and events?

2. Why is Angkor considered one of the world's greatest civilizations?

3. How do Angkor, Srivijaya, Pagan, Sukhothai, and Malacca differ in their impact on modern Southeast Asia?

4. How did Western colonial rule differ from one Southeast Asian country to another? How did American imperialism in the Philippines differ from British, French, and Dutch colonialism in other Southeast Asian nations?

5. Why were the transitions to independence difficult for the Southeast Asian nations that had been colonized?

SUGGESTED READINGS

The standard textbook for understanding recent Southeast Asian history is David J. Steinberg, ed., *In Search of Southeast Asia* (University of Hawai'i Press, Honolulu, 1987). Steinberg has chosen famous scholars to discuss the major issues of Southeast Asian history, including colonialism, nationalism, and the region's move to independent status. A comprehensive history that includes the early years is D. G. E. Hall, *A History of South East Asia* (4th ed., St. Martin's Press, New York, 1981). For an interesting analysis of Angkor, see Ian Mabbett and David Chandler, *The Khmers* (Blackwell Publishers, Cambridge, Massachusetts, 1995). A new and important book by Anthony Reid is *Charting the Shape of Early Modern Southeast Asia* (Silkworm, Chiang Mai, 1999).

4

CULTURE

It is impossible to comprehend Southeast Asia without understanding the unique mix of values, beliefs, and attitudes that constitute the region's cultures. This chapter outlines the Southeast Asians' styles of religion, their notions about authority and personal relationships, and their family structures and home life. It also introduces some of the region's best-known literature, music, and celebrations. This chapter's discussions must be viewed in the context of Southeast Asian diversity, as there are variations to all the generalizations. Yet, despite the differences, there are many features that are shared across much of the region.

Religion

Buddhism, Islam, Animism, and Catholicism are the primary religions represented in Southeast Asia (see Chapter 2 for details on each). In practice, the local versions of these religions are syncretic, combining elements of many belief systems. Thus, the Thai version of Buddhism is closely intertwined with spirit worship and with elements of Hinduism. Similarly, the Islam of Indonesia, Malaysia, and the southern Philippines has adapted aspects of Hinduism, Buddhism, and Animism. The Catholicism of the Philippines is very different from that in the United States, Latin America, or Europe. Even in areas where people share the same religion, the rituals and customs of one village may differ greatly from those of a neighboring village.

Buddhism

Some analysts explain the behavior of Southeast Asians in terms of their religious beliefs. For example, the Thai emphasis on superior-subordinate relationships has been said to be based on the Buddhist concepts of merit and *karma*. Deference to authority is said to be explained by the Buddhist teaching that a person's lot in life is primarily a result of the virtue or immorality of his or her deeds in previous existences. People of high status are treated with respect because they are assumed to be good people who have obviously accumulated great merit in their past lives. These notions have been said to explain the political passivity of Buddhists in Thailand, Burma, and elsewhere. The Buddhist countries' low level of economic development (at least until recently) was similarly said to be rooted in a lack of greed and materialism, a mindset supposedly fostered by the Buddhist idea that desire and greed cause suffering. This devotion to religious pursuits was said to be demonstrated by the many magnificent temples in these countries.

Buddhadasa Bhukkhu

Thailand is a Buddhist nation with monks as the spiritual leaders. Buddhadasa Bhikkhu may have been the most influential of the monks.

Buddhadasa Bhikku was born in 1906 and died in 1993. In 1932 he founded Wat Suan Mokkhablarama, a beautiful forest monastery in southern Thailand. He founded Wat Suan after discovering that urban temples were not conducive to meditation and peacefulness. Much of Buddhadasa's fame comes from his aim to make Buddhism accessible to the layperson, combining traditional Buddhist teachings, Zen, science, and modern development. He was particularly eager to introduce friends, foreign and Thai, to the natural truth explained in the Buddha's teachings.

His works on Buddhism have been translated into many languages. He has taught thousands about the art of meditation and contemplation, featuring a technique of breathing as the focus of his teaching. Using his teachings, one can become sensitive to one's body, become calm, and learn to live in the present moment.

These explanations sound convincing, but they must be viewed cautiously. Buddhism is an important aspect of mainland cultures, but Buddhists have differing interpretations of their religion and display a wide range of motivations. Furthermore, deferential behavior was an operative force in Southeast Asia even before Buddhism was firmly established, though Buddhism may have strengthened this already existing behavior. We must be equally careful of religious explanations for economic behavior. The Buddhist who builds a temple may appear to be spiritually ascetic, but in his own way he may be as materialistic as the person who spends his money on material goods. Temple-building is a good way to accumulate merit, so the Buddhist donor may be trying to guarantee a more comfortable life in his next existence instead of striving for self-perfection or the quenching of desire. It is important not to judge by appearances.

Nevertheless, Buddhism contributes to the social fabric in a variety of ways. Buddhism provides a sense of national unity and identification that helps foster social stability and unity (the Thai often define themselves first and foremost as Buddhists). Buddhism's inherent tolerance, flexibility, and lack of rigid dogma may have encouraged the spirit of compromise that is a hallmark of the politics of Buddhist Southeast Asian nations, and the Buddhist emphasis on serenity and virtue may have mitigated the violence of rulers toward the ruled. (There are clear exceptions, as in Cambodia during the rule of the violent Khmer Rouge [see Chapter 6], but in that case, the rulers eschewed Buddhism.) Finally, Southeast Asian Buddhism is said to be attuned to the village environment, an agrarian society with relatively simple patterns of social, economic, and political interaction.

Modernization has placed considerable strain on these traditional patterns. Urbanization and industrialization have upset the Buddhists' ritual rhythms. In addition, the communist Vietnamese, Lao, and (for a time) Cambodian governments systematically tried to destroy the Buddhist teachings, harassing the monks and turning the temples into rice storage centers. Thus, modernization and oppressive regimes are making the future of Buddhism problematic. The irony is that Buddhism, with its emphasis on individualism, moderation, ethical values, and serenity, could be especially relevant and promising for human welfare in the fast-changing Southeast Asian world.

Figure 7. Buddhist temple in Bangkok

Islam

Islam in Southeast Asian is even more determining of behavior than is Buddhism. Indonesian self-identity is not simply a function of ideological or personal predispositions but is a function of deep-rooted religious and socioeconomic affinities. Indonesia is not formally an Islamic state, but the religion's many rules govern almost all aspects of life. The three variations of Islam (Santri, Abangan, and Prijaji [see Chapter 2]) are central to understanding Indonesian life, as political parties and socioeconomic interest groups are influenced by these religious divisions. In all social and political upheavals, the role of Islam has played an important role in determining winners and losers.

Islam is also important in Malaysia. In Malay villages Islam has provided social integration through communally shared prayers, rituals, rites, and festivals. A religious element is also central to Malaysians' political orientations. The ruling alliance has displayed a preference for moderate attitudes, beliefs, and values, but the principal opposition leaders are strict Muslims who link their religious doctrines to political objectives.

Islam has contributed to Malay ethnic solidarity, but it has also been a major reason for the communal split between Malay Muslims and Chinese non-Muslims. The term "communalism" refers to politics framed in terms of ethnic and religious differences. The tensions between the two groups have been primarily economic, but religious differences also underlie the bad feelings. It is difficult to find solutions to the problem, because religious and ethnic issues are often one and the same. In Malaysia, adherence to Islam provides opportunities not available to non-Muslims. The Chinese have much influence over business, but many professions are now reserved exclusively for Malay Muslims. Malays are also provided special privileges in government service, education, trade, and property. In addition, the increasing use of religion in politics, while popular among many Muslims, has alienated non-Muslims, as the Chinese in particular feel threatened by the religious emphasis.

Animism

Animism is ubiquitous in Southeast Asia, where it coexists with other religious traditions. Spirit worship offers an important and sometimes more satisfying alternative to the teachings of the mainstream religions. For example, in contrast to the Buddhist teaching of individual responsibility, spirit worship places the blame for suffering on malicious spirits rather than on the sufferers themselves. Southeast Asians propitiate the spirits by building spirit houses and by engaging in rituals that include chants. They also wear amulets or strings designed to protect them from malicious spirits. Spirit doctors are utilized to exorcize disease and evil. Meanwhile, astrologers are consulted for auspicious times to begin feeding rice to a baby or to promulgate new constitutions. In Thailand, the first name given to a baby is often an ugly one, such as Little Rat, to fool the capricious spirits into thinking the newborn is unloved so they will not covet the baby and take it away.

In many Southeast Asian nations supernatural beliefs play an important role in politics. For example, Indonesian President Sukarno (ruled 1949 to 1965) consciously surrounded himself with the trappings of the mystical world in order to endear himself to his followers through the suggestion of supernatural powers. His successor, President Suharto, adhered more conventionally to Muslim beliefs. Yet Suharto consulted traditional gurus and mystical leaders before making important decisions, and like Sukarno he cloaked himself in the symbols of the mystical world. For example, the decree naming Suharto president was titled Supersemar, an ingenious reference to Semar, an important mystical character in the Mahabharta epic. Semar regularly flouted aristocratic rule, and Suharto's identification with him was an attempt to enhance his own credentials as the people's leader.

In Malaysia, as in many other Southeast Asian countries, spirit worship and belief in magical powers are interwoven with the agricultural cycle. Ceremonies are held to drive the evil spirits from the fields and to find the most propitious time to begin planting. A person's entire life cycle is thought to be affected by magic. Rituals are performed to assure safe births and the correct naming of a baby. Also important are the rites of puberty and marriage and the arrangement of proper funerals. Many diseases are said to be caused by supernatural forces, and cures are carried out by magical practices.

Personalism and Authority Relationships

Personal ties between social superiors and inferiors are important to most Southeast Asians, and they are a fundamental element of social organization. This focus on personalism stands in contrast to the Western focus on laws and formal organizations. Personalism occurs in societies where there are marked inequalities in wealth and status and where institutions such as bureaucracies, political parties, interest groups, and the rule of law are not available. Southeast Asians form relationships with people of higher status to achieve benefits they could not have otherwise. Scholars call these hierarchical, face-to-face relationships "patron-client" ties. The patron-client ties are inter-linked and thereby help integrate the society at all levels.

These patron-client ties are not visible to the eye nor can they be precisely articulated even by those involved. Rather, the patron-client notion is an idealization that shows how societies are integrated. The belief that personal ties are important and effective causes Southeast Asians to seek the support of patrons higher in the socio-economic hierarchy who can assure them access to necessities such as food, education, housing, and a job. Meanwhile, patrons enhance their own status and influence by building client entourages among people lower in the hierarchy.

The patrons' need to provide benefits to their clients has been a major cause of corruption, as public office has been used for private gain and for the support of clients. In the 1970s, the clientele-ist nature of the Philippine society was especially evident in President Marcos's granting of monopoly privileges to selected followers. Yet weakening these patron-client ties is not necessarily a good thing. For centuries the traditional Filipino patron-client ties had bound together the rich and the poor in a mutually beneficial pattern. When Westernization weakened these inter-class ties, the still-poor Philippine peasants lost an important means of support.

There have always been other organizing elements in Southeast Asian societies, and they are increasingly important today. Alongside the hierarchical relationships there are clan ties and friendships among social equals. The organization of Southeast Asian societies has also been affected by formal laws, force (as in Burma and Vietnam), and the introduction of democratic procedures such as voting. Today modernization is weakening the importance of patron-client relationships as new government and private institutions provide services formally available solely from elites. Nevertheless, personalism remains an important element of Southeast Asian social and political organization.

Personalism and authority play out differently in each of the Southeast Asian cultures. In the Philippines, reciprocity is an important element of patron-client relationships. In these reciprocal relationships, there is a state of indebtedness between giver and receiver that is called *utang na loob* (debt of gratitude). One must repay an *utang na loob,* even with interest, but the repayment may be fundamentally different from the original debt. For example, a farmer who helped his neighbor till the field may receive a gift of cash in return. Failure to repay an *utang na loob* debt causes shame and embarrassment (*hiya*). Those who fail to meet their debt can be ostracized. *Utang na loob* is so strongly felt that Filipino bystanders may be unwilling to "interfere" when a stranger is in distress, so as not to place the afflicted person under obligation. For their part, the distressed persons may not even want help, because they do not want to incur *utang na loob* if they can manage without assistance.

Philippine personalism is also manifested in non-kin ties called *compadrazgo*. These ties usually involve godparents (*compadre)* who take special responsibility for children's welfare. The Catholic church originally intended the system to provide for children's spiritual upbringing, but *compadrazgo* has evolved into a reciprocity pattern in which a member of a higher-status family acts as a godfather and thereby provides support to a member of a lower-status family. The lower-status family develops an especially high degree of *utang na loob* toward the *compadre*.

The *compadrazgo* system was once a crucial element of Filipino political life, and it was exploited by both the *compadres* and the families. For example, a candidate for public office would be asked to sponsor a marriage or newborn baby in return for the family's support in elections. The family then had the right to seek patronage from its new *compadre*. Politicians were desirous of becoming sponsors as a way of ensuring a wide base of electoral support, and politics came to be based on the system of reciprocal personal relations. Formal institutions were often ignored, because Filipinos knew they could rely more effectively on interpersonal ties to have their needs met. Similarly, tenant farmers felt indebted to the landlords who had provided the farmers with jobs, so they carried out their *utang na loob* by voting for candidates favored by the landlords. With the advent of more democratic institutions, this system of sponsorship and obligation has become less influential, but the general notion is still found throughout the archipelago.

Related to personalism is the Philippine notion of *pakikisama*, or smooth interpersonal relations. Filipinos stress the value of being polite and nonconfrontational and look disdainfully on those who are rude. Community issues are often left unsolved because the people involved are reluctant to confront one another. Substance is secondary to style. For example, people who raise their voices publicly automatically lose face and legitimacy. The only people exempt from the expectations of *pakikisama* are individuals who are high enough in the hierarchy to act arrogantly without concern for the sensitivities of others.

Relationships in Indonesia, as in the Philippines, are founded on reciprocity. This is clearly seen in the Javanese tradition of *gotong rojong*, a term that means "mutual aid." *Gotong rojong* is the cornerstone of mutual cooperation among peasants as they help each other in the fields or as they engage in any other activities that require cooperation to succeed. *Gotong rojong* is an important aspect of village unity and it provides a sense of community. Just as Filipinos who forget their debts of gratitude may be shunned, so also may Indonesians who do not engage in *gotong rojong* suffer ostracism.

Also like the Philippines, Indonesia is a society where vertical alignments predominate and where there is a high degree of social stratification between patrons and clients. In Indonesia the hierarchical social system is known as *bapakisme*, or "fatherism." The Javanese, in particular, place much value on deference to people of superior status such as members of the aristocracy. Indeed, when Javanese meet, each automatically recognizes the other's relative status, speaking and acting accordingly. In *bapakisme* there is emphasis on the subordinates' automatic acceptance of their superiors' decrees. Subordinates accept superiors' decisions simply because they know their "proper" role behavior as followers.

In Indonesia, as elsewhere in Southeast Asia, the emphasis on authority and hierarchy contrasts with the Western stress on bureaucratic and industrial efficiency. It also contrasts with the Western notion that subordinates should question superiors' policies as a means of improving their effectiveness. Indonesians tend to distrust persons engaged in frenetic activity. In Java traditional authority does not require persuasion, rewards, or sanctions. Instead, the Javanese respect cultured persons of status who are *halus* (refined) and whose every desire is anticipated and obeyed by their subordinates and followers. Indonesians feel a debt to their superiors (*hutang budi*), a debt of moral obligation which strengthens the patron-client ties.

Patron-client ties are also important in Thailand, even though they are less prominent than they were twenty years ago. Patrons are expected to be compassionate and kind. They are to protect, compliment, and give practical support to their clients. In return, the clients are expected to act deferentially to patrons, performing their tasks efficiently with the least amount of trouble for their superiors. A traditional virtue in Thailand is *kreng jai,* or not wanting to trouble or embarrass another person. Because they feel *kreng jai,* subordinates often find ways to get their needs met without going directly to their patrons.

In Thailand, as in the rest of Southeast Asia, the patron-client relationship is not one of perfect balance, despite the reciprocal nature of the tie, because the client feels obligated to the patron. If individuals have great needs but few resources, the person who can supply what is needed attains power over the recipient. Therefore, the patron has the predominant power over the client. However, excessive demands by patrons may cause their clients to seek new patrons. In contrast to Indonesia, where authority patterns are highly stable, and to the Philippines, where the sense of shame (*hiya*) keeps ties relatively strong, the Thai move relatively easily from one set of bonds to another. Hence there is little commitment to any particular patron-client grouping. Both patrons and clients continually assess the advantages and disadvantages of the relationship to determine whether it offers the greatest possible rewards.

In Thailand, a striking aspect of the patron-client relationship is the leeway it allows for individual action. The Thai conform in the presence of their superiors, but at other times they do as they like. This tension between Thai "spontaneity" and "conformity" stems from the dual socialization process that Thai people experience in their formative years. In Thai families, the socialization process emphasizes freedom and individualism, but in the schools and the political system socialization emphasizes dependence and authoritarianism.

Authority relations are just as important in Vietnam and Singapore as they are in the rest of Southeast Asia. Vietnamese attitudes and beliefs have been shaped by the Confucianist philosophy that has pervaded Vietnam for centuries. Confucianism is also important to the predominantly Chinese Singaporeans, who brought the tradition from China when migrating to their small island-state. Confucianism stressed principles of government that emphasized centralized political authority. The emperor was at the top and a mandarin bureaucracy administered the state according to the emperor's whims. Traditional Vietnamese culture rested upon the notion of duties of the lower to the higher: the ruled to the ruler, the son to the father, and the pupil to the teacher. Individuals did not view themselves as independent and isolated persons, for they did not distinguish themselves as individuals from their position in the society. Obligations to superiors were the cement of the Confucian order. These obligations were translated into a deferential and unquestioning behavior toward those in authority that was very much like the *bapakisme* system in Indonesia.

According to traditional Vietnamese ideas, there is a universal moral order that remains in harmony as long as all persons carry out their duties by fulfilling the obligations of subordinate to superior and vice versa. The emperors are as obligated to rule according to moral principles as peasants are to follow their commands. When harmony does not exist, or when there are wars, pestilence, or natural calamities, the ruled may perceive that the emperor has lost the "mandate of heaven." At these times the personal virtue of the emperors is thought to be lacking, for otherwise the cosmos would not be out of harmony.

The Confucianist concept of the mandate of heaven is important for illuminating authority relationships in Vietnam. The cosmological beliefs of the Vietnamese are essentially conservative, since the mandate of heaven is lost or gained largely by fortuitous means that are beyond the control of individuals. On the other hand, this cosmological view can provide a rationale for rebellion, because when the emperors lack virtue and when society and the cosmos fall into disorder, the ruler's mandate is perceived as lost and his rule is called into question. The transfer of the mandate of heaven is proven by the rise of a new revolutionary government, totally in control, that replaces the previous regime's doctrines and leadership. The victory of the communist government in April 1975 was the most recent example of such a total change. The communist triumph caused authority relationships to shift rapidly and traumatically to the new communist rulers.

In this emphasis on hierarchical relations the Confucian social order is similar to other Southeast Asian societies. But other aspects of Confucian social organization are very different. The cosmological scheme based on *yin* and *yang* is unique to the Vietnamese, the Singaporeans, and the overseas Chinese, among whom it has suffused every aspect of life and thought. *Yin* and *yang* are two forces from which everything else in the universe was created. The two coexist and are necessary for each other. They are opposed but complementary. *Yin* emphasizes egalitarianism, femininity, flexibility, and emotion. *Yang* emphasizes male dominance, hierarchy, competition, and orthodoxy. When a balance exists between *yin* and *yang*, harmony is assured.

The world view of the Vietnamese is intimately associated with these cosmological notions of *yin* and *yang*. Just as a Confucian ruler can be undermined by the mandate of heaven, so also could people lose faith in *yang*-style authority if it is not balanced with *yin* flexibility. Most Americans did not understand this world view when the decision was made to send millions of soldiers to Vietnam in the 1960s and 70s. Ngo Dinh Diem, the leader of South Vietnam from 1954 to 1963, had a mystical belief in his *yang* model of Vietnamese society. He was Catholic rather than Buddhist, but he had been imbued with Confucianist views his entire life. He expected to be obeyed because he believed himself a morally superior person who had the mandate of heaven.

Diem never understood Saigon, a *yin* city filled with heterodoxy, opposition, a multitude of sects, and societal chaos. Diem made himself unpopular by attempting to thrust his *yang* brand of homogeneity and authority on Saigon. He also engaged in blatant nepotism and was blind to the rising rebellion against him. The *yin* forces of the intellectuals grew in Saigon and indeed throughout the southern region of Vietnam as oppositionists gave speeches and wrote books, articles, and poetry that were explicitly anti-Diem. Eventually, the opposition became so strong that even Diem's American backers became disenchanted with him.

Southeast Asia is changing rapidly as modernization has arrived. Westernization undermined the importance of patron-client relationships as it fostered the establishment of formal institutions that took the place of personal relationships. As the region becomes more a part of the global economy and western influences, notions such as *yang* and *yin* are also losing importance as determinants of daily behavior. Yet, despite their lessening importance, patron-client ties continue to play an integrating role in Southeast Asian societies.

Asian Values

The notion of Asian values is an argument that Asian society and politics should continue to be structured hierarchically. This notion was set forth by authoritarian Asian leaders such as Singapore's Senior Minister Lee Kuan Yew, Malaysian Prime Minister Mahathir Mohammad, the Burmese military junta led by Than Shwe, and former Indonesian President Suharto. They argued that the free competition of ideas and interests that marks liberal democratic politics is inappropriate for

Asians, who they said were less advanced and more interested in harmony and consensus. They argued that economic development must precede political liberalization, and they were critical of many features of Western society. They felt that with proper guidance from above, and with attention to traditional morality, Asians could have economic development without having to experience the materialism, sexual misconduct, racial discrimination, and high crime rates that these leaders associated with development in the West.

This stress on Asian values represents a radical change in attitudes. Just twenty years ago, Chinese leaders were arguing that Asia's Confucianism was responsible for China's backwardness and domination by the West. The Confucian values of harmony, family, order, hierarchy, and communitarianism were also said to be keeping the peasantry downtrodden and beholden to elites. But in the 1990s, when Southeast Asia was enjoying the world's highest economic growth rates, the argument was turned upside down. Confucian traditions were said to explain Asia's remarkable economic success. The values of education, thrift, obedience to the law, respect for authority, discipline, and anti-individualism were now said to be responsible for the high rates of growth. This new perspective won many adherents in Asia and elsewhere. Then in mid-1997 the Asian economic crisis challenged this theory; the very values touted as responsible for Asia's economic success were now viewed as the cause of the collapse of the area's economies. The Confucianist fad had come full circle.

To believe that Asian values were responsible for either the astounding economic miracle or the crash that followed, one would have to accept that Southeast Asia is essentially homogeneous. However, the most important characteristic of Southeast Asia is the area's great diversity of religions, histories, and governmental systems. Moreover, Confucianism is a complex philosophy, originating not in Southeast Asia but in East Asia, that can be interpreted in numerous ways. Confucianism does not assert that individuals have no rights, nor does it say that they must acquiesce to unrighteous rule. The ideas of Confucianism inhibit rebellion by supporting stability and harmony of the social order, but society's leaders must rule morally and in the best interests of the people. If they do not, the people have the duty to overthrow them.

It is condescending to argue that Asians are not "ready" for democracy and open government. That is tantamount to saying that Asians can cope only when guided by strong leaders, and is patently a rationale for dictators to retain their power. For example, the Burmese State Peace and Development Council (SPDC) leader General Than Shwe has stated that democracy and human rights are not a part of the Burmese culture and tradition. His assertion flies in the face of the will of the Burmese people. In 1990 more than 80 percent of them voted against the military and in favor of an opposition party supporting democracy (the military ignored the results and continued its oppressive rule).

Yet although some Southeast Asian leaders may be cynically using "Asian values" to perpetuate their own power, in another sense there may truly be cultural factors that impede the development of liberal democracy. For example, Aung San Suu Kyi, the leader of the Burmese democratic forces, has suggested that some Burmese values are antithetical to democratic ways. Much of what she says applies as well to other Southeast Asian countries. Aung San Suu Kyi says that while Burmese culture places great importance on being respectful to those in authority, there is also a tendency to be jealous of those elites. She believes that *anadeh*, the Burmese tradition of deferring to the interests of others so as not to offend them, fosters resentment, selfishness, and sometimes even vengefulness. People will say, "If only I had not been checked by my *anadeh*, this person would not have their power." According to Aung San Suu Kyi, this attitude creates factionalism, because once people come into power they become targets of resentment.

Aung San Suu Kyi has also suggested that Burma's political leaders do not know when to quit their positions of power. The transition from one set of leaders to the next is especially difficult in Burma. Military *coups*, assassinations, and fraudulent elections are examples of unsmooth transitions that undermine democracy's chances. "Life is in the leaving" is her way of explaining that leaders have a responsibility to exit gracefully and to set the stage for their successors.

But a society's world view is only one of the factors determining democracy's future in Southeast Asia. Rapid economic development, when its fruits are relatively equitably distributed, is equally important for enhancing democracy's prospects. So far, Southeast Asia's record on democratization is a mixed one. No Southeast Asian nation has been able to sustain democratic processes over a long period of time. There are often zigzags and missteps, with Thailand being an especially extreme example of frequent oscillations between authoritarianism (usually military) and democracy (see Chapter 6). In recent years Thailand, Malaysia, and the Philippines have had some success in establishing enduring democratic processes. But Vietnam, Laos, Cambodia, Burma, and Brunei have failed to establish democratic ways, while Indonesia and Singapore have vacillated between authoritarian and democratic norms.

Figure 8. Burmese family

The Family, Women, and Sex

The Family

Southeast Asian families have traditionally been close, as the welfare of the family group was and is considered more important than the desires of any particular individual. Whenever the "family" is talked about, the term refers to more than the nuclear unit. Families usually include not only the parents and children, but also the aunts, the uncles, the grandparents, and the spouses of the married children. Many of these extended family members may live within the same compound or even the same house. Each member is expected to contribute to the family's welfare. While the parents work in the fields or outside the home, other members have duties that include child care, cooking, and cleaning. Older children are expected to care for the welfare of younger family members, and a typical scene is one of children caring for their younger siblings.

In Southeast Asia, men hold the political and the public economic positions of power. Accordingly, Southeast Asian families are ostensibly patriarchal. The men are predominant, and the oldest male is considered the major authority, though the women also influence family decisions. All family members are defined in terms of their relationship to the family's male head. Especially in those areas where Confucianism was influential, the woman is the "wife" of the man, while the son and daughter are the "children" of the man.

Despite the formal dominance of men, the mother/wife has the principal responsibility for budgeting family moneys. In urban areas, though two-career families are becoming common, for most socio-economic classes the standard procedure is for the man to go to work, bring home his salary, and present it to his wife. The wife will then make decisions regarding the purchase of food, clothes, and property. There is controversy about just how much authority these budgetary responsibilities provide Southeast Asian women. Some analysts suggest that women's power over the purse strings provides them with high status. Others note that little real power is involved because the budgets rarely go beyond the purchase of essentials.

Figure 9. Vietnamese boys

Boys and girls are socialized differently. By the age of ten, a girl is expected to help with household tasks. At the same age, a boy is trained to do outside chores including tending the livestock. In the mainland, rural boys become Buddhist monks for short periods and are generally encouraged to be independent. Meanwhile, girls are taught to be dependent and stay close to the home.

Families rarely disintegrate, and divorce is still a rare event. Children often live with their parents even after marriage. When parents become elderly, it is accepted that the children will have the responsibility of seeing after the parents' welfare. Most Southeast Asians are shocked by the Western notion of nursing homes for the elderly. Few such institutions exist in the region, because families are deemed to have an obligation to take care of the older generation. Southeast Asians would lose face if they did not take care of their parents.

Veneration of ancestors is an important part of Southeast Asian culture, being viewed by the living as a means of assuring their own immortality. Houses generally include special shrines where the ashes of ancestors are stored. On the anniversary of an ancestor's death, special rituals are performed to show respect and to unify the heirs. Reverence for ancestors and parents is manifested in many other ways as well. For example, the young people rarely engage in behavior that could bring embarrassment to their parents, because it is considered unacceptable for youth to do anything that would cause their families to lose face.

Figure 10. Woman carving vegetables in a Vietnam market

Women

Despite the ostensibly patriarchal character of Southeast Asian families, women in Southeast Asia are generally not considered the "weaker sex." Especially in comparison to the women of China and India, they are perceived as having relatively high status. As noted above, Southeast Asian women have responsibilities for managing family budgets and influence on household decision-making. Though a woman is expected to be dutiful and obedient to her husband and his parents, this expectation is not nearly as important in Southeast Asia as it is in China or India. Women cultivate the fields, interact with townspeople, own factories, retain family stability, and discipline the younger generation. As the primary agents of family socialization, women are responsible for the education of the youth and for the formation of their values. In contrast to the Chinese focus on ancestral lineage traced through the father and grandfather, Southeast Asians generally have bilateral kinship systems. The mother's side and the father's side relatives are considered to be equally important, and women generally inherit an equal share of their parents' estate. Even in Malaysia and Indonesia, where the Islamic law favors male inheritance, the land is often divided equally among members of both sexes.

Prateep Ungsongtham Hata

Prateep Ungsongtham Hata was born in 1952 in Klong Toey slum, in Bangkok, Thailand. She suffered from all the deprivations famous in slums: malnutrition, disease, and hopelessness. Klong Toey is infamous in Thailand, lacking drainage, sewage, sanitation, and safe drinking water. Originally, Klong Toey housed the unskilled laborers who worked in Bangkok's port, but it then became a place where squatters looked for cardboard to shelter them from the rains.

Out of this squalid environment emerged Prateep, a vital, bright girl who was determined to make a difference. Despite being deprived of education and forced to work in dreadful conditions, she managed to save enough money to attend night school and eventually received a tenth grade certificate. She opened a school in Klong Toey and became a teacher of the poor. She attracted volunteer teachers and found time to attend college. Her work became known throughout Bangkok and soon her school received financial contributions.

In 1978 she received the Magsaysay Award, an honor in Asia equivalent to the Nobel Peace Prize. Prateep's Pattana (Development) Village Community School enrolled 700 children and became the heart of Klong Toey. With her award money she established the Duang Prateep Foundation. She won many awards from Thailand and internationally she attracted supporters. She oversaw numerous projects all designed to contribute to empower the community. At present, the Duang Prateep Foundation has a budget of nearly $20 million.

Southeast Asian families are getting smaller. For centuries, Southeast Asian women averaged six births each. In the past two decades, however, family planning programs in Thailand, Malaysia, Singapore, and Indonesia have succeeded in bringing down the rate of population increase to about half what it was just two decades ago. The number of children per woman has dropped to three, unless the first three children are female, in which case the woman continues having children until a male child arrives, because it is still considered important to produce a male heir. Per capita economic growth rates have been highest in the nations with effective family planning, and the people of these countries have consequently enjoyed a higher standard of living.

Sex

Most Southeast Asian societies are highly conservative about sexual matters. Sex is not considered a topic appropriate for discussion between men and women. Brides are expected to be virgins when they marry, and men and women do not show affection publicly. Young people often have little say in the selection of someone to marry. Instead, parents select a mate for their son or daughter through an arrangement with the parents of the chosen partner. One-on-one dating between boys and girls takes place only in the most urbanized and western locations, although the practice of dating is spreading as westernization becomes more and more an integral element of both urban and rural culture.

Alongside the conservative outlook there exists a sexual double standard. Premarital sex is generally deplored, but this rule is applied more strictly to girls than to boys, as a high value is placed on the virginity of unmarried young girls. Particularly among higher-status and upwardly mobile families, girls who are thought to have had sexual relations before marriage are criticized and even ostracized, while boys who have sex before marriage are not criticized.

A major blot on the reputation of Southeast Asia is the easy availability of prostitutes. Several Southeast Asian nations, including Thailand and the Philippines, have developed a negative reputation for their "sex services," especially prostitution by young girls. Many Thai men, both married and unmarried, have traditionally visited prostitutes. But in recent years Southeast Asian prostitution has become particularly infamous as a result of "sex tour" catering to men from European countries and from Japan, Australia, and South Korea.

It is difficult to explain this paradox of a large prostitution industry in the midst of sexually conservative societies that value female virginity. However, it must be remembered that only a small percentage of women engage in prostitution. It is also important to remember the double standard that promotes women's virginity and faithfulness while condoning extramarital sex by men.

In addition, the income from prostitution can be greater than that from other occupations, and many prostitutes send money to their families in the villages. In some Thai villages, the largest houses are known as *baan sopenee*, which means "the house owned by a prostitute." After they have served as prostitutes, the girls often return to their villages and attempt to live a normal life. Tragically, many carry the AIDS virus.

A related blot on the reputation of parts of Southeast Asia is the widely reported selling of young girls who come from poor households in the hill areas of Thailand, Burma, and Laos. Agents from large cities have journeyed to remote areas to entice parents to "sell" their female children by signing contracts that commit the children to working as "waitresses" or "hotel maids." When the girls arrive for work, they find that they are virtual slaves of pimps who force them into prostitution.

One result of prostitution has been a rapid increase in the number of persons who are HIV positive. Thailand has been called the "AIDS Capital" of Asia because of the high number of AIDS patients, which are estimated to be between five hundred thousand and one million in a total population of just over sixty million. AIDS is also increasingly found in Burma, Cambodia, and Vietnam, although it is not clear how many persons are infected.

Figure 11. AIDS Awareness poster in Vietnam
Death holds a hangman's noose over a prostitute and a drug user.

In Burma, the principal causes of AIDS are the sharing of dirty needles among drug addicts and prostitution along the border with Thailand. However, in Thailand AIDS is primarily a heterosexually fomented disease. About 75 percent of all Thai prostitutes are HIV positive. The Thai government has moved positively in the war against

AIDS, for example by encouraging the use of condoms, but it has also been complicit in the business of prostitution, perhaps because so many police and other officials are involved in the huge profits to be made.

Many Thai men continued visiting prostitutes even after the AIDS crisis began. This activity put their lovers and wives in increasing jeopardy. However, in the past ten years a major behavioral change has taken place. Thai men are no longer visiting prostitutes in such large numbers, because they fear catching AIDS and because their wives have made it clear that they will not sleep with husbands who continue going out. This change has brought the AIDS epidemic under some control.

The Home and Food

Southeast Asian cities are growing rapidly, but the majority of Southeast Asians still live in rural villages that are surrounded by rice fields or by other cropland. In many parts of the region rural houses were traditionally made of wood or bamboo and rested on stilts. But there were exceptions: stilts were not used by the Javanese, Balinese, Vietnamese, or Chinese, and in some areas, such as northern Vietnam, houses were built of concrete, mud, or brick instead of wood. During the monsoon season the stilts kept the house high and dry above the muddy and sometimes flooded earth. In the hot season, the house was cooled by breezes that blew through and under the home. The space between the house and the ground could be used for storage or as a shaded place to keep chickens or other domesticated animals. In many villages, the space under the houses might also be used for crafts such as sewing or basket weaving. Today the wood and bamboo are gradually being replaced by other construction materials. Many rural houses now have corrugated iron roofs that are considered more "modern." Unfortunately, these iron roofs cause the houses to be like ovens as they absorb the tropical heat. During storms they are extremely loud as the rain pounds on the roof.

In urban areas, the middle and upper income people are likely to live in houses made of concrete, while the poor live in hovels made of wood or thatch. Huge apartment houses and condominiums have also been built to house the rapidly growing populations. Middle and upper income Southeast Asians use air conditioners in their Western-style homes, because the concrete absorbs the heat and keeps the house hot day and night.

In earlier days, teak wood houses were common in both urban and rural areas. Traditional teak houses did not have glass windows or modern air conditioning. Instead, they were designed to let the air pass through. The teak houses have fallen out of favor lately, because the scarcity of teak and the very high price of the wood make them expensive. The open walls also make them unpopular; pollution has

Figure 12. Transplanting rice
Part-way through the growing cycle, young rice plants are uprooted and replanted farther apart.

Figure 13. Threshing rice

become such a ubiquitous part of urban life that people want to be able to close their homes from the smog, smell, and noise.

Southeast Asian agriculture has diversified its crops in recent years, but rice remains the staple food everywhere. Rice is generally eaten three times a day. In Thailand, the verb "to eat" is literally "to eat rice." Noodles are also popular, especially during the day and as snacks. Fish is the major source of protein. Rice is eaten with side dishes—including curries, fish, and vegetables—that are noteworthy for being quite spicy, at least to the Western palate. In urban areas food is eaten with spoon and fork; in more rural areas it is eaten with the hands; and in areas where the Chinese predominate it is eaten with chopsticks. In some parts of Southeast Asia, especially in Laos and northeast Thailand, glutinous rice is the principal food. This "sticky" rice is eaten warm or cold. It is rolled in the fingers and then dipped into sauces and curries.

In the poorest parts of Indonesia *sago* is substituted for the more expensive rice. *Sago,* which comes from a particular tree, looks like a smooth porridge after being cooked. In Indonesia, as in other areas of Southeast Asia, rice is served with side dishes such as curries, tofu, vegetables, fish, and *sate* (meat that is skewered on sticks). One of the most popular dishes in Indonesia is *nasi goreng,* a dish similar to fried rice that contains vegetables and meat. Another popular dish is *gado gado,* a vegetable salad served with peanut sauce.

Rice whiskey, wine, and local beer are drunk in large amounts throughout much of Southeast Asia. As a result, there is a problem of alcoholism, especially among men. On the other hand, Indonesians, Malays, and Bruneians drink little alcohol, because Islamic teachings forbid its use.

Education

Southeast Asians have long placed a high premium on education as a way to improve their status and their standard of living. Members of Confucian societies such as Vietnam especially valued education, because it was and still is considered essential for becoming a member of the elite.

Until recently, many Southeast Asian schools were located in the village temples and mosques. The teachers were monks or clerics. Students were supposed to be respectful to their teachers, and the role of religious leaders as teachers increased the students' feelings of veneration.

Today, few schools are located in temples or mosques, and almost all teachers are lay people. But teachers are still highly respected. Each year, Teacher's Day celebrations are held to provide students with the opportunity to show reverence towards those who have taught them. In these ceremonies the students present their teachers with gifts and bow before them. Southeast Asians who study in the United States or Europe are shocked to discover that students often interact with the faculty almost as equals, as this style of interaction would be inconceivable in Southeast Asia.

Public education used to be of limited availability in Southeast Asia, but lately the situation has improved dramatically. For the past three decades universal elementary education has been a ubiquitous part of Southeast Asian societies. More than 90 percent of youth are attending elementary schools, and literacy levels are also approaching 90 percent. Yet even today many poor students have trouble getting an education because they must work the fields with their parents to assure sufficient food for the family.

Southeast Asia is now home to several excellent universities. The best known among them include (but are not limited to) Chulalongkorn and Thammasat Universities in Thailand, Ateneo de Manila University and the University of the Philippines, the University of Malaysia, Gajah Mada University and the University of Indonesia, and National University of Singapore. Overall, however, the educational systems of most Southeast Asian nations are second-rate compared to those in the West. The region's schools rarely instill analytical skills or reward creative thinking. At all levels of instruction, from primary school to university, education is "traditional" in the sense that the rote memory system is still dominant. The students' deference to authority figures makes it impossible for them to question instructors or to offer points of view different from the ones that have been articulated by the teachers. Many Southeast Asian universities are akin to diploma mills, with students "paying their money, receiving their degrees." The colleges and universities of poorer nations such as Vietnam, Laos, Cambodia, and Burma have very few learning resources. Libraries at all but the best universities are bereft of up-to-date books, and computers can be found in only the most prestigious universities. Professors are hard to find outside the classroom, because the pay levels are so low that many of them have obtained better-paying work on the side as consultants for private corporations or multinational companies. In addition, too few of the region's students are earning degrees in engineering, technology, and the sciences, careers essential to Southeast Asia's economic development.

Literature, Theater, and Music

Before the early twentieth century, most literary works in Southeast Asia were written in verse rather than prose. Two of the most influential classical literary masterpieces were the great epics the *Ramayana* and the *Mahabharata*. These works, which originally came from India, have become important parts of the cultures of Southeast Asia, especially in Thailand and Indonesia. Also important (and also coming from India) are the *Jataka* stories about the Buddha's life and about his former existences.

The *Ramayana* is a cycle of stories about the life of Rama, an incarnation of the Hindu god Vishnu. In Thailand, where the *Ramayana* is known as the *Ramakian,* the story has been rewritten in Thai verse and has been used as source material for classical masked dramas and for a famous temple mural in the Grand Palace. In Indonesia, the *Ramayana* stories are frequently presented with shadow puppets (*wayang*) in an all-night performance.

The details of the complex *Ramayana* story differ from country to country, but the basic plot is the same. In the Indonesian version, a king named Dasarata wanted to give his kingdom to Rama, his first-born son by his wife Kausalya. The king's other wife reminds him that she had been granted two wishes, which she uses to have Rama banished and to have her own son crowned king. Rama and his wife Sita wander the forests, where a wicked giant finds them and complicates their lives. The giant eventually kidnaps Sita and imprisons her in his kingdom. Struggles and wars ensue. Aided by the monkey king Hanuman, Rama and Hanuman's monkey armies invade the giant's kingdom, where Rama kills the giant and frees Sita. Rama returns home in triumph, and at last he gains the throne. However, both Rama and the people suspect that Sita has not resisted the giant's advances. She proves her virtue in an ordeal by fire, but the suspicions complicate the rest of their lives.

Made Wianta

A Balinese painter, Made Wianta is one of Indonesia's most creative artists. His work has been influenced by Balinese traditional painting as well as Western forms. Born in 1949 in a small village on the island of Bali, Made Wianta grew up learning about the *Wayang Kulit* (traditional shadow puppetry) and the Hindu religion. In school he was superb in arts, including puppetry, acting, dancing, and *batik* painting. In 1975 he was invited to work in Belgium to give demonstrations of his painting which combined abstract influences with Balinese forms.

Upon his return to Indonesia Wianta became the nation's most famous painter. His paintings, now found throught the world, are unique, characterized by bright colors and fascinating geometric shapes. They are Balinese, yet they are also abstract, free of convention, and quintessentially creative.

The *Mahabharata* is India's other major literary contribution to Southeast Asia. One of the world's longest poems, it consists of some 90,000 stanzas. The epic holds a central place in Indonesian literature and is a major source of the country's mythology. The *Mahabharata's* origins are not entirely clear, but the poem may be based on complex dynastic struggles that took place among the leading families of India around the ninth century B.C. There are stories about sons born blind, children of semidivine origins, ruthless relationships among relatives, narrow escapes from death, passionate loves, great courage against overwhelming odds, wanton destruction of cities, and great wars.

In Indonesia, the *Mahabharata* is performed regularly as a *wayang* play. *Wayang* is a generic Indonesian term for "puppetry" and is also the word for this kind of theater. A central aspect of Indonesian culture, the popular *wayang* performances are a principal means of teaching religious and traditional ways. The most famous of the many variations of *wayang* is the *wayang kulit* ("shadow puppet play") of Java and Bali. The puppeteer tells stories by manipulating exquisite leather puppets behind a large white see-through screen. The audience sees the shadows of the puppets on the screen as it listens to the drama, which might last an entire day and evening.

The presentation of the *Mahabharata* as a shadow-puppet play is an important part of Javanese culture, as it symbolizes the history of the area and the spiritual values of the people. Shadow plays based on the *Mahabharata* are filled with fascinating heroes and villains, and they are so popular that most Indonesians (Javanese, in particular) know the details of each character. The puppeteers are highly respected men who have learned by heart the entire *Mahabharata, Ramayana,* or similar stories. The classical stories provide the source material for these performances, but within their traditional structure there is also much ad-libbing by the performers.

In the Buddhist societies of mainland Southeast Asia, stories about the Buddha are an important part of the culture. The Buddha's life is the subject of much religious art, as the account of his birth, enlightenment, teaching, and attainment of *nirvana* is portrayed in statuary and in magnificent temple murals. In many places it is possible to view the most important events in the Buddha's life from beginning to end simply by circumambulating the temple.

The *Jataka* stories about the Buddha's former lives are another significant part of the Buddhist cultures, and the stories were once important tools for teaching morality. The best known of the *Jataka* tales are the stories of the Buddha's last ten lives before obtaining Buddhahood. Special attention goes to the last of these ten existences, in which he was born as a king named Vessantara. In the *Vessantara Jataka* the future Buddha cultivates the virtue of generosity by giving his wife and children to a hermit, though owing to the power of his merit he gets his family back in the end. In northeast Thailand the *Vessantara Jataka* is recited every year as part of great temple celebrations.

In contemporary times there has grown up a literature that uses new forms of expression to explore Southeast Asian cultures and histories. Essays, short stories, novels, poems, plays, and song lyrics reflect the rich variety of the people's concerns and behaviors, with emphasis on family life, religion, modernization, and politics. Though the fame of the leading writers is not yet widespread among Western readers, much of the work is skillfully and engagingly written. Some observers have suggested that Southeast Asian authors such as Pramoedya Ananta Toer of Indonesia and Nick Joaquin of the Philippines merit serious consideration for the Nobel Prize in literature.

Francisco Sionil Jose

Author of numerous books, short stories, and poems, founding president of the Philippines PEN Center (an international organization of poets, playwrights, and novelists), winner of the 1980 Maysaysay Award for Journalism, Literature, and Creative Communication Arts, and owner of the Solidaridad Publishing House and the Solidarity Bookstore, Frankie Jose is the leading cultural icon of the Philippines.

Born in 1924 in Rosales, Philippines, Jose became the foremost Filipino novelist who writes in English. His books passionately describe aspirations for national sovereignty and social justice. In one of the best known of these works, the five-novel Rosales Saga, he writes about Philippine history through the lives of generations of the Samson family.

Jose has also been a social critic. He fought vigorously against the Marcos dictatorship and later characterized Cory Aqauino's government as incompetent. Yet, he remains optimistic about Filipino resiliency and about the future of liberal democracy in the Philippines, even though corrupt governments have continued to oppose agrarian reform, which Jose considers the single most important option for lifiting the nation from penury. He is convinced that in some future time it will be the anonymous Filipinos, "with mud on their feet," who will redeem his country from its present difficulties.

The traditional music of Southeast Asia takes many unique forms, using bamboo flutes, gongs, bronze drums, and both wooden and metal xylophones. The diverse performance types include formal orchestras, solo sessions, impromptu folk dances, and stylized singing contests. In recent years many Southeast Asians have studied Western classical music, and in all Southeast Asian countries new forms of popular music have developed that draw on both local and international influences.

In Indonesia the most popular musical form is the *gamelan*, a percussion orchestra whose name originates from the Javanese word "*gamel*," or "hammer." There are numerous local variations in the orchestra's composition and in the sounds produced. The main instruments sound similar to a Western xylophone, but there are also gongs, drums, and at times flute-like instruments. The music's intricate sounds and rhythms can have a mesmerizing quality. *Gamelan* music can be heard at religious festivals, ceremonies, or concerts. Though the *gamelan* is most strongly associated with Javanese culture, it is also found throughout the Indonesian islands and in nearby regions.

P. Ramlee

Malaysia's most renowned composer, director, actor, and singer was born in 1929 and died in 1973. Known throughout his career as P. Ramlee, Ramlee bin Puteh exemplified the popular culture of Malaysia, especially during the 1950s when his music could be found in every village and city. He also became the nation's most famous actor and film director.

P. Ramlee expressed modern Malay life in films and music. Rather than writing modern versions of traditional forms of Malay music, he wrote contemporary popular songs about Malaya and helped the world better understand Malay (and later Malaysian) cultural life.

Celebrations and Rituals

Celebrations and rituals play an important cultural role in all of Southeast Asia. Religious observances and major life events are important personal and social occasions. In addition, each nation has elaborate religious rituals, festivals, and other ceremonies that are far too numerous to mention individually. Major life-cycle events such as birth, marriage, and death are cause for elaborate ceremonies, even when the participants cannot really afford the high cost of feeding the many friends and associates who attend.

Weddings are often lavish and are an opportunity for the bridal couple's parents to show off their wealth. Funerals are also highly ceremonial. In the Islamic tradition, a body must be buried within twenty-four hours of death. The body is bathed, wrapped in white cloth, and then buried. In Buddhist and Hindu societies, cremation is more common than burial, and the cremation sometimes occurs many months after a death. The higher the dead person's status, the longer the wait before cremation.

Birthdays are also important. The birthdays of the nations' leaders are even made national holidays. In much of Southeast Asia the years of a person's life span are arranged in twelve-year cycles, with each year having the special name of an animal. Major birthdays occur on every twelfth year of a person's life, for example on the twelfth, twenty-fourth, thirty-sixth, forty-eighth, and sixtieth birthdays. These twelve-year groups are called cycles. For example, the thirty-sixth birthday is the completion of the third cycle.

People's characters are said to be shaped by the year in which they were born. Persons born in the Year of the Rat are said to be hard-working and ambitious. Persons born in the Year of the Ox are known for their patience and their concern for others. Tigers are thought to be sympathetic to others and deliberate in decision making. The Rabbit is considered friendly and trusting. The Year of the Dragon is especially auspicious, because people born in that year are said to be intelligent. The Year of the Snake is for wise and helpful people, while people born in the Year of the Horse are deemed artistic. Those born in the Year of the Goat are thought to be shy but loving. The Year of the Monkey is characterized by people who are creative, and people born in the Year of the Cock are hard-working and aggressive. People born in the Year of the Dog are said to be sympathetic and concerned about justice. Finally, the Year of the Boar features kind and loving persons.

Religious festivals are important communal events. In Indonesia, the Javanese style of religion revolves around a communal ritual called the *slametan*. Slametans are held to mark important moments such as housewarmings, harvests, circumcisions (performed on boys between the ages of seven and fourteen), and celebrations of good fortune (as when a sick person has been cured). Slametans provide a sense of well-being for the Javanese. They include parades, speeches, feasts, and community participation.

In the Philippines, people hold *barangay* fiestas to honor the patron saints of each settlement. Another important event is Holy Week, which celebrates the Passion of Christ and is marked by public processions on the evenings of Holy Wednesday and Good Friday. Celebrants parade through the town carrying images of the apostles and saints, most of whom are portrayed as Westerners. The processions also include floats featuring statues of saints dressed in fancy robes and surrounded by lights similar to Christmas tree decorations. In some places barefoot pilgrims may carry a heavy wooden cross, sometimes collapsing from the heat and the cross's weight. Meanwhile, flagellants beat themselves with thorn bushes and lashes as an act of penance.

In Thailand, Burma, Laos, and Cambodia, the traditional new year festival usually occurs in April at the height of the hottest season. Called *Songkran* (but known in Burma as *Thingyan*), this festival can last one to several days. The observance begins with merit making at the Buddhist temples. Birds and fish are set free to symbolize new life. In Burma and some other areas, the older people also wash the Buddha images as a means of making merit and paying respects. People then visit the village elders to show them respects. In turn, the elders wish the younger family members and friends good health and prosperity. Among the Thai and Lao, the *Songkran* festivals feature a unique way to celebrate the new year, as people pour water on each other. This practice is based on a traditional water-pouring rite to honor the respected persons in the villages. Today, the mood is more frolicsome, as entire buckets of water are thrown from cars, motorcycles, and bicycles at whomever is close by. Because *Songkran* occurs during the hottest season, the water throwing cools off those who are doused.

Also important in Buddhist countries is the Buddhist Lent period beginning in June/July, which is a season of several months during which the people are to be restrained in their behavior and many young men become temporary monks. The beginning and end of the Lent period is a beautiful time to visit Burma, because there are festivals of lights symbolizing the Buddha's return to earth. Candles are lit everywhere, entertainment abounds, and the Burmese visit all their friends and relatives.

The Burmese, Lao, Cambodians, and Thai also perform ceremonies designed to keep evil spirits away. One popular ceremony, called *bai sri,* is performed on special occasions, such as birthdays, and also for people who have been going through stressful times. The people who carry out this ceremony believe that each person has spirits within. To keep the good spirits intact, village elders or religious specialists bless white strings and tie them around the individual's wrist. The strings protect the good spirits, keep out the bad spirits, and help call back good spirits who have wandered.

DISCUSSION QUESTIONS

1. How have religions affected the cultural values of Southeast Asian citizens?

2. Do you agree that "personalism" in the form of patron-client relationships is at the heart of Southeast Asian culture? Why or why not?

3. How is Vietnam different from the Southeast Asian nations that had no Confucianist background?

4. Discuss the concept of "Asian values." Do you believe in universal principles that apply to all societies, or do different political and economic behaviors apply to different societies?

5. Southeast Asian nations are generally viewed as patriarchal, meaning that men dominate most sectors of society. Do you agree that men dominate, or do you believe that women are also playing prominent roles?

SUGGESTED READINGS

An important book on the political culture of Southeast Asia is Lucian W. Pye, *Asian Power and Politics: The Cultural Dimensions of Authority* (Harvard University Press, Cambridge, Massachusetts, 1985). Ghulam-Sarwar Yousof has written extensively on Southeast Asian drama. Especially important is his *Dictionary of Traditional South-East Asian Theatre* (Oxford University Press, Kuala Lumpur, 1994). For a better understanding of Indonesian culture see Benedict R. O'G. Anderson, *Mythology and the Tolerance of the Javanese* (Cornell University Southeast Asia Program, New York, 1996). Students interested in religion should read Robert C. Lester, *Therevada Buddhism in Southeast Asia* (University of Michigan, Ann Arbor, 1973). Also important is Donald K. Swearer, *The Buddhist World of Southeast Asia* (SUNY, Albany, 1995). A classic is James L. Peacock, *Indonesia: An Anthropological Perspective* (Goodyear Publishing Co., Pacific Palisades, 1973). Ronald Provencher has written a superb overview of the region in *Mainland Southeast Asia: An Anthropological Perspective* (Goodyear Publishing Co., Pacific Palisades, 1975). A fascinating view of Malaysia is Douglas Raybeck, *Mad Dogs, Englishmen, and the Errant Anthropologist: Fieldwork in Malaysia* (Waveland, Prospect Heights, Illinois, 1996). For an understanding of gender roles in the region, see Penny Van Esterik, ed., *Women of Southeast Asia* (Center for Southeast Asian Studies, Northern Illinois University, 1996).

5

VILLAGE LIFE

Until recently the vast majority of Southeast Asians lived in rural villages. The villagers had widely varying ethnicities, traditions, and economic statuses. Many villages were isolated, as good roads were few and travel times were long. Cultures and behaviors could vary greatly from village to village. As they say in Indonesia, "*lain desa, lain adat*" (different village, different customs).

Despite these differences, certain similarities can be seen. Traditionally, rural villages were typically made up of some one to four hundred households, with the family being the basic unit of social organization. Agriculture was generally the center of life, and rice farming was the main means of livelihood. Most of the farmers were poor, while a minority of landowners were disproportionately well off. (the farmers are sometimes also called "peasants"). Villagers have been economically at the mercy of the elements. Droughts, floods, volcanic eruptions, and typhoons can bring disaster to subsistence-level peasants and their small farms. Villagers are also at the mercy of powerful people such as urban and rural landlords, urban business people, moneylenders, and public officials.

Up until the past several decades, many Southeast Asian villagers were caught in a vicious cycle of poverty. Machinery, pesticides, and fertilizer were not yet in widespread use, so farmers were forced to live a subsistence life. Debilitating diseases sapped the farmers' energy, labor-intensive farming methods resulted in low levels of productivity, and enervating weather conditions threatened the harvests. The lack of surplus crops kept farmers from earning capital, and the lack of capital precluded savings and investment. Birth control was not yet practiced, and the farmers' economic situation was worsened by the large numbers of mouths that had to be fed. Arable land became less available as populations expanded, and family farms shrank as they were divided among the children.

For many villagers, the need for subsistence was the basic motivation for economic and political decisions. The villagers perceived their world as having only a constant quantity of available resources, so they were competitive in their attempts to maximize their interests. Even in their relations with peers, the isolated rural poor were likely to exhibit feelings of distrust. They were often individualists, withdrawn and self-reliant.

Poverty also caused many villagers to be committed to the status quo and to traditional methods of farming. This conservative trait stemmed from a "safety first" principle in which subsistence-oriented farmers, preoccupied with survival, tried to avoid economic disaster instead of taking risks that might maximize their average yearly income. Instead of thinking like adventurous entrepreneurs, they typically preferred arrangements with social superiors that would enable them to survive times of bad harvests.

In the past several decades the conservative and withdrawn nature of Southeast Asian peasants has begun to change. Since the 1960s the "Green Revolution" has swept over much of the region as many farmers have adopted and adapted new technologies such as pesticides, fertilizer, and machines. The once traditional and subsistence-oriented farms have become part of a cash economy that has replaced the traditional barter economy. However, only the wealthiest and least isolated farmers have been able to take fullest advantage of the modern technology. As a result, the richest farmers have increased their wealth, while the poorest continue to struggle. In the past three decades all economic classes in rural Southeast Asia have improved their standard of living. Yet the gap between the rural rich and poor has increased.

As Westernization and the cash economies have taken hold, more and more villagers are leaving their families and moving to cities in search of work. Just a few decades ago, it was unthinkable that Southeast Asian families would be separated, but increasingly that is the case. Many rural youth go to the cities to seek their fortune. Others are simply trying to cope with the ubiquitous problem of too many people living on ever smaller parcels of farmland. Migration to the cities has led to increased alienation among the young, as in the urban environment they no longer have the security and support of their families.

Throughout history Southeast Asian villagers have been kept at arms' length from the economic, political, and social sources of power. For most of the twentieth century a large part of the cultivated land area of Southeast Asia has been under the control of a landed elite, and it remains so today. The tenant-farmers who now comprise a majority of the rural people have had relatively few means to improve their lot. The essence of the relationship between landlord and tenant was the lack of equality between the two. Theirs was a "patron-client" relationship established on the principle of reciprocity between "superior" and "inferior." Landlords provided cash payments, favors, and incentives, but they fixed the quantity of crops the tenant-farmers could keep. At the same time, because the landlords also had a responsibility to meet tenants' basic needs, the clients' employment, housing, and educational needs were met in return for their deference to their benefactors.

Contrary to conventional wisdom, peasant life has not been altogether static. Despite the powerful forces against change, Southeast Asia has witnessed a great transformation in recent times. An important engine of change is the rapid population increase. The rural peoples of Southeast Asia have doubled their population in just thirty years. Although family planning has been successful in Thailand, Indonesia, Singapore, and Malaysia, in other nations the high population growth rates have caused millions of rural peasants to leave their overpopulated farms to seek work in urban areas. Just decades ago, land was available throughout the region. Today, land is scarce. Farmers have been forced to move to less fertile areas, such as the higher areas of hills and mountains, in a desperate attempt to find land they can till.

The introduction of cash economies into the rural areas is another factor affecting the villages. Interpersonal relationships have changed as market needs have begun to predominate and rural economies have become more specialized. The customary bonds of peasant society have broken down. Teachers, officials, landlords, and entrepreneurs such as rice-mill owners and moneylenders have gained more influence over village resources. Traditional patron-client patterns have given way as the new entrepreneurs, who are often outsiders, have narrowed the scope and style of the exchange between patrons and clients. The new ties are more distant and formal than the relatively comprehensive and personal ones of the traditional patron-client relationships.

As the central government has become more involved in the daily affairs of the rural people, new social groups have arisen that did not exist even forty years ago. These new groups—including kinship-based organizations, ethnic organizations, farmers' associations, political parties, and non-governmental charitable and activist organizations—facilitate attainment of the people's demands and are therefore part of the growing move toward decentralization and responsiveness. At the same time, national leaders have improved communication networks and increased their own capacity to mobilize the peasantry. The region's governments have built roads and radio stations, so that today few areas of Southeast Asia are entirely isolated from the central authorities. The nations' leaders control the television, radio, and media communication channels and thereby control the kind of information heard by rural peoples. In turn, villagers have gained easier access to market towns, provincial capitals, and national capitals, where they learn urban and "Western" values. The central governments have also established development programs in rural areas. For example, they have improved access to electricity, built schools and irrigation systems, and fostered a widened market for village crafts produced for export.

All of the Southeast Asian nations except for Brunei have developed political parties that campaign in rural areas to elect candidates. Party organization usually revolves around personalities rather than ideologies or party loyalties, but in some countries the national party has built strong networks extending to the citizenry, even in rural areas. In communist Vietnam and Laos, the communist party apparatus extends to every village, while in capitalist Singapore, a single highly organized party controls both the state administration and most of the public interest groups. Party organizations are still weak in Thailand, Indonesia, and the rural Philippines, but even in these countries they are increasingly influential in bringing the central authorities into contact with rural peoples. The 1999 parliamentary election in Indonesia is an example of the new phenomenon of central authorities interacting with villagers. For the first time, Indonesian government officials went to rural areas to campaign for votes. As they campaigned, they toured existing development projects and committed themselves to new ones.

To provide more detail and analysis of Southeast Asian rural life, this chapter will focus on three representative nations—Thailand, Vietnam, and Indonesia. The three nations differ in several ways. Thailand and Vietnam are mainland nations, while Indonesia is part of island Southeast Asia. Vietnam is under communist rule, while Thailand and Indonesia have encouraged the development of fully capitalist economies. Thailand is Theravada Buddhist, Vietnam is Mahayana Buddhist, and Indonesia is predominantly Muslim. Thailand was uncolonized, Vietnam was once dominated by the French, and Indonesia was ruled by the Dutch colonists. In addition, the villages of each country show the unique effects of local histories, cultures, and government practices.

Thailand

Thailand contains about 50,000 villages organized into some 5,000 "clusters" known as communes. Rural Thai villages often look like sleepy communities that are irrelevant or at least peripheral to events in Bangkok. However, behind the facade of an isolated, traditional, static, rural community is a vibrant social and political life that is every bit as fascinating as Bangkok, the traditional center of national politics. The apparent isolation of the villages is also misleading, as there is much interaction between the villagers and the people who live in towns and cities. Teachers, Buddhist priests, merchants, landowners, and village political leaders all have ties to people both in the villages and in the towns and cities. As Thailand has modernized, an increasing number of persons have also been participating in development projects and have become members of organizations such as farmers' groups, irrigation associations, temple committees, and farm cooperatives.

Thai villages are led by headmen who are usually elected to their position by the villagers. Any male resident is eligible, so long as he is between the ages of twenty-one and sixty, is neither a monk nor a civil servant, and has lived in the village for at least six months. In recent years women have also been eligible to be the elected heads of villages, though female headmen are still extremely rare. Headmen owe their reputation to their unique personal qualities, their extensive clientele, their relatively high level of education, and their important contacts outside the village. Headmen attend village meetings, settle private and public disputes, officiate at temple fairs, entertain visiting guests and officials, and advise villagers on registration and tax procedures. They also initiate, plan, and implement village projects. They meet with higher level officials to discuss policy issues such as whether to build a school, repair a road that has washed away in the rains, or refurbish a Buddhist temple. They also decide about the formation of youth groups, construction of a midwife center, and the establishment of an irrigation canal. Headmen are "middlemen" between villagers and government officials. They see their role as a link between the villagers on the one hand and the district, provincial, and national officials on the other. The headmen are in an unenviable position, because in their role as middlemen they are subjected to conflicting pressures from both sides.

Almost every Thai village has a self-sufficient subsistence economy, irrigated rice-farming, a central Buddhist village temple, several influential kinship groupings, and religious ceremonies that include the worship of spirits. At the same time, each village is somewhat unique. The principal factors influencing village structure and behavior are the village's resources, proximity to main roads and urban centers, kinship patterns, internal cohesion, government programs, and local leadership. As these factors combine into various patterns, a village takes on its own identity.

Because Thai villages vary so greatly, it is difficult to provide an example of a "typical" village. The following list of characteristics is drawn from a composite of many different kinds of villages. Thai villages are surrounded by lush rice fields (though the farms increasingly include other crops) and the communities consist of some hundred to two hundred houses that are built on stilts in order to remain above the water line when the monsoons flood the plains. The houses are often grouped in compounds, with extended families living together. Most homes are surrounded by coconut and banyan trees. Chickens and water buffalo escape the heat by remaining in the shade under the houses. The men, women, and older children are in the rice fields during most of the day, while older residents and the very young stay at home. Within the village boundaries is a Buddhist temple that serves as the religious, educational, and social center of the village. Most villages now have electricity. A majority also have running water. In villages that do not have these amenities, water must be fetched from a well outside the village.

In the more remote Thai villages, located on dirt roads that have no public transportation, electricity is unusual and there are few ongoing development projects. In such villages there is usually one mandatory project where official money is spent. For example, all available money might be spent to repair the road to the district office each year. In many remote villages almost all of the villagers support production of a particular item for market. One village might make the rattan baskets that wet market vendors use to store fruit. Another might paint umbrellas and then send them to tourist stores in a nearby city. A third might manufacture shirts, make silver trinkets, or carve wood statues. These activities help bring in money that keeps the village above the bare subsistence level.

Village group activity is based on a web of loose, reciprocal, *quid pro quo* relationships. In only a few of the village groups is the villager's involvement mandatory. The Buddhist temple and the school are symbols of the community, but they do not necessarily symbolize, or demand, any special community spirit. This is not to say that there is no "community"; rather, the community is based on personalized relationships rather than on formally organized collective activity. The farmers rarely work alone in their fields. Children work alongside their parents, while neighbors and kin help each other in an informal mutual aid system. Farmers who receive assistance are expected to help others in turn, though no formal record is kept of who worked for whom or for how long.

Most of the Thai continue to be *kreng jai* about contacting officials. That is, they are shy and reluctant to bother persons of higher status. As a result, there is little direct contact between villagers and government representatives. Many officials have neither the time nor the inclination to make a full day's trek to villages located off passable roads, while few villagers have the money, time, or confidence to go to the district office. In addition, because political relationships are generally personalistic, villagers rarely have access to formal organizations that could contact officials on their behalf. They rely instead on patron-client ties to influential people. This network of patron-client ties is what integrates Thailand and makes it work—at least until modernization overwhelms traditional ways.

And change has certainly happened. At one time, each village represented a truly separate community centered on the Buddhist temple. Today, the administrative "village" is often an arbitrary subdivision of a peasant community. In north and northeast Thailand, the natural peasant social and economic communities appear to be isomorphic with the administrative structures. In those areas the village is an important arena of social interaction, and the village headman is a relatively influential figure. However, in the central delta region there is little correlation between the village's administrative system and its political and social system. Discrete, integrated, self-governing villages have largely disappeared from these areas, mainly because the rapidly growing population has caused housing clusters to overlap, while the commercialization of agriculture has resulted in large farms that straddle more than one village. The delta villages continue to elect "headmen," but the village as recognized by the administrative system has little relationship with the people's patterns of life.

Vietnam

As in the rest of Southeast Asia, villages are the heart of Vietnamese society. Wars have defined much of Vietnamese history, and much of the fighting has been done by rural villagers. Vietnam has suffered countless invasions from foreigners, such as the Chinese, and the Vietnamese peasants have also rebelled frequently against their own leaders. In the colonial period, the French took away the traditional independence of the villages, and the change sparked intense and violent struggles by villagers to regain control over their country. The American war in Vietnam (1960s to 1975) is only the most recent major war; in the course of that conflict several million Vietnamese became casualties.

Vietnamese villages are strikingly different from those in Thailand and Indonesia. For many centuries, especially in the north, houses were built with concrete, mud, or brick rather than with thatch or wood. Family compounds were prevalent. The buildings of the compound were arranged in a circle with an open courtyard in the center. Each village in Vietnam was built around a multi-family group of people that usually had a common respected ancestor. Most villages contained a *dinh*, a sacred building that houses the relics (some believe the spirit) of the famous ancestor. The village's important documents and ceremonial paraphernalia were also stored in this building. The villagers would gather in the *dinh* for ceremonies, parties, and meetings.

During the pre-French era, the Vietnamese emperor owned the land, and private ownership was unknown. Despite his formal control of the land, the emperor did not become involved in the villagers' daily decisions. Indeed, a famous Vietnamese saying states that the emperor's power stops at the village gate. In the time of the emperors, the village was governed by a Council of Notables with support from the village functionaries and the chief. To be a council member, one had to be male, have some education, and have good family contacts. Decisions were ideally arrived at through discussion and consensus, though Vietnamese villages were usually characterized by factionalism.

Vietnamese villagers were rice farmers. They often grew two crops of rice each year, a spectacular achievement that kept the nation self-sufficient in food. As in the rest of Southeast Asia, each Vietnamese village also produced a particular craft item as a way to increase income. Basketry, weaving, tailoring, wood carving, and blacksmithing are examples of these distinctive village activities. Yet, despite the income from the crafts, farming was viewed as the higher status work.

The religious beliefs and practices of the Vietnamese villagers drew on multiple sources. Rural people in particular integrated animism and ancestor veneration into their more formal Buddhist religious beliefs. For hundreds of years, villagers prayed both to the *bodhisattvas* (the Buddhas-to-be of Mahayana Buddhism) and to ancestors. Confucianism, the most important secular philosophy of urban people, was less important among rural villagers, yet its stress on family values and on respect for authority fit well with village life.

There were contradictions among the values promoted by the several traditions. For example, Confucianism stressed men's superior status, while Buddhism was more egalitarian. Confucianism was more intellectual, while animism promoted astrology and magic as important aspects of life. Buddhism was fatalistic and counseled villagers to accept their lot in life, while Confucianism taught that hard work, education, and skill could get persons to a higher status.

Confucianism provided the intellectual framework for integrating the village with the rest of the country's social and political system. In the days before colonialism, even young men from poor backgrounds were supposedly able to earn high-level government positions. In practice, however, the required education was more expensive than most farmers could afford. In truth, Confucianism was often made an additional barrier against social mobility. The mandarins (scholar-officials) who taught Confucianism and administered the country wanted to keep their power intact. They set forth the view that the mandarin's exalted position was worthy of praise and his decisions not to be questioned. As the mandarins demanded higher taxes, more compulsory labor, and more recruits to fight their wars, the gap between the rulers and ruled began to grow and villagers were more and more exploited.

Beginning in the late nineteenth century, the French colonialists drastically changed the village system, thereby undermining social stability and fomenting mass rebellions. The French changed the rules on owning land, forcing villagers into tenant relationships with wealthy farmers. They also attempted to bring "order" by thrusting French law on villagers. In addition, the French continued the burdens of mandarin-style rule by further increasing taxes, forcing farmers into *corvée* labor to build huge construction projects, and generally treating villagers as second-class citizens. The result was catastrophic. Village traditions were undermined, and the villagers were left with few resources. In just eighty years of colonialism, a mere 3 percent of the people came to own most of the land. The economic and administrative changes introduced by the French turned villager against villager while giving the French a degree of control over village affairs that the emperor had never enjoyed.

In 1954 the Vietminh nationalists drove the French from Vietnam and placed the north's administration in the hands of the communist revolutionaries. The American war that followed in the 1960s and 70s changed village life still further. The war forced millions of farmers to evacuate their villages, especially in the south. The displaced villagers moved to the cities, to refugee sites, or to "secure" villages controlled by the South Vietnamese government. Two million people, mostly male, were killed out of a total population (north and south combined) estimated at about fifty million as of 1975. As the men went to fight, the villages became dominated by the women, who both during the war and in the immediate post-war years were forced to take care of families and farms.

In 1975 the communist triumph united the country under a single regime that moved rapidly to socialize the entire economy through the expropriation of land and the nationalization of industry and business. Under communist rule, the southern Vietnamese villages lost even more of their autonomy and freedom from the central government. The communist administration went into the villages looking for persons who were deemed untrustworthy, forcing these people into "re-education" camps where many were imprisoned for years. Private land ownership was frowned on. Agricultural collectives were established, as the people were told to make personal sacrifices for the collective good. These changes produced an agricultural disaster, because the villagers refused to grow rice as long as they did not receive a decent profit. The southern economy declined, inflation rates skyrocketed, and unemployment reached over 20 percent. Famine threatened some 10 million farmers.

In 1986 the Vietnamese government finally began to realize the extent of the disaster. It recognized that the ideal of "personal sacrifice for the sake of the collective good" had failed to take hold. To overcome the crisis, the government proposed major reforms. It agreed not to dictate its socialist policies to the village. It also ended collectivized agriculture and gave farmers the legal right to sell their produce on the free market. As a result of these reforms, the economy strengthened and Vietnam reemerged as a major rice exporter. Inflation abated, and economic development began to take hold.

Indonesia

It is impossible to generalize about Indonesian villages because the nation is characterized by such far-reaching diversity. Both in the uplands and in the lowlands, farming practices differ depending on location, weather, topography, resources, and population. Nevertheless, there are some features that are common to most of the communities. For example, rural Indonesians believe in the importance of community discussion and consensus in making group decisions. It is imperative to reach *mufakat* (consensus) so that everyone is generally satisfied with the solution to a problem. *Mufakat* is achieved through *musjawarah* (open discussion of an issue) that involves all the villagers. Through this process, villagers believe they reach a community spirit of *gotong rojong* (mutual aid) in which the villagers receive mutual benefits. These cultural traits of mutual aid through discussion and consensus are being lost in urban areas, but they remain an important part of the rural lifestyle.

In rural Java the fundamental social unit is the nuclear family household, though in practice many newly married couples live with their parents. Parents provide equal inheritances to all their children, and they pass on most of this wealth before they die. For example, newlyweds often inherit such things as land, a house, and household goods. Many Indonesians marry young. Boys marry at ages 17 or 18 and girls at ages 15 or 16 (though according to Indonesian law the minimum age for marriage is at least 16 years). The newlyweds normally desire to set up independent households, but many of them cannot afford the expense, so they live with the bride's parents until they can establish a separate residence. The advantage of living with parents is that expenses can be shared and resources pooled, including labor for working the fields, collecting firewood, and cooking. The majority of divorces occur in the first year of marriage, whereas few occur after three years. When a couple divorces, the young husband and wife each retain the property given by their own parents.

Like villages elsewhere in Southeast Asia, Indonesian villages are undergoing rapid and fundamental changes. For example, education has become more widely available. During the period of Dutch colonial rule, only the very rich could afford to send their children to school. Hence, illiteracy rates were strikingly high. At present mass education has filtered to virtually all areas of Java and also to most of the areas in the outer islands. The amount of schooling depends on social class and the ease of getting to the schools, but for both girls and boys the overall average is just over six years.

Indonesian villages have also experienced improved standards of living. Beginning in the 1960s, Suharto's New Order regime emphasized economic development and opened the country to Western and Japanese businesses and values. Virtually everyone's standard of living increased and rice yields doubled in just one decade. However, Indonesian villagers remained poor by Western standards. They also lost an important public voice as many rural political organizations were closed down as part of the New Order's authoritarianism.

Today, the traditional model of rural farmers producing purely for subsistence is a thing of the past. A "Green Revolution" has occurred in eastern Java. Similar changes have happened in the rest of Indonesia and indeed throughout all but the poorest nations of Southeast Asia. Cash crops are now grown everywhere. Pesticides, fungicides, fertilizers, and tractors are in widespread use. Even in the highlands, which were once devoted to *swidden* agriculture, farmers have shifted from subsistence cultivation to capital-intensive commercial agriculture. However, it is the wealthy who have taken best advantage of the new technologies, so the gap between the rich and poor has widened.

Indonesian village life is slower and more oriented to tradition than is urban life. The big cities now feature shopping malls, discos, fancy hotels, movie theaters showing Western cinema, and more secular values. The nation's leading universities and private schools are also in the big cities. As education has become more widely available and as economic development has progressed, Indonesian villagers are increasingly moving to the cities for higher education, for excitement, and in order to gain separation from families they consider too restricting. Many also are seeking work—in transportation, trade, government, tourism, and related enterprises—that pays better than farming. The urban migration has its drawbacks, as the exodus of men in particular is contributing to higher rates of divorce. Nevertheless, the flow of people continues. Since President Suharto's 1998 resignation, the excitement of a more open society has been drawing still greater numbers of people to the cities, even as hopes rise for a more democratic society in the villages.

DISCUSSION QUESTIONS

1. How have patron-client relationships affected the average villager?

2. How do Thai, Vietnamese, and Indonesian villages differ?

3. How have Southeast Asian villages changed over the past decades? What would you say is the most important consequence of the recent changes?

4. Discuss the implications of recent economic development. What are the costs and the benefits for the rural villagers and urban migrants?

SUGGESTED READINGS

James C. Scott has written a fascinating book on how Southeast Asian villagers make their demands known to the elites. See his *Weapons of the Weak: Everyday Forms of Peasant Resistance* (Yale University Press, New Haven, 1985). For a wider view of the whole of mainland Southeast Asia, see Charles F. Keyes, *The Golden Peninsula: Culture and Adaptation in Mainland Southeast Asia* (University of Hawai'i Press, Honolulu, 1995). Important for understanding island Southeast Asia is Ben J. Wallace, *Village Life in Insular Southeast Asia* (Little, Brown and Co., Boston, 1971).

6

RECENT HISTORY AND POLITICS

Eleven diverse nations comprise Southeast Asia. The diversity among these eleven nations is one of the things that makes the region so fascinating. Because of the widespread differences among the eleven countries, it is difficult to generalize from one nation to the next. Nevertheless, the Southeast Asian nations have faced common issues, on which each has taken a different approach.

Since independence, the Southeast Asian nations have faced issues of national integration as they struggle to form effective governments that can win popular support (or at least legitimacy) while being strong enough to address problems and make difficult decisions. Most of the nations have also wrestled over the choice between civil government and authoritarian government. Not only have some countries moved back and forth between the two forms of government, but there is also an ongoing debate over which of them best meets the region's needs. In addition, Southeast Asian leaders have had to consider how best to promote economic development that benefits the people as a whole while addressing especially the needs of the least privileged.

This chapter summarizes the recent historical and political issues faced by each Southeast Asian country. The nations are dealt with separately because of the widespread differences among them. We begin with a recent event that touched nearly the entire region, because it appears in several of the country-by-country narratives.

From the 1960s to the 1990s the nations of Southeast Asia experienced some of the world's fastest economic growth. But they were hit hard by the Asian economic crisis that began in Thailand in 1997 and then spread to other countries. The crisis was a surprise. Most analysts had been captivated by the region's stunning record of high economic growth. However, those growth rates had masked a situation of imprudent governmental supervision, visionless political leadership, pervasive corruption, and business practices that lacked transparency. Borrowed money was being spent on real estate speculation and on poorly considered investments in industries and luxury projects that offered meager returns.

In 1997 and 1998, Southeast Asian nations paid the price for these practices. The Thai government devalued its currency, and other governments soon followed suit. Thailand, Malaysia, Indonesia, the Philippines, and other nations quickly slid into deep recessions marked by high unemployment, inflation, bank failures, stock market crashes, business bankruptcies, and declines in foreign investment. In much of Southeast Asia, the crisis caused the number of people living in poverty to skyrocket. Urban wages decreased and there were not enough people wanting to buy the farmers' food. The rich lost huge fortunes in the crashing stock market.

With their economies in collapse, the people of the region became restive. The most dramatic case was in Indonesia, where people went to the streets to protest the 33-year-old Suharto government. The demonstrations, which led to Suharto's overthrow, reminded the region that while many Southeast Asians may be willing to put up with harsh governments that meet the economic needs of the people, they are not so willing when the economy sours.

By the end of 1999, virtually all of the nations hit by the crisis had taken positive steps to correct the underlying weaknesses. The crisis eased as the governments reluctantly accepted the demands for reform that were being made by the International Monetary Fund and other international organizations. Governments budgeted more carefully, and trained technocrats were hired to get the economies back on track. In response, stock markets rebounded and foreign investment began to flow back into the region.

The economic crisis was not the only significant event in this period. In the 1990s communist Vietnam and Laos were opening their economies and diversifying their diplomatic relations. Thailand was taking steps to institutionalize a fuller dimension of democracy. Indonesia overthrew its military government. The region's eleven nations were also taking steps toward fuller cooperation. If anything, the crisis showed how important Southeast Asia was becoming in world affairs, because for a time it was feared that the crisis would bring down the economies of East Asia and even the United States.

The following eleven sections recount major events in the recent histories of Southeast Asia's eleven nations. Each section retells the country's origins, surveys recent politics and significant leaders, describes the current form of government, and takes note of economic successes and failures. As you read, observe the similarities and differences among the countries. Consider their historical backgrounds, their ethnic makeup, the dynamic changes in their diverse forms of government, and the varied results of their efforts to develop strong, growing economies.

Brunei

Brunei (officially named Negara Brunei Darussalam) is the least known of all the Southeast Asian nations. The country is located on the northwestern side of the island of Borneo, where it is surrounded by the Malaysian states of Sarawak and Sabah. Its population numbers just over 300,000. The nation has an exceptionally high per capita income (over $20,000) due to its plentiful oil resources.

Brunei was once a powerful state that dominated most of northwest Borneo and benefited from the trade that passed through the area. But in the late nineteenth-century Brunei lost most of its territory to British adventurers and businessmen (who established the present-day Malaysian states of Sarawak and Sabah until finally the sultanate was reduced to about the size of Delaware. At the turn of the twentieth century the tiny remains of this once-sizable polity accepted protection within the British Empire.

Brunei was one of the last Southeast Asian nations to gain independence. Great Britain granted internal self-government in 1959, and in 1963 the sultanate was invited to join the Federation of Malaysia (see sections on Malaysia and Singapore in this chapter). But Brunei chose to remain under British rule, and it remained a British colony until 1984, when it finally took over its own foreign and military affairs.

Since independence, the nation has been stable, largely because the fortune earned from the nation's oil and gas reserves has allowed Brunei to meet the needs of its people. The government has created a welfare system that provides free education and health care. It also provides subsidies for housing, funerals, and pilgrimages to Mecca. There is no income tax. But because this system is built on the great wealth brought in by the sale of oil and gas, Brunei is an anomaly from which it is impossible to generalize about any aspect of Southeast Asia as a whole.

Brunei is known as the nation with the world's wealthiest leader, the Sultan of Brunei. Sultan Haji Hassanal Bolkiah Mu'izzaddin Waddaulah is an absolute monarch whose legitimacy derives from his heredity, not from popular elections. The sultan embodies every aspect of Brunei. He controls billions of dollars, and it is impossible to know what money is his personally and what is the state's. He lives in a palace with 1,700 rooms. He also controls the small armed forces. There is no semblance of democracy in this oil-rich state. There are no political parties and there is no meaningful representative parliament. The sultan controls all communications, including newspapers and television. Brunei's absolute monarchy is increasingly anachronistic in Southeast Asia.

Burma (Myanmar)

With fifty million people and a magnificent geography including mountains, a long seacoast, fertile and verdant valleys, and picturesque cities and towns, Burma is potentially one of Southeast Asia's most vibrant and important nations. Ever since achieving independence in 1948, Burma has been seeking to become a *pyidawtha*—a peaceful, happy, and prosperous country. The goal has not yet been achieved. Instead, contemporary Burma has suffered continuously from ethnic disunity, economic stagnation, political instability, and governmental oppression. The overriding purpose of the various governments has been to perpetuate the positions of those in power.

Burma became unified in its current form fairly recently. Separate polities had existed earlier in Arakan (on the west coast near India), in the Irrawaddy delta region (once ruled by Mon peoples speaking a language related to Khmer), and in the Shan states of the northeast. But from time to time most or all of present-day Burma was united under a single ruler, and some of those empires were powerful. In the late eighteenth century one of these empires destroyed the Siamese capital at Ayuthaya and even controlled portions of northeast India. Its conquests led to conflict with the expanding British empire in India, and over a sixty-year span in the nineteenth century the British acquired Burma in the course of three separate wars.

Burma became independent in 1948. The Burmese struggle for independence was led by the Thakin movement, a group of anti-British nationalists headed by Aung San, a fiery nationalist who had received training in Japan. During World War II, the Thakin movement initially received support from the Japanese, but it turned against Japan as the occupation became increasingly repressive. The Thakin movement served as the core for the Anti-Fascist People's Freedom League (AFPFL), a united front group opposed to the Japanese that included key members of minority groups, leading elements of the Burmese National Army, the communists, and the socialists. AFPFL forces cooperated with the British to oust the Japanese and then turned against the British in the struggle for independence.

When negotiating Burma's independence, the British initially wanted to divide the country into "Burma proper" and the "border areas." The portion inhabited primarily by ethnic Burmans would be given full self-government, while the outlying areas inhabited by minorities would remain under British rule. Aung San opposed this proposal, because he wanted independence for the whole of Burma. Negotiations continued, and the British eventually agreed to Aung San's demands. Aung San was expected to be the country's first head of state, but he was assassinated in 1947, thus becoming the nation's martyred hero. When independence was granted in 1948, the first parliamentary government was led by U Nu.

Aung San

Aung San, the father of Burmese independence, was assassinated in 1947 before he was able to step into the presidency of newly independent Burma. Formerly a leader of the Burmese Communist Party, he fought for a short time alongside the Japanese army, but he soon realized that Japan's occupation of Burma was even harsher than that of Great Britain, the country's formal colonizer. Disillusioned, he declared war on Japan and received the support of British generals. After the war, he negotiated Burma's independence from Great Britain, but before independence had been granted he died at age 32 at the hands of his political rivals.

Aung San's fame as a nationalist later helped propel his daughter, Aung San Suu Kyi, into the leadership of the democratic movement against Burma's military dictatorship. She has led the opposition from 1988 to the present despite being under house arrest most of the time.

The newly independent Burmese governments faced several serious problems. The first was ethnic strife and civil war. The period extending from 1948 to 1958 was known as the time of troubles. Well-organized minority ethnic groups, especially the Karen and Shan, opposed the government's insistence on a unified national state, advocating instead the establishment of autonomous states for each group. The minority groups were supported by communist insurgents or, in the case of the Shan rebels, by Chiang Kai-shek's Koumingtang army. The government eventually used military force to suppress the separatist movements, but some of the insurgencies never entirely died out.

The second major problem after independence concerned the poorly trained civil service, which was not able to carry out government programs effectively. President U Nu's government had proclaimed a socialist policy that required effective centralized administration, but the Burmese bureaucracy foundered, resulting in severe political and economic disturbances such as inefficiency and corruption. By 1958 the political condition of Burma was so chaotic that U Nu voluntarily turned the nation's administration over to a caretaker military government led by General Ne Win, who had once worked with Aung San in the independence movement. Ne Win's government restored a semblance of law and order, and it reorganized the bureaucracy to make it more efficient. The military government stabilized the cost of living and suppressed the black market. Exports increased and corruption was at least temporarily halted.

Despite the military's success, the electorate chose in 1960 to return U Nu to leadership. The popular U Nu was committed to democratic means and Buddhist passivity, and he was an example of Buddhist piety. But corruption returned and the new government was ineffective. When U Nu announced a plan to make Buddhism the state religion, uprisings increased among the ethnic minorities, many of whom were led by non-Buddhists. At the same time, U Nu upset the military by proposing a federation plan that was intended to provide the hill groups with more autonomy. The military believed that the proposed federation would increase disunity and intensify the internal armed conflicts. The military also perceived U Nu's civilian government to be weak, lacking in unity, and dependent upon Western-style political institutions that were incompatible with Burmese culture.

On March 2, 1962, Ne Win led a military *coup d'etat* that deposed U Nu and began an era of military rule that continues at the present time (2004). Ne Win disbanded the parliament, banned political parties, arrested U Nu for his failure to modernize Burma, and restricted civil liberties. He established a military-dominated Burmese Revolutionary Council, consisting of seventeen military leaders, that set forth a program of radical economic and political policies called the "Burmese Way to Socialism." The military's program of socialism included the nationalization of major industries, schools, rice mills, businesses, and financial institutions. The Burmese Way to Socialism became a political-ideological end justifying any governmental means, including suppression of human rights. Parliamentary democracy was rejected as incompatible with the aims of the new state. Instead, the Revolutionary Council conferred all legislative, executive, and judicial powers on General Ne Win.

To mobilize support for the new socialist program, Ne Win established the Burmese Socialist Program Party (BSPP). The BSPP was intended to reach down to the village level along hierarchical lines, with all power centered at the party's military-dominated top echelon. The people were to be organized in peasants' and workers' councils that functioned to legitimize army rule and to communicate directives from the top down.

Ne Win's government moved toward a neutralist foreign policy that took the form of isolationism. The government refused foreign aid and investment, abrogated treaties, restricted the flow of tourists, and rejected all forms of Westernization. Unlike other Southeast Asian nations, Burma did not accept or encourage the Western model of development. Instead, the government pursued an isolationist policy that separated the country from the Western-dominated global economy.

In January 1974 Burma became the Socialist Republic of the Union of Burma. Ne Win discarded his military uniform and became the "civilian" president of the new government. The BSPP ruled with little internal or external opposition. Nevertheless, there were periodic revolts against the government by citizens who were incensed by the country's stagnant economy, its isolation from the world, the dearth of democratic rights, and the closed universities and schools. The economic stagnation was particularly galling because Burma was a nation rich in natural and human resources and because Burma's neighbors, particularly Thailand, were prospering. Thus, while the ongoing ethnic insurgencies continued to fester, the citizens of Burma's cities periodically protested the government's failures. The most significant demonstration occurred in 1988, when thousands of Burmese rose in wrath against the dictatorship.

An immediate cause of the 1988 demonstrations was the Ne Win administration's decision to declare valueless some 80 percent of the money then in circulation. The demonetization adversely affected the entire population, both rich and poor. The demonstrations were precipitated by a March 1988 incident in a tea shop, where students and other patrons were squabbling over the choice of music tapes being played. The police arrived, a student was killed, and thousands of schoolmates later returned to avenge their colleague's death. The incident ended horrifyingly when 41 students suffocated to death in the heat of a police wagon into which they had been jammed. The demonstrations and strikes that ensued forced Ne Win to announce his resignation as BSPP Chairman. Unfortunately, Ne Win's replacement was U Sein Lwin, who is known as the "Butcher of Burma," because of his violent repression of dissidents in 1962, 1974, and 1988. His unpopularity led to his downfall after just a few weeks and he was replaced by Maung Maung, a more moderate leader. But in September 1988 the hardliners regained control, as General Saw Maung crushed the demonstrations and restored the military to power in a *coup* that was followed by mass arrests and violent repression. Saw Maung established the State Law and Order Restoration Council (SLORC), consisting of generals loyal to Ne Win, which became an all-powerful, much-despised government entity. Its acronym was often sneered at, as the word "slorc" sounded like a repressive agency. To appease public opinion, SLORC agreed to multi-party elections in 1990, certain that the government could and would control every aspect of the elections through its power over the media and officials.

With unexpected approval from SLORC, an opposition party emerged in late 1988 that was eventually known as the National League for Democracy (NLD). In an extraordinary turn of events, a woman named Aung San Suu Kyi (the daughter of the independence hero Aung San) had recently returned from her home in England to take care of her ailing mother in Burma. Aung San Suu Kyi began making speeches about the need for freedom and democracy. The crowds listening to her grew daily, until she became the leader and symbol of the democratic movement. The military was frightened by her unexpected and astounding popularity, and in July 1989 they placed her under house arrest for having been "manipulated" by communists and foreign intelligence agencies. SLORC also attempted to minimize the opposition's influence by means of censorship and harassment. Nevertheless, the NLD won the May 1990 election by a landslide, taking more than 80 percent of the seats in the *Pyithu Hluttaw*, Burma's legislature.

Despite their resounding defeat at the polls, the generals refused to allow the transfer of power. They declared the elections null and void, arrested the winners, and isolated Aung San Suu Kyi. They have retained their illegitimate power until the present. In 1992, General Saw Maung resigned from his position as the nation's leader (he was said to have gone crazy), and he was replaced by Army Chief of Staff General Than Shwe. Little was heard from Burma during these years, although in 1991 Aung San Suu Kyi won the Nobel Peace Prize for her courageous stand against the dictators. In 1997 Burma was admitted to ASEAN (the Association of Southeast Asian Nations), an inter-governmental organization that was originally founded to counter North Vietnam but which today works to facilitate regional cooperation. Also, in 1997, in a cosmetic attempt to improve its international image, SLORC officials renamed the ruling council the State Peace and Development Council (SPDC). SPDC is a junta of about 19 high-ranking military officers led by a ruling troika. The three dominant leaders include Senior General Than Shwe, who is the troika's leading figure and military commander-in-chief. Lieutenant General Khin Nyunt holds the post of prime minister, and General Maung Aye is deputy military commander and heir apparent to Than Shwe. General Ne Win, the former dictator and mentor to the troika, died in 2002.

The SPDC has refused to share power in the governance of Burma. The leading democratic oppositionist, Aung San Suu Kyi, has been kept under house arrest for occasional short periods of several months during which it would become clear that she still retained the admiration and support of the Burmese people. SPDC officials claimed that only the military could assure political and economic stability in Burma. That claim is belied by the terrible economy, which has left almost all Burmese in a state of impoverishment. Already stagnant under Ne Win and SLORC the economy has gotten even worse under the SPDC. Even rice is no longer plentiful, and malnutrition is a severe problem. In the late 1990s, the economy improved briefly but the positive effects were temporary.

The SPDC has stayed in power by suppressing any potential threats. Dissidents are jailed or executed, and peasants are forcibly relocated to areas where they will be less influential. Military officers have replaced civilians at all levels of the bureaucracy. The government allows no freedom of assembly, and it has closed the universities and banned political parties. There has been no elected parliamentary body since the opposition's victory in the nullified elections of 1990. The press is totally controlled by the generals, and the daily English-language paper is considered one of the dullest in the world. The only news allowed in the media is "good news" about the generals visiting various factories and pinning hero medals on workers. Burmese citizens are not allowed to subscribe to foreign publications, and all e-mail and internet communication must go through the government.

Burma remains an anachronism and a beautiful country run by autocrats. Visitors to Rangoon speak about the magnificence of the Schwedagon pagoda, perhaps the most ethereal place on earth, and the stunning temples at Pagan are among the most remarkable in the world. The Burmese continue to wear the traditional *longyi*, a sarong-like skirt for men and women. Monks wear saffron-colored robes. The rivers and mountains are gorgeous. Yet, amidst this grandeur is a government that is exploitive, corrupt, and abuses the people's rights.

Cambodia

The name Cambodia is derived from the word Kampuchea, the country's traditional name in the Khmer language (the terms Khmer and Cambodian refer to both the language and the people). Cambodia traces its history back to the great Angkor civilization that once dominated mainland Southeast Asia, but since the late fifteenth century, Cambodia has been a small, relatively weak nation. Today it is about the size of Illinois and has some eleven million citizens.

The French granted Cambodia's independence in 1954. Independent Cambodia was initially a constitutional monarchy ruled by King Norodom Sihanouk. In 1941 the French had placed Sihanouk on the throne because they considered him "accommodating." However, he became an ardent nationalist and was responsible for winning Cambodia's independence. In 1955 he abdicated the throne, in favor of his father, in order to enter politics and form his own political party, Sangkhum Reastr Niyum (People's Socialist Community). His abdication meant that he was henceforth referred to as Prince Sihanouk. Sihanouk dominated Cambodian politics until he was overthrown in 1970. Under his rule, Cambodia enjoyed relative stability and peace at a time when neighboring nations were suffering from warfare and internal strife. Cambodians were exceedingly poor but they were not oppressed by the government.

In 1970 Sihanouk was overthrown by a military *coup* led by General Lon Nol, the armed forces chief. Sihanouk's downfall stemmed from the presence of North Vietnamese and Vietcong forces who were using the "Ho Chi Minh Trail," located partially in Cambodia, to transfer troops and supplies to southern Vietnam. In response, the United States was secretly bombing Cambodian territory. The Cambodian *coup* leaders believed that Sihanouk had welcomed these foreign incursions. They were incensed that Cambodian territory was being used by alien (Vietnamese) forces. (Sihanouk denied that he had acquiesced to the activities of the Vietnamese troops, and he also denied having approved the American bombing.) The military *coup* leaders also accused Sihanouk of engaging in corruption and of not providing sufficient mobility for ambitious elite Cambodians, who resented the total control Sihanouk wielded over policy-making. In addition, Sihanouk's relations with the United States had become acrimonious, mainly because the American government did not trust him and his on-again, off-again policies toward the Vietnam war. Because of his royalty, Prince Sihanouk retained the loyalty of the rural masses, but the peasants wielded little influence over the outcome of power struggles in the capital city of Phnom Penh. Sihanouk had failed to institutionalize the political system, and politics had become exclusively a function of his own desires and whims. When he displeased enough members of the elite, he became unable to retain his position as the country's leader.

From 1970 to 1975 the military was the dominant institution in Cambodian politics. Led by General Lon Nol, it oversaw a five-year period of war and governmental ineptitude. The economy collapsed, and the nation once known as "an island of tranquility in a sea of chaos" was torn asunder. The Lon Nol government was incapable of resolving the economic crisis, the pervasive corruption, and the growing power of anti-government insurgents led by the communist Khmer Rouge (Red Cambodians). Even Sihanouk voiced support for the rebels from his exile in China, thereby providing them with legitimacy. The government was unpopular with the rural people, and as a result the rebel forces grew in influence and controlled ever-larger portions of the country.

In April 1975 the Khmer Rouge rebels took control of Phnom Penh. Under the leadership of the secretive Pol Pot, the new regime immediately began a program of radical social restructuring. The cities were emptied, money was banned, the family structure abolished, schools closed, Buddhist temples destroyed, and books burned. The Khmer Rouge silenced the citizenry through draconian measures such as strict discipline, terror, mass executions, and isolation. Teachers, intellectuals, government leaders, and professionals were particularly targeted.

Pol Pot's purpose was to "purify" Cambodia by ridding the nation of every form of decadence. A follower of Mao Tse-tung, he wanted to turn Cambodia into a perfectly egalitarian society of peasants in which everyone worked the fields. He believed that education was best done holding the plow. He ended every form of life he considered bourgeois, including marriage, religion, education, and family. Under Pol Pot, Cambodia became the most closed society on earth. An estimated one in four Cambodians was killed or starved during this four-year period of Khmer Rouge rule.

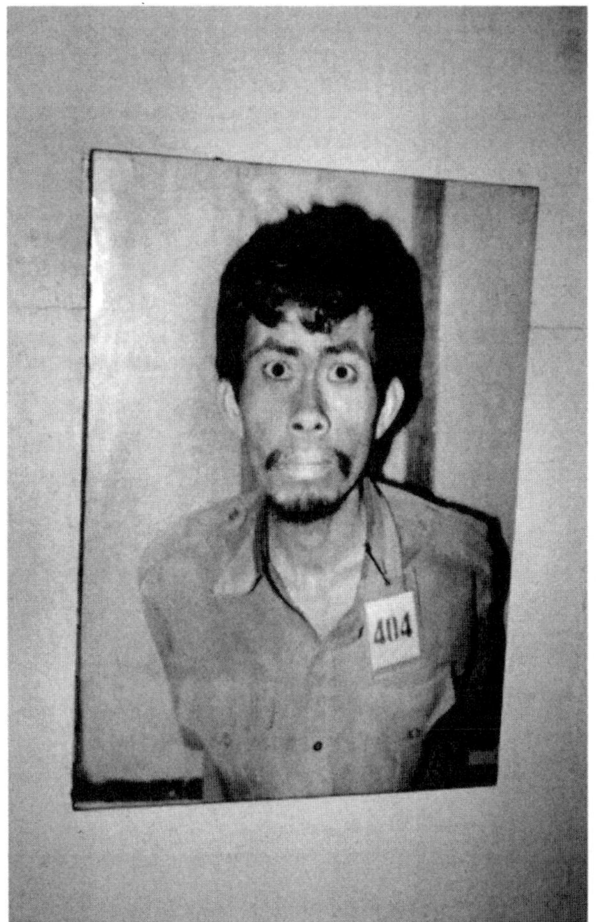

Figure 14. A victim of the Khmer Rouge
Photo displayed in the former Tuol Sleng Prison (now a museum).

On Christmas Day 1978, the Vietnamese invaded Cambodia, overthrew Pol Pot's regime, and set up a new government that was soon headed by Hun Sen. Vietnamese troops occupied Cambodia from 1979 to 1989, a galling situation for Cambodians who historically detested and feared the Vietnamese. Nevertheless, Hun Sen's government undid the most onerous policies of the Khmer Rouge. The cities were repopulated, money was reintroduced, families were reunited, schools were reopened, and Buddhism was allowed to function. However, the new government faced severe problems. Virtually all the educated Cambodians had been executed, so there were few officials, doctors, engineers, or industrialists to help build the country. Corruption proliferated. Finally, in 1991, the United Nations assumed a direct role in supervising Cambodian affairs. An international task force helped write a constitution and organized elections that took place in 1993.

Figure 15. Khmer Rouge torture
Memorial paintings in a Cambodian village.

Death in Cambodia

As Buddhists, Cambodians believe that death is merely the end of one existence and the beginning of another. Hence, there is little outward expression of grief. Mourners wear white clothing. Funerals are attended by family and friends and include cremation. During the genocidal Khmer Rouge regime that lasted from 1975 to 1979 an estimated one in four Cambodians was killed.

The 1993 elections favored Sihanouk's son, Prince Ranarridh, but Hun Sen refused to relinquish his position as prime minister. The United Nations then agreed to a co-premiership for Hun Sen and Prince Ranarridh. Sihanouk returned from exile to become the nation's king, but because of his advanced age and precarious health he played only a minor role in the country's affairs. The co-premiership arrangement lasted only a few years, and in 1998 Hun Sen ousted Ranarridh by means of a *coup d'etat*. Elections held later in 1998 brought Ranarridh back from exile to lead the National Assembly (the nation's legislative body), but

Hun Sen retained the post of prime minister and continued to be the most powerful man in Cambodia. The United Nations had attempted to establish a government that balanced power between the executive and legislative branches, but Cambodia had again become an authoritarian nation dominated by Hun Sen.

Chea Samy

The tradition of Cambodian classical dance was nearly eradicated by the Khmer Rouge, who were determined to stop any cultural activities considered traditional. When the genocidal Khmer Rouge were ousted in 1979, one of the surviving women went on to revive Cambodia's famous classical dancing. This woman, Chea Samy, had been born in 1919. At age five she became a dancer in the royal palace serving during the reigns of King Sisowath and King Monivong. While in the palace, she met her husband-to-be, who turned out to be the younger brother of Pol Pot, the despised leader of the Khmer Rouge.

Like all Cambodians in 1975, Chea Samy had been sent to the rural areas where she collected manure for fertilizer. Neither she nor the local Khmer Rouge realized that she was married to Pol Pot's brother because Pol Pot used a false name and isolated himself even from most of the Khmer Rouge. To survive she told the Khmer Rouge that she had been a vendor in the market.

When she and other Cambodians were liberated from the Khmer Rouge in 1979 Chea Samy began teaching children Cambodian classical dancing. With the help of musicians who had survived the Khmer Rouge, she gradually rebuilt the national classical ballet. She died in 1994, knowing that her nation's ancient arts had a future.

The July 27, 2003 elections resulted in a victory for Hun Sen and his ruling Cambodian People's Party. The CPP won 73 of 123 seats in the National Assembly, while Funcinpec, led by Prince Ranarridh, won 26 seats and the Sam Rainsy Party won 24. Because Hun Sen's Party did not win two-thirds of the vote, he was forced to forge a parliamentary coalition with the opposition. However, his personal domination over virtually every aspect of Cambodian politics and economics remained intact.

Throughout the 1980s and 1990s, the Khmer Rouge had conducted a resistance based in the mountains of western Cambodia. In the late 1990s the resistance suddenly fell apart. The once-powerful Pol Pot, now an old man, was brought before a "people's tribunal" ironically chaired by his Khmer Rouge colleagues. He was denounced by his former Khmer Rouge supporters and placed under house arrest, but he died in April 1998 without ever having expressed remorse or guilt. He asserted that he had a clear conscience.

The problem of how to govern Cambodia effectively has been one of the thorniest issues in the politics of contemporary Southeast Asia. The Cambodians' phenomenal resilience is the best hope for recovery from the horrific trauma the nation has suffered from the 1960s to the present. Their resiliency will continue to be tested by the persistently authoritarian administration and the weak economy.

East Timor

East Timor is one of the poorest areas in Southeast Asia. For centuries the island of Timor was isolated and neglected, ruled by a traditional system of local chiefs. Portugal dominated the eastern half of the island since the 1600s but it was only about 100 years ago that Portugal took direct administration. During World War II, East Timor became known internationally because the strategic location of the island was of importance to the Japanese as well as the allied powers, especially the Australians. East Timorese overwhelmingly sided with the Australians in the war.

When Indonesia became independent in 1949, East Timor remained a Portuguese colony. In the 1970s Timorese political parties emerged, the most important being the pro-independence Fretilin. In 1975, sensing that East Timor was close to receiving independence from Portugal, the Indonesian army invaded, and on July 16, 1976, Indonesia declared East Timor to be its 27th province. The Indonesian military justified the invasion by arguing that East Timor was geographically and culturally part of Indonesia. But the East Timorese desire for self-determination endured, and over the years periodic uprisings took place against Indonesia. Over 100,000 Timorese were killed in the ensuing battles. Despite the horrific war which devastated East Timor, there were few official condemnations of Indonesia. Nevertheless, in 1996 East Timorese Catholic Bishop Carlos Belo and Spokesperson Jose Ramos-Horta won the Nobel Peace Prize for their courageous stand against the Indonesians.

As long as Suharto remained president of Indonesia, the hopes for East Timorese independence were minuscule for it was at his direction that the invasion has taken place. However, when Suharto was overthrown in 1998, his successor, President Habibie, allowed a referendum in East Timor to decide its future. Almost 80 percent of the East Timorese voted for independence in the 1999 vote. However, elements of the Indonesian military then began a dreadful rampage that resulted in the deaths of one in four East Timorese, and destroyed much of the island. The United Nations sent troops in to bring order, but the country's infrastructure had already been destroyed. Despite this tragedy, East Timorese pressed forward to form a constitution and a provisional government. The first presidential elections were held in

April 2002 and the country was officially declared independent in May under the leadership of Xanana Gusmao, a former prisoner of the Indonesians. It is the world's newest democracy.

The future of East Timor is ambiguous. On the one hand, the country is a functioning democracy with competing executive, legislative, and jusicial branches of government, and this would seem to bode well for the country's future. On the other hand, its economy is one of the poorest in the world. Much of the infrastructure was destroyed by Indonesian troops, and despite the substantial reconstruction efforts since 1999, the people's standard of living is low. The total GDP (PPP) is under $500 million, and the per capita income is about $500 per year, a tiny fraction of those of other nations throughout the world. There are few paved roads and no railway system. Foreign trade is almost nonexistent, and the local economy depends primarily on agricultural products such as coffee, rice, maize, cassava, soybeans, and various tropical fruits. There is virtually no telephone system. Computers are not to be found. Three-quarters of the population is without electricity, and half is without safe drinking water.

Indonesia

The Republic of Indonesia is a relatively recent invention. Before the advent of Dutch colonial rule, the Indonesian archipelago had been home to a dizzying array of polities, including states based in Java (including the Shailendra dynasty, Majapahit, and Mataram), Sumatra (Srivijaya, Aceh, Siak, and other states), Sulawesi, Borneo, and elsewhere. There were trading relationships among the islands, but the region had never been unified under a single ruler.

In 1602 the Dutch East India Company established a trading post at Batavia (now Jakarta), and it soon gained control of the spice trade originating in the Moluccas (Spice Islands) in the eastern end of the archipelago. At first the Dutch expanded their territorial control only gradually, concentrating attention on Java, the Moluccas, and other centers of commercial importance. But in the nineteenth and early twentieth centuries they rapidly extended their rule over the rest of the archipelago. In some places the Dutch takeover was relatively easy, but in others, especially in Aceh (in northwest Sumatra), resistance to Dutch rule was strong.

The Dutch East Indies contained such a wide variety of peoples, cultures, and languages that it is remarkable that a single nation could ever have been created out of them. However, nationalists led by Indonesia's future president Sukarno resolved to create a unified and independent Indonesian nation. The nationalists created a national flag and a national anthem. They also created a national language, *Bahasa*

Indonesia, which was based on a form of Malay already being used by traders and merchants.

During World War II the Japanese encouraged Indonesian nationalism, and the most prominent nationalist leaders collaborated with the Japanese occupiers. When the war ended, the nationalists sought immediate independence, and in 1945 they declared the formation of the Republic of Indonesia, with Sukarno as president. The Dutch ignored the declaration and over the next four years they gradually reoccupied most of the country. But they could not subdue the people, and their use of force increasingly angered the international community. The Dutch finally agreed to a settlement, and on December 27, 1949, Indonesia formally gained its independence.

Independent Indonesia faced a broad array of problems. World War II and the four-year independence struggle had devastated the country economically and politically. The nation's roads, communications, electricity, and ports were non-existent at worst and ineffective at best. Moreover, Indonesia was geographically, linguistically, ethnically, and socially heterogeneous. Indonesia's new leaders were trying to fashion a nation-state out of more than 100 ethnic groups, speaking over 200 languages, who were scattered among thousands of islands stretched out in a 3,000-mile-long archipelago.

Post-independence unity relied primarily on the leadership of President Sukarno (who, like many Indonesians, used only one name). Sukarno dominated Indonesian politics for two decades until he was overthrown in 1965. His first concern as president was national unification and solidarity. In order to facilitate national unity, Suharto proclaimed an ideology of Pancasila, five principles that were intended to provide the spiritual and philosophical basis for a secular Indonesian state. Though Indonesia was 85 percent Muslim, large portions of the country were inhabited primarily by people who followed other religions, and the government felt it wise that these people not feel threatened.

Pancasila

Pancasila refers to the five principles that are the foundation of the Indonesian state. The principles include a belief in one supreme god, humanism, nationalism, national sovereignty, and social justice. The most important aspect of Pancasila is the lack of direct reference to Islam, an omission intended to enable persons of all religions to follow the precepts. President Sukarno was the first leader to set forth Pancasila, but the principles have subsequently been embedded in Indonesia's constitution. More recently, under President Suharto, all political parties were forced to make Pancasila their sole guiding philosophy.

In the decade following Sukarno's rise to the presidency, a classic struggle arose between the "solidarity makers" and the "administrators." The "solidarity makers" emphasized nationalism and ideological purity, while the "administrators" concentrated on pragmatic approaches to the problems of economic restoration. Sukarno led the nationalists, while his vice president, Hatta, led the administrators. Although the solidarity makers prevailed under Sukarno's leadership, they failed to institutionalize an effective day-to-day administrative system. This failure led to government inefficiencies that left the people's economic needs unmet.

The period of 1949 to 1956 was the era of "liberal democracy," when political parties flourished, parliamentary government was established, and relatively free elections were held. However, democratic institutions did not "fit" Indonesian cultures, which traditionally placed little value on political representation or group formation and which lacked the personal trust that is essential for democracy to flourish. As a result, political parties became destructive of national unity because they revolved not around political issues or interest group representation but rather around prominent individuals who were primarily concerned with perpetuating their own high-level positions.

In 1959 Sukarno responded to the government's ineffectiveness by proclaiming "guided democracy," an authoritarian style of leadership that drew on the traditional Indonesian village procedures of making decisions by consultation and discussion (*musjawarah*) while searching for unanimous agreement (*mufakat*). Guided democracy was presented as a return to traditional political patterns and an answer to the failure of the Western style of electoral politics. Sukarno expressed contempt for Western-style "50 percent plus 1 democracy," which he saw as a polarizing system. However, some scholars have argued that guided democracy was really a mask to disguise Sukarno's aim of perpetuating his personal power and the power of the elites.

In the end, guided democracy was no more effective than liberal democracy. During the late 1950s and early 1960s, both the military and the communists gained influence. By 1965 Indonesia faced economic chaos and political instability. Flagrant corruption at every level of the bureaucracy had drained the budget. The transportation industry had collapsed, unemployment was rampant, and inflation (estimated at 600 percent per year) was running out of control. Sukarno was also moving Indonesia toward an alliance with the People's Republic of China, a development that worried the conservative military. He was outspokenly hostile to the West, especially to the United States, and in 1965 he withdrew from the United Nations. Internally, he sought to balance the right-wing military with an equally powerful left-wing peasantry as a way to make himself Indonesia's supreme arbiter.

Sukarno armed peasant farmers with weapons provided by China, and with his off-and-on encouragement the Communist Party of Indonesia (PKI) became the largest communist party outside the communist bloc. In the midst of all this activity Sukarno began showing signs of weakness. On one occasion in 1965 Sukarno collapsed while giving a speech, leading many to begin thinking about a post-Sukarno period.

On September 30, 1965, dissident members of the military attempted a *coup*. Within hours of the *coup* attempt General Suharto assumed command of the army and took control of the situation, moving swiftly to determine which military units remained loyal to the army's leaders. Indonesian analysts have presented three basic interpretations of the *coup*. The first suggests that the *coup* was an internal army affair devised by junior officers independent of outside influence. A second interpretation, advanced recently, suggests that General Suharto had a hand in the *coup* plotting. The third interpretation, the one advanced by Suharto and his conservative supporters, held that the army rebels were colluding with Sukarno and the Communist Party of Indonesia (PKI) to set up a socialist state to be led at least initially by Sukarno. This interpretation was used as justification for a two-year bloodbath that resulted in the deaths of an estimated half a million persons who were suspected of being communist. Indonesia's Chinese community was particularly hard-hit, because many Indonesians suspected that the country's indigenous Chinese community was loyal to China rather than to Indonesia. The question of who staged the *coup* may never be solved, and the precise role of the PKI, the army rebels, President Sukarno, and even General Suharto may never be known. The evidence is inconclusive and contradictory, and almost all of the leading *coup* participants were murdered or executed in the months after the event.

Gestapu

Gestapu is an acronym for the Indonesian words that mean September 30 Movement. On that date, a group of dissident military officers kidnapped leading Indonesian generals and then killed them. These dissidents claimed they were acting to preempt a *coup* by the generals themselves. Inexplicably, General Suharto was not among the generals targeted. He mobilized army troops and put down the *coup* after just two days of struggle. Suharto's supporters claimed that President Sukarno and the Indonesian Communist Party (PKI) had plotted the *coup*, but the evidence is inconclusive, so we may never know if the claim is true. In the long run, the *coup* played into the hands of the military, because in its aftermath the communists and much of the Chinese community were decimated, while the military took power under Suharto's leadership.

After the *coup* had been suppressed, Sukarno was confined to his palace at Bogor, in Java. Suharto took on more power with each passing month. He formally became president only in 1968, but he had taken effective control much earlier. Suharto banned the PKI, arrested pro-Sukarno officials, ended the close relationship with China, and rejoined the United Nations. He also proclaimed a New Order for Indonesia that emphasized authoritarian government, economic development, and political stability.

Suharto's New Order took firm control of the country. Political freedoms were curtailed, political parties circumscribed, and elections held solely to anoint Suharto's supporters. Under Suharto, the military essentially had power over every aspect of Indonesian society. Suharto placed military personnel in crucial administrative positions all the way from the national level to the provincial and district level. The military also controlled the media, and no opposition to their rule was allowed.

The military set up a political party, Golkar, which was a federation of organizations committed to Suharto. For the next 30 years Golkar dominated every election. Due to Golkar's control of the partially elected, partially appointed People's Consultative Assembly (MPR, from the Indonesian name *Majelis Permusyawaratan Rakyat*), the MPR elected Suharto president of Indonesia no fewer than six times, casting a unanimous vote all six times. The MPR was in theory the nation's law-making body, but in practice it was a rubber stamp for Suharto's policies.

Though it imposed political restrictions, the new regime quickly improved economic conditions. By 1970 the runaway inflation had been brought under control. Foreign investment, exports, and oil earnings increased significantly. The average Indonesian's standard of living also rose substantially. The New Order improved Indonesia's infrastructure, expanded health and educational facilities, and rationalized the formerly chaotic governmental system. Meanwhile, the army took on itself the role of *dwi fungsi* (dual function), combining its national security role with an interest in economic development efforts.

Dwi Fungsi

Since General Suharto's advent to the presidency of Indonesia, the military has insisted on a policy of *dwi fungsi*, which translates into English as "dual function." The purpose of the policy is to show that the military has a role not only in national security but also in the country's internal development. The military has played this dual role ever since the late 1960s, and in 1978 the People's Consultative Assembly gave the policy formal recognition. *Dwi fungsi* legitimated the military's desire to run both foreign and domestic politics during Suharto's New Order regime.

Suharto's policies were deemed highly successful both by most Indonesians and by outside analysts, who noted the end of inflation, the high rates of economic development, and the slowing of the population growth rate from 2.2 percent per year to 1.6 percent. Yet things were not entirely rosy. For example, by 1998 Indonesia's population had climbed to 210 million, making Indonesia the fourth most populous nation in the world. Sixty percent of Indonesia's people lived on the island of Java, the most densely populated area of the world (Java is about the size of New York state but has seven times the population).

The New Order ended abruptly and unexpectedly. In 1998, Suharto was seventy-eight years old. Due to his age, and because of the rising tide of democratization throughout the world, controversy had arisen regarding his future as a leader. Criticism centered on three main issues. Opponents criticized his family's and friends' domination of indigenous business and industrial conglomerates in the entertainment, construction, telecommunications, and oil businesses. They also criticized the government's authoritarian nature and its disregard for human rights. A third complaint related to the financial crisis of 1997 and 1998 that led to a drastic reduction in many Indonesians' standard of living.

On May 20, 1998, after ten days of student-led antigovernment demonstrations, Suharto resigned as president in favor of his hand-picked vice president, B. Jusuf Habibie. Habibie had the support of the military, and he put forth economic policies designed to resolve the crises of currency devaluation, inflation, and unemployment. He also laid the groundwork for more democratic elections, but he later had trouble presenting himself as a democratic reformer because he was perceived as Suharto's *protégé*.

On June 7, 1999, Indonesians voted in the fairest, most democratic election the country had experienced since the 1950s. Voters elected 462 representatives to the People's Consultative Assembly (MPR), where they joined 238 appointed representatives of the armed forces, provincial legislatures, and other societal groups. The elections featured several democratic reforms. Though the MPR was still partially appointed, Habibie had given the election real meaning by increasing the proportion of elected members. In addition, to assure election fairness, a dozen nations sent monitors to Indonesia, making it difficult for the ruling Golkar party to commit fraud.

Fully forty-eight political parties fielded candidates, forty-five more parties than had been allowed under Suharto. The most popular of the four major candidates was former President Sukarno's daughter, Megawati Sukarnoputri. Her Indonesian Democratic Party of Struggle ran on a secular-nationalist platform that received much support from poor people in both rural and urban areas. Megawati was popular as a symbol for everything Suharto was not, but she had virtually no administrative experience and her campaign was bereft of policy pronouncements. The second major candidate was Abdurrahman Wahid, also known as Gus Dur, who was head of the Nahdlatul Ulama, a 37-million-member Muslim organization. Despite his position as a religious cleric, Wahid was considered a secularist in national politics because he was opposed to the notion (then being voiced by some Muslim leaders) that Indonesia should become an Islamic State and enforce Islamic laws on all its citizens. His National Awakening Party was immensely popular, but his poor health undermined popular support for him. Third was Amien Rais, an intellectual and the leader of Muhammadiyah, a 23-million-member Muslim organization. His National Mandate Party campaigned on a platform of ethnic and religious inclusiveness, moral regeneration based on the precepts of modernist Islam, and abolishment of corruption, collusion, and nepotism. His party was immensely popular, because the Muhammadiyah organization had ties to a huge network of schools, hospitals, orphanages, and mosques. The fourth major candidate was B. Jusuf Habibie. He led the government party, Golkar, which in the public mind was tied closely to the Suharto presidency. This perception helped Habibie with people who remembered the New Order as a time of stability and economic growth, but it hurt him with people who remembered Suharto's presidency as a time of dictatorship and human rights violations.

In the June election Megawati Sukarnoputri's political party won the largest number of votes. Though her party did not win a majority, the Assembly was expected to name her as Indonesia's new president. Instead, the Assembly named Abdurrahman Wahid as president and Megawati Sukarnoputri as vice president, while Rais became chairman of the Assembly. Wahid had won majority support in the MPR by forging a coalition with Islamic leaders (many of whom opposed a female president) and with members of the Golkar party.

Upon taking office in October 1999, President Wahid moved quickly and decisively to democratize the nation after its three decades of military dictatorship. Indonesia's new president faced tremendous challenges. His first challenge was to professionalize the armed forces by confining its functions to defense, a difficult task following 35 years of military rule. President Wahid began the process by appointing a civilian as defense minister.

The second challenge was economic. Suharto and his cronies had plundered the nation, engaging in rampant corruption, shipping billions of dollars out of the country, and turning many important industries over to friends and relatives. Indonesia was considered one of the most corrupt nations in the world. Its banking system was in tatters, and in many industries free competition was nonexistent because of the nepotism practiced by Suharto and his family. It will take years to undo the damage, and there was world-wide skepticism about the nation's capacity to reform, but the new administration began a vigorous campaign to improve the country's image. Immediately after the election, President Wahid traveled to the other Southeast Asian nations and to the United States in an effort to show that Indonesia was becoming a country in which foreign investments would be secure.

Third, and perhaps most importantly, President Wahid faced a crisis of national integration. In a 1999 referendum approved by President Habibie, the people of East Timor had voted overwhelmingly (78 percent) to become an independent nation. In 1976 East Timor had been forcibly annexed by Indonesia, and this action was followed by a civil war that led to the deaths of one in four East Timorese. The success of the East Timorese independence movement sparked independence demonstrations in other areas where there had been festering separatist sentiment. Especially noteworthy were calls for independence in Aceh (in northwestern Sumatra) and in Irian Jaya (western New Guinea). Critics of the latter two movements pointed out that East Timor had been colonized by the Portuguese rather than the Dutch and had therefore never been an integral part of Indonesia, whereas Aceh and Irian Jaya were traditionally and inherently Indonesian. But the Acehnese and Irianese separatists argued that under former Presidents Sukarno and Suharto the two areas had faced decades of social injustice and military abuse. Acehnese separatists noted in addition that Aceh had been an independent empire before Dutch colonialism, and they argued that it should return to that status. The Irianese similarly noted their territory's differences from the rest of Indonesia. Unlike Aceh, Irian Jaya had never been a unified independent nation prior to colonialism, but its people had also not been part of the Indonesian nationalist movement. The Dutch acquired western New Guinea later than the rest of the archipelago, and they kept control of the area (then called Netherlands New Guinea) when they withdrew their forces from Indonesia in 1949. Only after military threats by Sukarno did the Dutch turn the territory over to Indonesia in 1963.

In addition to these separatist movements, the problems of national integration showed themselves in a rising tide of communal violence. During the economic crisis, Chinese merchants had been blamed for the country's economic troubles and many of their shops had been burned. Stresses were also growing between people who wanted to keep Indonesia a secular state, in which members of all religious traditions could feel at home, and those who wanted to make it an Islamic state ruled by Islamic law. Churches were burned in Java, and in the eastern Moluccas (where Christians are a large proportion of the population) armed warfare broke out between the Christian and Muslim communities.

Abdurrahman Wahid proved to be a weak president who was unable to solve the archipelago's numerous crises. Struggling with his failing health, he had little energy to devote to administration, while the nation seemed on the verge of breaking up into small pieces. Separatist movements fought for autonomy in Aceh at the western tip of the island pieces. Separatist movements fought for autonomy in Aceh at the western tip of the island of Sumatra, and in Irian Jaya (West Papua) in the far east of the nation. The economy remained stagnant. The legislative body (MPR) twice censured Wahid, and it formally ousted him in July 2001. Megawati Sukarnoputri, the vice president, was named president. Some Indonesians were outraged that the MPR named a woman to the top position in the country, and some saw her as a puppet of the military. But she remained popular not only for her outspoken opposition to Suharto before 1998, but also because her father Sukarno is remembered as a supporter of the poor.

In 2003, Indonesia continued to face internal and external crises that threatened its stability. As with many Southeast Asian nations, Indonesia's leaders looked for a balance between authority and civil liberties, economic growth and traditional culture. In addition, they sought to balance the acceptance of Islam as the bedrock of Indonesian culture with an avoidance of Muslim extremists. Their overall performance fell short of the ideal, as the gap between the elites and the masses, between urban and rural areas, and between landlords and peasants have widened rather than narrowed. To many, the huge archipelago now seemed ungovernable. Yet, a semblance of political order remains, providing some hope for Indonesia's future.

Laos

Contemporary Laos is still a rural, subsistence agrarian society. The nation is isolated and landlocked, and its almost six million people are divided among more than forty ethnic groups. Laos might best be described as a quasi-nation, because it emerged from maps drawn by European colonialists rather than from any indigenous sense of common territory, history, or nationhood. Laos has witnessed constant warfare among contending factions, and it has also suffered interventions from external powers such as Thailand, Vietnam, China, France, and the United States.

Laos has long suffered problems of poverty, poor education, external encroachments, and ethnic factionalism. But the country was not always so weak. From the fourteenth to the sixteenth century the area of present-day Laos and northeast Thailand was dominated by the Lao state of Lan Xang (pronounced lahn sahng) centered on Luang Prabang and Vientiane. However, dynastic quarrels in the eighteenth century led to separate kingdoms in Luang Prabang in the north,

Champassak in the south, and Vientiane (the present capital) in the central area. In the years that followed, Thailand and Vietnam periodically plundered the Lao states, and in the 1890s the French colonized the area. The French colonialists created a semblance of unity, and they allowed a few elite Lao families to consolidate their positions of power, but they did little to modernize or integrate the nation. As a result, Laos emerged from colonial rule divided, isolated, and stagnated.

The Japanese ruled Laos from 1941 to 1945, although the French administered many of the governmental affairs. When the Japanese departed, the Lao elites split into left-wing and right-wing factions. The left-wing groups initially emphasized nationalism. They first took the form of the Lao-Issara, or "Free Lao," but later they regrouped as the communist-led Neo Lao Hak Sat (NLHS), or "Lao Patriotic Front." This latter group fostered the Pathet Lao revolutionary movement, a coalition of communists, intellectuals, and anti-monarchists that would eventually take control of the country. In the late 1950s the left-wing groups controlled the northern and eastern highlands, while the right-wing groups established themselves in the lowlands to the west. In the capital, numerous *coups d'etat* took place as power passed back and forth between rightists and a mediating faction of neutralists (the United States usually favored the rightists).

In the late 1960s the escalation of the war in Vietnam changed the nature of the struggle within Laos. Growing numbers of southward-moving Vietnamese soldiers used the Lao mountain paths (the famous Ho Chi Minh Trail) to escape bombing attacks in Vietnam. Laos itself eventually became the target of massive American bombing. On a per capita basis, Laos became the most bombed country in history (one ton of bombs per person). Meanwhile, with United States support, right-wing groups held power in Vientiane. In the late 1960s and early 1970s, the United States dominated every aspect of the Lao government, including providing 90 percent of its budget.

In 1975, the Pathet Lao took full control of the country. By this time the NLHS had renamed itself the Lao People's Revolutionary Party (LPRP). Its politburo members were disciplined, dedicated communists. They abolished the 622-year-old monarchy and established the Lao People's Democratic Republic. Kaysone Phomvihan, the party's secretary-general, became the country's new prime minister, and Vietnamese troops were allowed to station themselves in the country. About 70,000 Lao citizens were sent to prison or to reeducation camps on suspicion of associating with the previous regime. Civil servants and technocrats with connections to the vanquished pro-American government were purged. Many of the country's wealthy elite families fled to Thailand. The United States broke formal diplomatic ties but retained a low-level mission in the country.

The new Lao government launched a number of ambitious programs. For example, it emphasized education and built primary schools in isolated areas. Instructional supplies were minimal, yet the percentage of literate adults increased. As in Vietnam and Cambodia, the new communist leaders banned Buddhism and traditional cultural ceremonies, and they instituted a socialist economic system that included collectivization of land and factories. Laos did not experience the kind of bloodbath suffered by the Cambodians under the Khmer Rouge, but life was harsh nonetheless. The new government's economic policies were ineffective, and the people's standard of living deteriorated. Many Lao peasants refused to give up their land ownership, and in the absence of financial incentives they refused to grow crops. Laos increasingly depended on Vietnam and the Soviet Union for economic aid, and hundreds of thousands of farmers, teachers, government officials, skilled technocrats, and highlanders fled the harsh conditions by crossing the border to Thailand. The refugee exodus left the nation bereft of its most productive and experienced people. More than 270,000 of these refugees, especially members of the Hmong and Lao ethnic groups, would later resettle in the United States.

In 1979, after it had become clear that the government's economic policies were failing, the leaders set forth a New Economic Policy (NEP) that returned land to the peasantry and allowed for small-scale capitalism and private trading. International investment was welcomed, and Laos slowly began to become part of the international capitalist order. Breaking from its economic dependence on Vietnam and the Soviet Union, Laos looked to new nations for help with its development. Japan soon became the largest aid donor, and Thailand became a major trade partner. Yet Laos experienced little economic progress.

In the early 1980s, Vietnamese forces withdrew from Laos, and later in the decade the Soviet Union (then evolving into post-communist Russia) ended its large aid program. Despite these changes, the Lao political system remained closed. Only candidates from the Lao People's Revolutionary Party were allowed to run in the elections. President Kaysone's death in November 1992 provided an opportunity for Laos to usher in a new generation of leaders more in tune with the international movement away from communism and toward democracy, but the Communist Party's new secretary-general, Khamtay Siphandone, was a conservative who had little desire to imitate the West. In 1998 Khamtay was also elected the country's president, making him the most powerful person in Laos since Kaysone, who likewise held both the top communist party position of secretary-general and the top state position of president. The elected National Assembly continued to be communist controlled, and the LPRP's politburo continued to be the effective ruling body.

Over the years, the United States repeatedly pressed the issue of the "missing in action" (MIA) American soldiers who had been lost in Laos during the war in Vietnam. Officially, 528 American servicemen are listed as missing, though most scholars believe that all are dead. The United States also pushed Laos to curb trafficking in the drugs, mainly opium, that were being produced in the country. As of 1999, the United States had an aid program that was contingent on the Lao government ending its support for the drug export trade.

Today, Laos remains a forgotten country with a small population, a lack of strategic importance, a nonexistent military capacity, and an impoverished citizenry. In 1997, Laos was admitted to ASEAN, an organization facilitating regional economic and political cooperation, but the slow-moving Lao economy was hurt yet again when the economic crisis of 1997 induced Southeast Asian nations to reduce their investments in Laos. In 1998 the Lao Kip lost some 70 percent of its value against world currencies. Inflation reached 60 percent that same year. Since 1995 the Gross Domestic Product of Laos has grown about 3 percent per year, but that was slow compared to neighboring countries such as Thailand. In 2003 Laos was still ranked as one of the world's poorest countries.

Malaysia

In the first years of the new millennium, Malaysia wore an aura of progress, and many Third World leaders looked to the country as the "model of success." Malaysia's twenty-four million inhabitants were envied, and they were proud of their country's accomplishments. At least until the 1997 economic crisis, Malaysia boasted impressive economic growth rates, a centralized but semi-democratic government, and a relatively high standard of living for virtually every socio-economic class. However, at the end of the decade Malaysians faced a period of travail as their economy was battered by the regional financial crisis and their politics were beset by factionalism within the dominant political alliance.

The European presence in Malaysia began when the Portuguese took control of Malacca in 1511. The city later passed to Dutch control, and then to the British. By the early nineteenth century the British also controlled Penang and Singapore. At first the British preoccupied themselves with commerce, but they found themselves increasingly involved in local affairs, and in the late nineteenth century they took formal control of the entire Malay peninsula (also known as "Malaya"). Both the British and the local Malay rulers encouraged immigration by Chinese and Indian laborers to help develop the peninsula's rubber and tin resources. Many of these workers stayed permanently, forming ethnic communities that persist today with distinctive languages and cultures.

The Second World War brought dramatic changes. The occupying Japanese governors exploited Malaya's rich natural resources, such as tin, rubber, and oil. They also oppressed the indigenous Chinese. By turning the Malays against the Chinese, the Japanese created an antipathy between the two groups that has persisted ever since. The war years were extremely disruptive. By 1945, when the returning British attempted to restore order, the economy was devastated, the currency worthless, and crime high.

In 1946, Great Britain separated Singapore from Malaya, and in 1948 the British instituted in the peninsula a new government called the Federation of Malaya. Hereditary sultans continued to rule in each of the nine states, while the senior sultan became the *Yang di-Pertuan Agong* (Paramount Ruler), a rotating position that passed to a new sultan every few years. Malaya's legislative council was initially an appointed body, but by 1955 it became an elected legislature.

The formation of the Federation of Malaya was followed by an insurrection, known as "The Emergency" (1948–1955), that was led by communist Chinese guerrillas who wanted immediate independence and who believed that the rights of the Chinese were being unfairly restricted in the federation structure. British land owners were murdered, and the uprising further estranged the Chinese and Malay communities. The insurrection eventually petered out as the government responded with effective counter-insurgency measures such as economic development and amnesty programs. The insurrection was also undermined by a general improvement in the Malaysian economy.

The overriding characteristic of Malayan politics has been its communal nature. The term "communalism" refers both to the nation's ethnic diversity and to the tensions that arise from the differences between the communities' cultures, traditions, and religions. Ethnic Malays are slightly less than 50 percent of the population, and the Chinese are about one-third. The rest of the population includes Indians, aborigines, and Europeans. The Chinese have disproportionate economic influence, while the Malays view themselves as *bumiputera* (sons of the soil) who merit special political rights and economic protections to balance the business prowess of the recently arrived Chinese and Indians.

To cope with the severe tensions among the nation's ethnic groups, an Alliance party system was devised in 1952. The Alliance included leading representatives of the United Malay Nationalist Organization (UMNO), the Malayan Chinese Association (MCA), and the Malayan Indian Congress (MIC). The political leaders who participated in the Alliance were responsible for explaining and justifying the Alliance's decisions to their respective ethnic communities and for securing compliance from the members of those communities. The Malays were granted a privileged position in the political system, while the Chinese remained predominant in economic activities. The dominant ethnic political party was therefore the UMNO, which was led by Tunku Abdul Rahman, the "father" of Malayan independence and the nation's future prime minister. The Alliance brought stability to the potentially explosive political situation, mainly because the Alliance leaders were ideologically moderate and because each ethnic group perceived its interests to be served best by such a system. In somewhat modified form the Alliance has remained the primary institution of Malayan politics down to the present day.

Bumiputera

Bumiputera is a Malay word meaning "sons of the soil." The term differentiates the Malays and other indigenous people of Malaysia from the Chinese and Indians, who are viewed as sojourners. The Malaysian government intended for *bumiputeras* to gain from an "affirmative action" program meant to provide more opportunities to the Malay people, especially in the economy. Corporations were to open their doors to Malay people, scholarships were earmarked for Malays, and certain professions were reserved exclusively for the non-Chinese. The notion of *bumiputera* suggests the high degree of tension among the different ethnic groups in Malaysia. In Indonesia, where a similar concept exists, indigenous people are known as *pribumi*.

In 1957 the Federation of Malaya was granted independence, though Britain continued to rule the Borneo dependencies of North Borneo (Sabah), Sarawak, and Brunei. The British also retained the self-governing colony of Singapore. Independent Malaya had a parliamentary form of government, with the *Yang di-Pertuan Agong* (a position still rotating among the nine sultans) continuing to serve as head of state.

Yang di-Pertuan Agong

Malaysia's monarchy differs from that of every other nation. The "king" of Malaysia is known as the *Yang di-Pertuan Agong*, or "Paramount Ruler." The holder of this position is usually the senior sultan of one of the nine states of peninsular Malaya. The title rotates among the nine sultans and each monarch serves only five years. The *Yang di-Pertuan Agong* used to have the right to sign or not sign laws, but in 1994 the Malaysian parliament amended the constitution so that bills would automatically become law within thirty days, even without the *Yang di-Pertuan Agong*'s signature.

Despite his exalted title of paramount ruler, the *Yang di-Pertuan Agong* does not set forth or administer the country's policies, as real power lies in the hands of the parliament and especially the prime minister. The *Yang di-Pertuan Agong*'s exalted but limited position is similar to that of the King of Thailand or the Queen of England.

In 1963 the leaders of Great Britain and Malaya agreed to merge Malaya with Sabah, Sarawak, and Singapore in a new Federation of Malaysia (note the change of spelling). Singapore's urban and industrial economy was expected to balance rural Malaya's agricultural economy, while the large population of Singaporean Chinese was to be offset by the addition of the Malays and other indigenous peoples of Sabah and Sarawak. Furthermore, Singapore was to be granted wide-ranging autonomy in its domestic affairs.

Sarawak and Sabah

In 1963 the British dependencies of Sarawak and Sabah (both on the island of Borneo) joined the Federation of Malaysia. Sarawak is about the size of Illinois and has a population just under 2 million. Some 50 percent of its people are Iban and other groups native to Borneo, 20 percent are Malay, and 30 percent are Chinese. Together with the Malays, the Iban and other indigenous groups are considered *bumiputera* (making this category 70 percent of the population) and are given special privileges in the Malaysian communal system. Sarawak is known for distinctive Iban longhouses where some 50 families live under one roof.

Sabah was known as North Borneo until 1963. It has a population of about 1.5 million (82 percent Malay and other *bumiputera* and 16 percent Chinese) and is the home of Mount Kinabalu, one of the highest mountains in all Southeast Asia.

The Federation of Malaysia lasted only two years in this form. In 1965, Singapore was asked to withdraw. The prime minister of Singapore, Lee Kuan Yew, was calling for a "Malaysian Malaysia" with equal participation from all areas and ethnic groups, a vision that contrasted with Tunku Abdul Rahman's design for a "Malayan Malaysia" in which special privileges would continue to be reserved for the politically dominant (but economically weak) Malay ethnic group. Lee Kuan Yew was also attempting to strengthen Singapore's influence in Malaysia's national political arena, and his Singapore-based People's Action Party (PAP) was campaigning for seats outside Singapore. Tunku Abdul Rahman considered Lee Kuan Yew's political activities a direct threat to Malay political dominance and to the Alliance system that he headed. Therefore, in 1965 he requested that Singapore leave the federation.

The ouster of Singapore did not resolve the ethnic problems in Malaysian politics. The 1969 national elections showed rising support for opposition parties outside the Alliance, raising questions about the Alliance party's capacity to govern effectively. Communal riots erupted in the capital city of Kuala Lumpur, inspired by Malaysians who believed that it was time for a change in the country's leadership. Scores of persons were killed and hundreds injured.

In reaction to the violence, the ailing Prime Minister Tunku Abdul Rahman ordered Deputy Prime Minister Tun Abdul Razak to establish a National Operations Council (NOC) and declare martial law (Tun Abdul Razak became prime minister the following year). The government disbanded the parliament, curtailed civil liberties, and pushed through a series of Sedition Acts that extended the Malay community's rights still further by setting aside for Malays a proportion of positions in higher education and in certain businesses. The government prohibited discussion of "sensitive issues" such as the prerogatives of the Malay rulers, the special rights for the Malays, and the official (and paramount) status of the Malay language.

A limited form of parliamentary government returned to Malaysia in 1971. The government effectively became a one-party system in which the legislature acted as a rubber stamp for the leader of the dominant UMNO party, who continued to be the country's prime minister. By 1974 the Alliance coalition had expanded into the National Front, a coalition consisting of an even larger number of ethnicity-based parties, but UMNO continued to play the leading role. In 1976 Prime Minister Tun Razak was succeeded by Tun Hussein Onn, who in 1981 was succeeded by Dr. Datuk Seri Mahathir bin Mohammad, Malaysia's first commoner prime minister (the honorifics Tunku and Tun mean "prince" and indicate aristocratic heritage). By the year 2003 Dr. Mahathir had been prime minister for twenty-two years, having won ten general elections as leader of the National Front parties.

Mahathir has been Malaysia's most influential and controversial national leader. By 2003 his Malaysia had become one of Southeast Asia's most successful nations, boasting a standard of living second only to Singapore's. He was responsible for backing the construction of the world's tallest building, the Petronas Towers in Kuala Lumpur. He also built research parks, an international airport, a new government center, and Southeast Asia's leading road system. He is deemed brilliant by his supporters, who give him credit for the strong economy he has presided over since 1981.

Yet Mahathir has also ruled with a strong hand, taming the bureaucracy, the political parties, the judiciary, the press, and the sultans, all of whom had once challenged his leadership. Mahathir became a spokesman for the notion of "Asian values," which he said were superior to "Western values." He claimed to be moving Malaysia toward a more "Asian-style democracy," but in fact he had created an authoritarian system with himself in full command.

Mahathir's control was not threatened until 1997, when the Asian economic crisis undermined his presumed invincibility. The crisis threatened his "Vision 2020" program, a plan for making Malaysia one of the world's leading industrialized nations by the year 2020. He blamed outsiders for the financial debacle, but internal political controversy soon followed. In 1999, Mahathir had a falling out with Deputy Prime Minister Anwar Ibrahim, Mahathir's main rival and a fellow member of the National Front. Anwar was removed from office and sentenced to jail in 1999 for alleged sedition and sodomy. Mahathir's critics claimed that Anwar had been sacked because he dared to speak against Mahathir and because his popularity was increasing, and the case became a *cause célèbre* during the November 1999 elections for parliament. Despite the scandal, Mahathir's National Front won a resounding majority, lengthening its record of never having lost.

At the end of October 2003, when he was age 77, Dr. Mahathir formally retired from office. His designated successor was the deputy premier, Abdullah Ahmad Badawi. Badawi officially became head of the ruling political party, which names the prime minister, stepping into a position that has been dominated by Mahathir for more than two decades. In contrast to the outspoken and charismatic Mahathir, Badawi is relatively unknown, so it is not known if he will lead Malaysia in new directions. Whatever his own ambitions it will be difficult for Badawi to emulate Mahathir who built an export-oriented economic powerhouse, achieved a stable society amidst a bifurcated ethnic and religious population, found a balance between Islamic identity and fundamentalist Islam, and established an illiberal democracy in which patronage flourished and democratic rights were subordinated.

The Philippines

The Republic of the Philippines is Southeast Asia's "showcase of democracy." Some seventy-seven million people live in this diverse archipelago of multiple ethnicities and languages. The formal structures of government are based on the American model of separation of powers, with a president, congress, and judiciary each independent of the other. Yet the Philippines has also gone through periods of unrest and authoritarian rule, and behind the facade of democracy is a society driven by class differences and a state in which an oligarchy of a few rich families dominates the economy and politics.

The Philippines has had longer experience with democracy than any other Asian nation, as the Philippine Revolution of the 1890s was Asia's first nationalist struggle. In that effort, the Filipinos liberated themselves from Spanish rule. Inspired by the ideas of the great Jose Rizal, they planned to form a democratic government. However, in the aftermath of the Spanish-American War (see Chapter 3), the United States attacked the Philippine Republic and forced the Philippines to become its colony.

Jose Rizal

Jose Rizal is the Philippines' most famous patriot. A brilliant writer, he struggled against Spanish colonization as a reformer rather than a revolutionary. Yet the Spanish imprisoned him for four years and then executed him for treason in 1896. Rizal was of mixed Chinese and Filipino ancestry. His death strengthened the revolutionaries, and by 1898 the Philippines had effectively achieved independence from the Spanish. That same year the United States intervened and established a new colonial regime that lasted until 1946.

Even while it was an American colony, the Philippines had a form of democratic rule, as members of the elite competed for positions in the legislature. In 1935 the United States granted the Philippines commonwealth status with limited self-government, promising full independence within ten years. The Second World War intervened, but independence was granted shortly afterward in 1946. The United States retained sizable military bases and took a special interest in the nation's affairs, but the country was truly independent. During the early post-independence period, the Philippine elections featured two political parties, the Nacionalista and the Liberal, which competed on a roughly equal basis until President Marcos proclaimed martial law in 1972. The most remarkable president in this period was the popular Ramon Magsaysay, who proposed a number of reforms meant to improve conditions for the country's poor farmers.

Ramon Magsaysay

The Philippines' most popular president served from 1954 to 1957. His popularity came from his frequent trips to the *barrios* (villages) and slums, where he was viewed as the "people's president." He lived simply and did not become involved in corruption. Sadly, he was killed in an airplane accident before his term was completed. He was strongly opposed by the elite landowning interests who controlled the legislature, so his land reform bills and development proposals were not passed. Even though he upset the Filipino elite, he was considered pro-American; after his death, documents were produced showing that Magsaysay had received financial support from the American Central Intelligence Agency.

Ferdinand Marcos was elected president in 1965 and reelected in 1969. He proposed a comprehensive development program, with emphasis on road building. The Philippine Congress refused to vote in the tax increases to finance his projects, yet by the end of his first term Marcos could boast of an improved economic climate for both industry and agriculture. Despite these improvements, the political system was still beset by the problems of graft, corruption, and the dominance of a few wealthy families who controlled the Senate and much of the bureaucracy. Marcos was fully at home in this pattern of corruption, and many considered his 1969 reelection victory to have been "bought."

The period from 1969 to 1972 was characterized by a terrible law-and-order problem. Private armies clashed, guns were available to everyone, and crime was rampant. The communist-led New People's Army (NPA) was gaining ground. In addition, in the southern islands an increasingly intense civil war raged between Muslims and Christians. In the midst of all this turmoil there continued to be a grossly unequal distribution of wealth and land.

Moro National Liberation Front (MNLF)

At one time the Muslim Moros were a majority in Mindanao and the other southern islands, where they resisted the Catholic Spanish colonizers for many years. Over the years successive governments in Manila have sent Christian settlers to Mindanao and other southern islands, and today the Moros are a majority in only a few provinces. Ever since Philippine independence, the Muslims of the south have been fighting to create a separate state. In the late 1960s this movement became led by the Moro National Liberation Front headquartered on Mindanao. Negotiations between the Moros and the Manila government have been plagued with tensions and lack of trust, though from time to time autonomy has been promised and cease-fires proclaimed.

In September 1972 Marcos proclaimed martial law, ending the longest period of multi-party democratic rule in modern Southeast Asia. He abrogated the constitution, severely repressed civil liberties, and imprisoned numerous political opponents, including his major rival, former senator Benigno Aquino. Marcos justified the crackdown by saying it would enable him to improve government efficiency, decree meaningful land reform, reverse the rising crime rate, expand the economy, end oligarchic rule, and preempt the appeal of the communist-led New People's Army (NPA). He achieved none of these goals, succeeding only in ending the longest period of democratic rule in modern Southeast Asia. However, another important reason for the move was that Marcos was constitutionally barred from seeking a third term as president, and he desired to retain his power. He retained political power for the next fourteen years.

Martial law did not solve the serious problems of Philippine society. The crime rate dipped only briefly. Economic stagnation continued. The civil war in the southern islands was not resolved, and meaningful land reform did not take place. The huge gap between the rich and poor remained. In Marcos's later years the Philippines experienced negative economic growth at a time when neighboring Southeast Asian countries were developing rapidly. Corruption continued, with Marcos and his immediate family the most obvious beneficiaries. Ferdinand Marcos amassed billions of dollars, while his wife, Imelda Marcos, gave lavish parties and went on expensive shopping tours abroad to buy jewelry, clothing, and shoes. Despite these shortcomings, the United States government backed Marcos because he was strongly anti-communist and an ally of the United States.

During his martial law regime, Marcos often held referenda, which he controlled, that called for him to stay in power. But by 1983, he had lost the support of most Filipinos, including the influential moral leader Cardinal Sin, Archbishop of Manila and leader of the Catholic Church. Filipinos' disillusionment with Marcos was brought to a head by the 1983 assassination of Senator Benigno Aquino. Aquino had been imprisoned for his opposition to Marcos, but he had later been freed and allowed to go to the United States for a heart bypass operation. When Aquino returned to the Philippines, he was shot the moment he stepped from the airplane down to the tarmac. The government was universally believed to have had a hand in this assassination. The event stirred up long-suppressed grievances against Marcos and led eventually to the famous 1986 People's Power revolt.

Benigno Aquino

Benigno (Ninoy) Aquino was born into a rich landowning family in Tarlac Province. He was the nation's youngest senator, was the principal opponent of President Ferdinand Marcos, and, as leader of the opposition party, was expected to be the next president. When Marcos proclaimed martial law in 1972, Aquino was imprisoned and then exiled to the United States, where he underwent a heart bypass operation. Though he believed he would be put back in prison if he returned home, Aquino flew back to Manila in 1983. As he stepped off the plane onto the airfield, he was murdered by a Marcos security guard. Following his assassination, his wife Corazon Aquino rallied the opposition forces and defeated Marcos in the 1986 elections. She served one term as president.

Under severe pressure from the public, Marcos called "snap" elections to be held in early 1986. The announcement was a surprise, and the election was to be carried out quickly. Marcos was confident that he could control the campaign machinery and ensure himself another lopsided victory. But his plans were threatened by the rising popularity of Corazon "Cory" Aquino, the widow of the martyred Senator Aquino. She proclaimed a "people's campaign," and as she toured the country she spoke simply and effectively. In a stunning climax, she unexpectedly won the popular vote for president. Election monitors from the Philippines and around the world attested she had won, but Marcos proclaimed himself to have been re-elected president. The reaction to this piece of thievery was a spontaneous popular uprising called People's Power, a non-violent civil disobedience movement that included people of all classes: students, farmers, nuns, shopkeepers, and both rural and urban residents. The spontaneous People's Power movement soon included even former Marcos associates such as Defense Minister Juan Ponce Enrile and armed forces head Fidel Ramos. A stalemate emerged as both Marcos and Aquino took the presidential oath of office. Throughout this period, American policy makers were divided, though President Reagan continued the official line of supporting Marcos. At the last moment, Reagan changed policy and informed Marcos that the United States would no longer support him. Marcos, his family, and his cronies fled in American helicopters to exile in Hawai'i, where Marcos died three years later. Corazon Aquino was now the country's undisputed president.

President Aquino had a new constitution drafted, ended the most flagrant corruption by removing Marcos's cronies from the directorships of state enterprises, defeated six *coup* attempts by dissident army leaders, and restored basic civil liberties such as the writ of *habeas corpus* that gives protection against unjust imprisonment. During her administration the American military presence was ended in 1990, when after intense debate the Philippine Senate rejected renewal of the Military Bases Agreement with the United States (Aquino stayed neutral but supported the final decision). The economy also improved. From the negative growth rates of Marcos's last years the economy rebounded to positive growth, and by the time Aquino stepped down business was expanding 6 percent per year. On the downside, Aquino failed to address poverty and did not change the socio-economic system in any fundamental way. The nation's economy continued to be dominated by a few wealthy families, and the gap between the rich and the poor remained one of the largest in the world. Aquino was reluctant to move on land reform. She was a member of the Cojuangco family, one of the country's richest dynasties, and meaningful land reform would have hurt her family and its closest friends. Aquino also failed to promote population control, because she was a loyal Catholic and the Church opposed family planning. In the early 1990s the country had a population growth rate of 2.8 percent, one of the highest in the world.

Abiding by the new constitution's limit of a single presidential term, Aquino did not seek re-election. She was succeeded by her *protégé* Fidel

V. Ramos, the army chief who had turned against Marcos in 1986. Ramos's victory was achieved with just 24 percent of the total vote, as the constitution does not require a run-off among the top vote getters. Ramos had little personal charisma, but his popularity ratings were consistently high because most Filipinos considered him an effective president. Ramos instituted important economic reforms, promoted an open market system, and exemplified personal honesty.

Ramos did not designate a preferred successor. In the 1998 elections he was succeeded by Vice President Joseph Estrada. Estrada was popular with rural Filipinos but disdained by intellectuals and urbanites who felt he was insufficiently intelligent and savvy to be president. Estrada won because of his charisma as a former movie star, because he eloquently supported the rights of the poor, and because he pledged to "clean up" criminal elements.

Estrada began his six-year term auspiciously. He enjoyed a majority in both houses of the Philippine Congress. Furthermore, the 1997 economic crisis had not affected the Philippines as strongly as it had Thailand, Malaysia, and Indonesia, at least partially because the country's economy was already a disaster. During his first two years as president, Estrada's rhetoric favored the poor but he did not succeed in producing policies that alleviated their difficulties.

In 2000, Estrada was accused of gross corruption and his personal life was vilified, especially regarding the special attention to his lavish gifts to his minor wives and mistresses. Impeachment proceedings began in the Philippine Senate where evidence was produced indicating that Estrada had been involved in illegal gambling activities and had accepted public monies for private gain. Despite the allegations, Estrada remained popular among many classes, who viewed the trial as the elite's attempt to undermine and overthrow their champion. Vice President Arroyo was the daughter of former president Diosdado Macapagal and a dozen of the Filipino establishment.

In January 2001 the impeachment trial collapsed when the Senate voted 11 to 10 not to allow bank documents to be shown to the Senate. Though technically an exoneration of Estrada, the move actually triggered the end of his administration. Hundreds of thousands of Filipinos demonstrated against Estrada, the military and much of the governmental officialdom rose against him and he was forced to leave Malacanang Palace, the traditional home of the president. The Supreme Court declared that the office of president was vacant, and that the vice president could legally assume the presidency. Although Vice President Gloria Macapagal-Arroyo had resigned her cabinet post months before to protest against the Estrada administration, she nevertheless replaced Estrada.

Estrada was arrested and faced charges of economic plunder, a charge that landed him in prison. Arroyo was immediately confronted with a restive citizenry, economic malaise, and separatist movements throughout the archipelago. At first, Arroyo announced that she would not run for a new term. However, she changed her mind and was re-elected to a six-year term as president in June of 2004.

The Philippine economy has improved notably in recent years. Under Marcos, the Philippine economy had been a model of what not to do, as the Philippines was left out of the region's economic miracle. President Marcos and his family had stolen a tremendous amount of wealth and put it into foreign bank accounts, where it was unavailable for productive investment in the Philippines. He also undermined market forces by setting incompetent cronies up in business and then providing subsidies that relieved them of the need for accountability and efficiency. Presidents Aquino and Ramos began correcting the effects of this mismanagement. By 1998, inflation was under control, economic growth rates were respectable (running about 6 percent), and the infrastructure had improved. In the cities fewer brownouts occurred, and in the roads there were fewer potholes.

Land reform has been one of the most significant political issues during recent administrations. In recent years manufacturing has become the country's major producer of wealth, but agriculture continues to be important in rural areas. Fertile land is scarce, and multinational corporations and wealthy landowners own the bulk of the best land. About half of the Philippine farmers are tenants, while the other half own their own land. Wealthy landowners hire tenant farmers to grow cash crops such as rubber, coffee, fruit, and palm oil. The success of the less affluent farmers is determined by the amount of rainfall, the availability of irrigation, the price of fertilizer, and the availability of credit. The average farm size nationwide is about seven acres, relatively small by world standards, and even many "large" landowners do not really have huge farms. There are but a few *haciendas* whose holdings number in the thousands of acres. These major land holdings include the famous Hacienda Luisita owned by the wealthy Cojuangco family (of which former president Aquino is a prominent member).

Despite the persistent inequalities of farm income there has been very little land reform. Presidents such as Marcos and Aquino have proclaimed land reform a central policy goal, but nothing substantive has ever been done. The land tenure problem is a complicated one, and reform efforts require effective leadership if they are truly to improve the lot of rural Filipinos. For reform to work, there must be careful planning that addresses comprehensively the complex issues of land ownership, availability of capital, profitable crops, cooperative associations, and transportation and infrastructure (electricity, roads, and markets). A meaningful land reform effort will also require deft diplomacy and tenacity, because it will entail a fundamental change in power relationships throughout the Philippines.

A unique aspect of Philippine rural life is the millions of Filipinos living and working overseas, mostly in the United States. Filipinos are the largest overseas labor force in the world. The country's high levels of underemployment and unemployment send people abroad in search of work, while the emigrants' widespread fluency in English helps them get jobs. The overseas workers send remittances to their family members back in the Philippines, many of whom live on farms. These remittances are the country's largest source of foreign exchange and are an important reason why rural Filipinos have been able to subsist.

The contemporary Philippine political system is formally democratic, with institutions of government that mirror those of the United States. Civil liberties are now protected and elections are free. There is no freer press in all of Southeast Asia. Yet in practice many areas of the Philippines remain oligarchic, ruled by a self-perpetuating elite of landed families. The 1998 election of the populist President Estrada might have been expected to signal a move away from elitism and toward a larger role for the masses. However, his replacement was the more elitist Arroyo, and so it is not clear whether Philippine politics can and will move in new directions.

In the post-September 11, 2001 era, the Philippines became of greater interest to the United States as the Philippines was considered a "front-line" state in the war on terrorism. President Arroyo, like President Bush in the United States, asserted that terrorism transformed the nation fundamentally and had to be taken into account regarding virtually every policy.

Singapore

Singapore ("Lion City," from the Malay words *singa,* meaning lion, and *pura,* meaning city) is Southeast Asia's most prosperous city. Its per capita income of $22,680 (PPP) is the highest of any Asian nation except for Japan. Singapore is efficient, bustling, technologically advanced, low in crime, clean, and antiseptic in both a positive and negative sense.

Formerly known as Temasek, Singapore is located on the southern tip of the Malay peninsula at the entrance of the Strait of Malacca, an important water passage where trade has flourished for centuries. When British merchants docked in 1819, Singapore was a small fishing village unknown to most of the world. The British colonial administrator, trader, and adventurer Sir Thomas Raffles persuaded the sultans who administered the island to cede it to the East India Company, and by 1824 Britain had assumed direct sovereignty. By 1867 the Straits Settlements (Malacca, Penang, and Singapore) had been given the status of a British Crown Colony, with an administration based in Singapore.

From this base in the Straits Settlements, the British would later extend control over the rest of Malaya. Raffles was responsible for many of the policies and reforms that moved Singapore toward its eventual prosperity. By the mid-1800s, Singapore had become a small city populated by a multitude of ethnic groups, including Chinese, Indians, Malays, and Europeans.

Sir Thomas Stamford Raffles

Thomas Raffles is known as the "founder" of Singapore. He landed there in 1819 and founded a trading center that soon became an important port for the British empire. At that time, Singapore was essentially a swampy fishing village of about one thousand inhabitants, but its status as a tax-free port helped the colony to grow rapidly. Raffles visited Singapore periodically to assure improvement in the conditions in which the people lived. Slavery was outlawed and gambling ended. Today, the nation's leading luxury hotel is called The Raffles.

Under the British, Singapore became a major trade center for ships sailing between Europe and Asia, and it eventually boasted one of the world's most modern ports. The new *entrepôt* drew immigrants from China, India, and Malaya. The Chinese who came to Singapore were primarily artisans, laborers, and merchants. They initially lived wretched lives of poverty, but many of them later became entrepreneurs, corporate executives, and owners of small businesses. Some of the Chinese also became bureaucrats. The (mostly Hindu) Indian immigrants from present-day India, Sri Lanka, Pakistan, and Bangladesh became involved in clothing trades and in the civil service, especially in the Ministry of Foreign Affairs. Malays worked in low-level positions; few moved up the ladder to high-level positions.

The Second World War brought great hardship. As the home of a major British military base, Singapore was an obvious target for the Japanese. The British made a major mistake when they organized Singapore's defense, because they assumed an attack on this important maritime base would come from the open sea to the south. Instead, the Japanese invaded from the Malayan peninsula to the north. After fierce fighting and bombing, the Japanese soldiers under the leadership of Japanese General Yamashita captured Singapore and renamed it *Syonanto*, or "Light of the South." The Japanese occupation was hard on the island's residents, because the new rulers demanded reparations of food and money and inflicted extremely harsh conditions on the Singaporeans.

Following the 1945 defeat of the Japanese, the British began to promote self-government. In 1946, Singapore was made administratively separate from Malaya, and responsibility for its governance was transferred to the London Office. The first measure of self-government came in 1955, when parliamentary elections produced a coalition government. In this election a small number of seats were won by the small but rapidly rising People's Action Party (PAP) led by Lee Kuan Yew, who won one of the seats. Lee was a brilliant lawyer who had graduated at the top of his class at Cambridge University, and this election marked the beginning of his rise to power.

In 1957 an agreement for formal autonomy was made, and in 1959 Singapore gained full control of its internal affairs, although the British continued to handle defense and foreign policy. In 1959 Singapore held its first truly meaningful parliamentary election. The PAP won in a landslide, and Lee Kuan Yew became prime minister. The PAP's victory frightened British investors, because at the time its membership included some communists. However, Lee soon purged the party of its extreme left wing, and he won the support of the British by pursuing moderate policies.

In the early 1960s, Lee desired to affiliate with the newly formed Federation of Malaya. Lee wanted the merger for several reasons. He felt the merger would assure economic stability in both units by balancing Singapore's trading economy with Malaya's agricultural one. He also felt the new arrangement would gave Singapore better protection against communist advances. With a population of only 1.5 million, Singapore felt impotent against a possible invasion from communist forces, in particular from China with its almost one billion population. Malayan Prime Minister Tunku Abdul Rahman agreed to the merger, and in 1963 the two nations joined together with the former British colonies of Sarawak and Sabah in the Federation of Malaysia. But the Malayan leader had second thoughts when Lee began talking more and more about a "Malaysian Malaysia," with the clear implication of a more significant role for Singapore and for the ethnic Chinese. The Tunku believed that a "Malayan Malaysia" was best for the federation, the implication being that Malays should continue playing the principal political roles. This conflict was not resolved, and in August 1965 the Tunku ousted Singapore from the federation.

Suddenly Singapore had again become an independent city-state, and Lee's PAP was the sole effective political party. The nation responded to the challenge by embarking on an intensive economic development program that rapidly raised the standard of living. Today Singapore's citizens enjoy the highest per capita income in Southeast Asia. Lee oversaw a parliamentary system similar to Great Britain's, with legislators elected to five-year terms. Multiple parties were allowed in theory, but Lee's PAP overwhelmingly won all the elections since 1965.

Compared to the administrations of the other Southeast Asian nations, Lee's had a dearth of corruption. He was the consummate

Confucianist leader, meeting the needs of his people while ruling strictly but fairly. The PAP's success stemmed from the party's superior organization and its ability to meet the people's economic needs. But it also relied on harsh oppression of opposition groups. Lee denigrated Western-style democracy as inappropriate for Singapore, extolling instead the virtues of "Asian values" that emphasized the importance of strong authoritative leadership (see Chapter 4). When Lee stepped down as prime minister in November 1990, he did not really give up guidance of the nation. His *protégé* Goh Chok Tong became Singapore's new prime minister, while Lee remained involved as "senior minister," a position that enabled him to remain the nation's most influential leader. In 2003 Goh Chok Tong announced that he would step down as Prime Minister and support Lee Hsien Loong as his successor. As the son of Lee Kuan Yew and the choice of Goh, Lee Hsien Loong had no competition for the nation's highest office. His many years as a government minister provided him with extensive experience, but his relationship to Lee Kuan Yew was the crucial factor in his rise to power.

Today, Singapore is governed by an elected parliament headed by a prime minister. In addition, every six years a directly elected president is selected from a slate of candidates who (according to the constitution) must have distinguished themselves in government or corporations. The president can veto bills and can keep the budget balanced by refusing to spend money that has been appropriated by parliament. All political parties in Singapore agree on the virtue of capitalism. Minor parties differ from the ruling PAP only in their views on the implementation of specific policies.

Singapore's political system is corporatist, which means that all the nation's political institutions and interest groups are run by the regime in power. For many Singaporeans, the PAP is the state. Most interest groups are controlled by the government, usually through the PAP, and only groups affiliated with the government have access to the state's immense resources. In addition, PAP control of the media enables the party to trumpet government accomplishments while remaining silent about any shortcomings. Technically, Singapore has a multiparty system, but the dominant PAP is not a political party in the Western sense, and there is rarely genuine competition for parliamentary seats. Ironically, though the PAP is anti-communist and favors free competition in commerce, its tight discipline and control over the nation's politics resembles the modus operandi of communist parties. Nevertheless, the government of Singapore is "soft authoritarian" in that it is decidedly paternalistic but not totalitarian (that is, it does not seek total control over every aspect of society).

With the exception of a two-year downturn in the mid-1980s, and a year-long recession in 2000–2001, Singapore has consistently posted the region's highest growth rates, sometimes reaching 10 percent. International trade has been the secret to Singapore's immense success. The nation has developed a telecommunications system second to none in the world, and foreign investment has grown every year. Singapore's exports have also grown, as the nation's products have developed a reputation for low price and high quality.

Today, the nation is a center for international banking. Its infrastructure is considered the best in the world. Singapore's high levels of economic development, combined with societal stability, make it a prime area of interest to international investors. That is both Singapore's greatest accomplishment and its curse. Singapore has the reputation of being a "sanitized" city, not only because it is physically clean and attractive, but also because it lacks room for non-conformity and has many rules governing the minutiae of public behavior. The price Singapore has paid for its economic status is a lack of meaningful popular participation in the affairs of state and a sterilized society that has lost much of its soul.

Because of its small size, it is impossible to generalize from Singapore to the rest of Southeast Asia. The city-state's economic accomplishments are impressive, but its methods are not a useful model for Southeast Asian nations to emulate, because its economic and political conditions are so different from those of the other countries in the region.

Thailand

Modern Thailand traces its history back to the Siamese kingdoms of Sukhothai and Ayuthaya. The head of state, King Bhumibol Adulyadej, is a member of the Chakri dynasty, which was founded more than 200 years ago and has reigned in Bangkok ever since. The Chakri kings ruled as absolute monarchs until 1932, when a *coup* ushered in a period of alternating civilian and military governments. After this event the Chakri monarchs continued to be head of state, but they had greatly reduced powers. Siam (renamed Thailand in the late 1930s) was never formally colonized, though in the early twentieth century the government had foreign advisors and for several decades Europeans had the right to trial under their own countries' laws and judges.

Thailand emerged from World War II in remarkably good shape. The government had acquiesced to a virtual Japanese occupation, but the Thai had continued to administer the nation and the people had suffered few social, economic, or political hardships. Rice was in abundant supply, and since Thailand was already a sovereign nation, its stability was not threatened by a debilitating struggle for independence.

Thai governments have always been highly centralized, with all administrative power stemming from the capital. Until recently,

Thailand's post-war history has been dominated by the military, but there have also been periods of civilian government. Civilians took power in 1944, when it was already evident that Japan would lose the war. The military was stripped of effective power, and the country held its first elections in ten years. However, in 1947 the military retook power, and a succession of military generals ruled for the next 26 years. The three most important leaders during this period of military dominance were Phibun Songkram (prime minister from 1948 to 1957), Sarit Thanarat (1957 to 1963), and Thanom Kittikachorn (1963 to 1973). These three generals sought legitimacy for their governments by placing prominent civilians in cabinet posts. All three stressed economic development and anti-communism, practicing a benevolent yet authoritarian style of rule much like that of the paternalistic and autocratic kingdoms of Sukhothai and Ayuthaya. Yet, although they sometimes held elections and otherwise permitted the appearance of democracy, overall they abrogated the democratic rights of the people as they sought to perpetuate their power. The military rulers were also involved in corruption. For example, when he died in 1963, Sarit (the Thai use first names when referring to individuals) had a personal fortune of $150 million, at a time when per capita income averaged only about $200 per year. He had also given automobiles and homes to more than fifty mistresses.

Given that politics in Thailand has been almost exclusively an affair of high-level elite cliques vying for power, the Great Tragedy of October 14, 1973 stands as an extraordinary development. On that date, large numbers of the citizenry demonstrated against the military government. Violence erupted, but the demonstrators stood firm. In just a few days the military government dissolved and the top leadership fled the country. King Bhumibol Adulyadej appointed a caretaker government that issued a new democratic constitution and held elections for a new government.

A multitude of planned and accidental events converged to bring about this momentous change. A major underlying factor was political and economic mismanagement, along with the perception that the military was increasingly ruling in its own self-interest. Furthermore, the military was becoming disunited while students were becoming organized, aroused, and capable of winning broad popular support for their calls for constitutional government. Many in the military refused to follow their superiors' orders to mow down the students, because the king supported the students and his word was revered.

The events of October 1973 ushered in a period of democracy that lasted three years. The civilian governments were besieged by severe problems. Laborers took advantage of the new freedoms by demanding higher wages. Crime and communist insurgency increased. Inflation rose and the price of oil skyrocketed as a result of the rising cost of petroleum from the Middle East. Students split into factions and could not agree on goals. Communism took command in the neighboring countries of Vietnam, Laos, and Cambodia, giving hope to armed insurgents who were already active in remote parts of Thailand. The administrations of Prime Ministers Seni Pramoj and Kukrit Pramoj were free of corruption, but their policies and administrative efforts were not successful enough to stem the rising sentiment against civilian rule, which was perceived as inherently weak and ineffective.

In October 1976 the military overthrew the democratic government, proclaimed martial law, and abrogated the constitution. Police and military forces stormed Thammasat University, killing hundreds of pro-democracy students. The *coup* was popular, as many people viewed the civilian government as weak and the military as strong. The economic situation in the kingdom was too much for the average Thai, who breathed a sigh of relief when the military returned to power. Initially, the *coup* leaders appointed a former judge, Thanin Kraivichien, to serve as prime minister. But his rule was so repressive that even the military could not tolerate him, and he was soon replaced. The military remained dominant for a decade, during which time the government was led by generals or former generals, the most prominent being Kriangsak Chomanand (prime minister from 1977 to 1980), and Prem Tinsulanond (prime minister from 1980 to 1988).

Figure 16. Election campaign posters in Thailand

Under Kriangsak's and Prem's rule, communist insurgency was curtailed, the economy strengthened, and a new semi-democratic constitution was established. Prem in particular demonstrated the balancing act that was Thailand's form of semi-democracy. During his administration, several national elections were held, but the winning parties always asked Prem to continue as prime minister, even though he himself never stood for election. They also allowed Prem to appoint the most strategic cabinet positions. As a former general, Prem had the support of the military. At the same time, his honesty and relatively liberal policies made him popular with the people, and he also enjoyed the strong support of King Bhumibol. The Kriangsak and Prem administrations functioned as a transition to a fully elected government led by Chatichai Choonhavan (prime minister from 1988 to 1991), the leader of the nation's largest political party and himself a former general. The strong economy kept Chatichai in office for three years, until the military again took power.

In 1991, the military staged another *coup d'etat*. This time the *coup* was not popular, because most of the Thai (and most scholars of Thailand) felt that the days of military rule were over. Realizing that they did not have the support of the people, the generals put a respected civilian, Anand Panyarachun, into the position of prime minister. A new constitution was written (the sixteenth since 1932), but it was undemocratic in that it gave too much power to the appointed Senate (the upper house of parliament) and too little to the elected lower house. When elections were held in 1992, pro-military parties formed a coalition and invited Suchinda Kraprayoon, the military chief, to serve as prime minister. Suchinda lasted in power only a few months.

Anand Panyarachun

Anand Panyarachun served as Thailand's prime minister on two occasions: the first following a 1991 military *coup d'etat* against the civilian government, and the second following the popular uprising against General Suchinda Krapayoon's 1992 installation as prime minister. Anand was honest, efficient, progressive, and internationally respected. Before becoming prime minister, he had served as Ambassador to the United States and the United Nations. His reputation for honesty was further enhanced by his conduct in office, and the people generally regarded his leadership as the best the country had known. He demoted the military leaders who were thought responsible for the violence of 1992. In his short administration he reformed the tax system, privatized some state enterprises, and supervised elections that were free of fraud. Anand had no political ambitions, and he returned to private life after normalizing the nation's political system.

The people rose in wrath against the new government, which was perceived as corrupt and anti-democratic. The military responded violently, and widespread rioting broke out in the capital. Order was not restored until the king lectured the opposing leaders on national television and told them to work out a peaceful solution. Suchinda soon resigned, and Anand Panyarachun was once again appointed prime minister (this time appointed by the king). Anand's deft handling of the top position made him highly admired, but he had no political ambitions, and he left office once he had organized elections.

In the second 1992 election, the pro-civilian parties prevailed. The new coalition chose Chuan Leekpai, leader of the Democrat Party, to be prime minister. Chuan, a civilian from a middle class family, was known for his impeccable honesty and his commitment to the needs of the people. Chuan attempted to democratize a corrupt, military-dominated political system. To an extent, he succeeded. He led the country from September 1992 to May 1995, becoming the longest-serving elected civilian prime minister in Thai history. But his democratization efforts also produced his downfall, as his coalition collapsed over controversies about decentralization.

Chuan's term was followed by the ineffective administration of Banharn Silapaarcha, leader of the Chat Thai party. Banharn had served six terms in Parliament and former minister of agriculture, industry, interior, finance, and transportation. He was also a billionaire business executive and a masterful user of political patronage. His election was viewed as a triumph for "money politics." His short-lived administration (1995–96) was characterized by corruption and lack of direction. New elections in 1996 were won by the New Aspiration Party whose leader, Chavalit Yongchaiyut, became prime minister. The Asian economic crisis began under his administration with the devaluation of the *baht* (the Thai unit of currency). Chavalit seemed unable to resolve the crisis and was replaced in 1998 by Chuan Leekpai, the head of the opposition Democrat Party who assumed the post of prime minister for the second time. Chuan also proved unable to resolve the crisis. A new election in 2001 saw the rise of Thaksin Shinawatra, a telecommunications mogul and leader of the Thai Rak Thai (Thais Love Thais) party. As the richest man in the country, he was deemed by the people to be incorruptible and his candidacy was highly popular. Although more than a dozen parties contested the election, Thaksin is the first prime minister of modern times to lead a party that received the support of the majority of voters.

No sooner had he been elected when, ironically, the supposedly incorruptible Thaksin was brought to trial on charges of corruption. But in August 2001 in an eight-to-seven decision, Thailand's highest court acquitted him on charges of corruption. Thaksin had been alleged by the constitutionally mandated National Counter-Corruption Commission to have hidden assets while serving as a cabinet member in 1997. He was accused of transferring shares worth billions of *baht* to his family, servants, and close friends. Thaksin claimed he had no knowledge of the transfer of assets. His position no longer threatened, Thaksin moved to end the economic crisis and to set forth programs designed to help the rural poor. He established a program of inexpensive medical care, gave loans and grants to villages, and cancelled or postponed debts owed by farmers. He also established an asset-management agency to reduce corporate debt. Thaksin's critics complained that these programs were unaffordable and smacked of rank populism. However, economic growth was renewed and Thaksin has continued to enjoy highly favorable poll support, especially in the rural areas.

After September 11, 2001, Thaksin was initially reluctant to join the United States in its anti-terrorism crusade. Thaksin was reluctant to be viewed as an American "lackey" and he did not want to upset Thailand's minority Muslim population. His position was strongly criticized both by American officials and by local politicians who portrayed him as a xenophobic nationalist. However, Thaksin soon joined the anti-terrorism coalition, visited the United States, and portrayed himself as an international leader.

Ever since 1932, when the absolute monarchy was overthrown, Thailand has had difficulty establishing a systematic process for transferring power. Successions have taken place primarily by *coups d'etat*, sometimes violent ones, and politics continues to focus on the military, politicians, and business elites. But recently steps have been taken to create more enduring democratic institutions and processes. A new power is emerging based on the rising middle class, a more educated segment of society that has arisen as a result of the nation's rapid economic development. The Thai middle class generally opposes military rule and may be responsible for the new direction toward stronger democracy.

The 1997 constitution, the seventeenth in sixty-five years, was unprecedented in its emphasis on reform and democracy. The new constitution takes power away from the bureaucracy. Constitutional courts now have supremacy in determining judicial affairs, and the Senate is no longer appointed. The constitution also provides for accountability and transparency. Candidates for office must indicate their assets and liabilities, and the Counter-Corruption Commission must examine assets and liabilities both before and after the politician has served in government. This provision is weeding the corrupt "godfathers" out of the political process. The Electoral Commission has also been given new power to reject election results if there is evidence of electoral fraud. During the 2000 Senate elections, in some districts the commission required as many as four separate elections before it accepted the results.

The new laws on elections also seek to reduce factionalism and corruption within political parties. The old system elected members of parliament from multi-member plurality districts. Candidates often competed against members of their own party in the quest to be among the district's highest vote-getters. This intra-party competition bred factionalism and weakened the party leaders' control over individual members of parliament. The new constitution addresses this problem by providing for 400 seats of the 500-seat lower body to be elected from single member districts. The remaining 100 seats are filled by proportional representation from nationwide party lists.

While the 1997 constitution represents significant progress, Thailand still faces serious problems that threaten its transition to full-fledged democracy. First, the economic crisis that ravaged the society in 1997–98 undermined the people's support for their government's leaders. Second, the nation has a dismal environmental record, and as a result of deforestation has suffered droughts, flooding, and pollution. Third, AIDS has hit with a vengeance, costing Thai society billions of dollars in medical bills and lost time. Fourth, Thailand continues to be challenged by the opposing forces of tradition and modernity. As the nation becomes Westernized, many of the traditional values have been lost. The result is more alienation and a widening generation gap. Additional challenges include a need for educational reform, a lack of skilled engineers and industrial technicians, a rising gap between the rich and poor, environmental degradation (such as deforestation and the traffic and pollution in Bangkok), child labor, legal and practical discrimination against women, and mistreatment of ethnic minorities.

Despite these problems, in recent years Thailand has been politically stable. There are a number of reasons for this increased stability. First, Thailand has successfully ended internal insurgencies by more effectively meeting the needs of the people. Second, the kingdom is free from serious outside threats to its security. China and Vietnam, for example, are now major traders with Thailand. Third, rapid economic growth has enriched many of the people. A rising middle class is the heart of a stable society. Fourth, the armed forces are being professionalized. Fifth, the monarch is a moderating influence on the Kingdom. Sixth, family planning has been successful. And seventh, Thailand is not a frontline state in the struggle against terrorism. These factors all work in favor of the vaunted Thai capacity to cope.

Vietnam

For many students of Southeast Asia, the name "Vietnam" calls up nightmarish images of a dreadful, unwinnable war fought by their parents and grandparents. The Vietnam War of the 1960s and 1970s was one of the great American traumas of the twentieth century. During the war, few Americans knew much about this nation on the other side of the world. Today, most Americans are still ignorant about the country's history, culture, and politics.

In the waning days of World War II, the insurgent forces of the League for the Independence of Vietnam, also known as the Vietminh, became increasingly active against the declining power of the Japanese occupation. When the Japanese surrendered, the movement sought to establish control of the country before the French could return.

In September 1945, the Vietminh leader, Ho Chi Minh, proclaimed Vietnam's independence and set up a provisional government headed by himself. Initially the French agreed that Ho's new Democratic Republic of Vietnam was in fact independent. However, the agreement broke down, and in 1946 a series of clashes initiated the eight-year-long French-Indochina War.

General Vo Nguyen Giap

General Vo Nguyen Giap was a close advisor to Ho Chi Minh and the Vietnamese revolution's leading military strategist. He is considered by many to be the most brilliant military general of modern times. General Giap gained fame for defeating the French, Japanese, and Americans, though his detractors noted that his victories came at a huge cost of millions of Vietnamese casualties. After the communist victory and takeover of southern Vietnam, Giap became an advocate for reform and renovation. He lost his position on the Communist Party politburo in the early 1980s, but he remained a hero to most Vietnamese.

Ho Chi Minh single-mindedly dedicated his life to achieving Vietnamese independence. He blended Marxism-Leninism with Vietnamese patriotism to create a nationalist force. It was he who was principally responsible for resisting French imperialism, organizing nationalist forces, establishing an independent government, and setting the foundation for defeating first the French and later the Americans. He proved that a well-motivated army could overcome huge material disadvantages. His indignation at humiliations imposed by the French, Japanese, and Americans was the catalyst for his revolutionary struggle. He was ruthless and willing to use any means to achieve full independence for his country.

The French had superior military technology and firepower, and they also received massive financial and military support from the United States. But the Vietnamese resistance kept gaining strength. In 1954, France finally admitted defeat after the battle of Dien Bien Phu, in northwestern Vietnam, where a supposedly invincible French force was annihilated along with its supposedly impregnable fortress.

Emperor Bao Dai

Vietnam's last emperor was influential from 1925, when he became emperor within the French colony, to 1955, when the throne ceased to exist. He administered the country under the French, collaborated with the Japanese, temporarily supported the Vietminh led by Ho Chi Minh, and was subsequently a reluctant supporter of Diem's Republic of Vietnam. Bao Dai lost the throne when Ngo Dinh Diem, the *protégé* Bao Dai had appointed the first president of South Vietnam, sponsored an anti-Bao Dai referendum that ended the monarchy. Bao Dai died in France in 1998, having gone into exile distraught about the communist takeover of Vietnam.

The Geneva Agreements of 1954 sought to separate the rival French and Vietminh forces by setting up a temporary military demarcation line at the seventeenth parallel. This line was not intended to be a political or territorial boundary, though it soon came to be treated as one. The Geneva Agreements also called for eventual national elections for the purpose of unification. The Vietminh, who had represented the Vietnamese at Geneva, were expected to win the elections because they controlled the political machinery in North Vietnam. However, there emerged in the southern part of Vietnam, especially in Saigon, an anti-Vietminh administration led by the strongly anti-communist and pro-American Ngo Dinh Diem. Diem had been placed in leadership by Emperor Bao Dai, but in 1955 Diem deposed the emperor and proclaimed the Republic of Vietnam with himself as the country's first president. With support from the United States, Diem consolidated his power and repudiated the Geneva Agreements' provision for unified national elections.

Diem's policies in the south became ever more oppressive, corrupt, and nepotistic. In the early 1960s (the date is not known precisely), an insurgent guerrilla force known as the Vietcong (Vietnamese Communists) emerged in the south. This group included peasants, workers, intellectuals, and Buddhists. The Vietcong were offended by Diem's attempts to control villages in South Vietnam, as his policies were contrary to the tradition that "the power of the Emperor stops at the village gate." At first there was no northern military involvement, but the North Vietnamese provided ever-increasing support until ultimately the Vietcong and the North Vietnamese soldiers were indistinguishable. To counteract the insurgency Diem relied on United States advisors, weaponry, money, and soldiers. Yet resistance to Diem continued to grow throughout the populace. When Buddhist monks arose against Diem and committed acts of self-immolation, the United States realized that Diem was a problem. In October 1963 President Kennedy supported a *coup* against Diem that resulted in Diem's death and led to a series of military juntas headed by Generals Khanh, Ky, Minh, Theiu, and others too numerous to list.

In August 1964 the United States Senate passed the Tonkin Gulf Resolution, which gave the American president authority to take all measures necessary to deal with North Vietnamese "aggression." That same year President Johnson ran for election on a platform that said his opponent, Senator Barry Goldwater, was a warmonger, and that American boys should not fight in Asian wars. Despite his landslide victory and his pledge not to escalate the war, Johnson rapidly got the United States more deeply involved. In February 1965 the United States began massive bombing to interdict North Vietnamese supply lines and to provide time for the south to strengthen its forces. Johnson also ordered a buildup of American military forces. By 1967, some 500,000 American troops were in Vietnam.

Tonkin Gulf Resolution

An alleged attack against American ships by North Vietnamese torpedo boats led to a United States Senate resolution in August 1964 that supported American retaliation and provided the president with full powers to respond. Only two senators dissented. The United States Senate never actually declared war against Vietnam, but the Tonkin Gulf Resolution stated that the president was authorized to "take all necessary measures to repel any armed attack against the forces of the United States." Lyndon Johnson interpreted this wording as authorization for full-scale military involvement in Vietnam. Years later, various reports made it clear that the alleged torpedo boat attack did not actually occur. In 1971 the Tonkin Gulf Resolution was repealed, but it was another two years before the United States disengaged from Vietnam.

In 1968 the massive Tet (Vietnamese New Year) offensive staged by Vietcong and North Vietnamese soldiers showed the ineffectiveness of the American war effort. On that date strong forces of Vietnamese insurgents rose up in almost every province of South Vietnam. The insurgents lost the battles, but their unexpected offensive caused the Americans to lose confidence in their ability to prevail. Still, because the southern military was factionalized and because corruption was rampant among its leadership, the United States took over more and more direction of the war, though protests grew more vocal back at home.

Stunned by the war's increasing unpopularity, President Johnson announced in 1968 that he would step down from the presidency instead of seeking re-election. Richard Nixon won the election later that year after proclaiming that he had a "secret plan" to end the war.

Doves

The "doves" who opposed the war argued that the United States was interfering in the domestic affairs of another nation. They viewed Vietnam not as two nations (North and South Vietnam) fighting an international war but as a single nation engaged in an internal civil conflict that should never have become a target for American involvement. The doves argued that the billions of dollars spent on the war should be used instead to solve the severe domestic problems that existed in the United States itself (this was a time of civil rights campaigns and of increased awareness of the poverty problem). The doves also said that the war was immoral. They cited horrific incidents, such as the My Lai massacre in which American soldiers had indiscriminately killed many villagers, and they said the United States should not be supporting corrupt, elitist, dictatorial regimes such as the one in South Vietnam.

After the election, the war continued as before. In April 1970 Nixon expanded the conflict further by sending troops into eastern Cambodia. The American Secretary of State, Henry Kissinger, had devised a plan to close the Ho Chi Minh Trail in hopes of shutting down the North Vietnamese supply routes to Vietcong and North Vietnamese forces operating in the south. Nixon justified the invasion by saying, "If when the chips are down, the world's most powerful nation acts like a pitiful helpless giant, the forces of totalitarianism and anarchy will threaten free nations and free institutions throughout the world."

Hawks

According to "hawks," the reasons for American intervention in Vietnam were persuasive. Of concern was the perceived national interest of the United States itself. Many American policymakers saw the fall of Vietnam to communism as one more stage of a spreading cancer that could eventually envelop America itself. South Vietnam was seen as a testing ground for communist wars of national liberation. The hawks believed that anything less than a committed effective stand against "communist aggression" would be tantamount to an invitation for further aggression in other parts of the world, and they believed American credibility as a world power was at stake. American policymakers also cited the commitment of four presidents and various treaties and agreements as proper justification for United States involvement.

The incursion into Cambodia encouraged the right-wing Cambodian military leaders who just two months earlier had overthrown Cambodia's long-time leader, Prince Norodom Sihanouk. But the invasion failed to shut down the North Vietnamese supply routes, and it spurred increasing military activity by the Khmer Rouge-led rebel groups who eventually took over Cambodia. Meanwhile, the invasion sparked massive new protests across the United States.

Shortly after the Cambodian invasion, President Nixon responded to the protests by proclaiming a policy of "Vietnamization," which meant gradually turning the ground war over to the Vietnamese soldiers while American bombers continued the air war. Vietnamization was popular in the United States because American soldiers began coming home. But for the Vietnamese the war continued to be catastrophic.

Figure 17. Martyred Mother Statue, near Saigon, Vietnam
Socialist-style statue memorializing mothers
of the soldiers killed in the war against America.

In 1972, the Paris Peace Accords set forth a peace process, but the South Vietnamese government rejected the accords because it believed they would strengthen the North. After massive bombing raids on Hanoi during the Christmas season of 1972, a new cease-fire agreement was signed in 1973 by United States Secretary of State Henry Kissinger and North Vietnamese Foreign Affairs Minister Le Duc Tho. The Americans were extricated from the war, and South Vietnam was left to fend for itself. In 1973 Kissinger and Tho were jointly awarded the Nobel Peace Prize, but Tho refused the prize on the grounds that Vietnam remained divided and, as a result, had not yet won a lasting peace. Over the next two years, intermittent fighting broke out between the northern and southern forces. In 1975 a North Vietnamese offensive sparked a sudden collapse of the South Vietnamese military. North Vietnamese troops moved rapidly through the south as the war ended in a communist victory.

The communists won the war for several sets of reasons. The first set of reasons had to do with the character of the competing regimes. Most Vietnamese, both in the south and the north, had never considered the Republic of Vietnam (South Vietnam) to be a legitimate government. Instead, the South was viewed as a lackey state of the United States. The more men and dollars the United States put into South Vietnam, the less authentic the Saigon government seemed. In contrast, the Democratic Republic of Vietnam (North Vietnam), despite being oppressive, was viewed as the country's legitimate government, because it had valiantly fought against the French to establish Vietnamese independence.

The second set of reasons for the communist victory had to do with the American military's difficulties adjusting to the kind of war it encountered in Vietnam. The Americans had attempted to fight a conventional war against an enemy who used guerrilla tactics and who blended in with the civilian population. This made it difficult for the American soldiers to know the difference between enemy and ally. The Americans also underestimated the strength of Vietnamese nationalism and the Vietnamese people's determination to push forward in the face of great odds. American soldiers were constantly amazed at the punishment that the Vietnamese were willing to withstand throughout some ten years of intensive warfare. The third reason for the communist victory was that the war never received the wholehearted support of the American public. Many Americans became convinced that the tremendous violence meted out by the United States military was disproportionate to the American government's stated goals.

Bao Ninh

Born in 1952 in Hanoi, Bao Ninh became Vietnam's most famous author. He was drafted in 1969 to fight in the American War and was one of only 10 survivors out of a group of 500 Vietnamese soldiers who served in the Glorious 27th Youth Brigade.

Bao Ninh's first and most famous book is *The Sorrow of War*. For many years the book was banned in Vietnam because it did not depict the North Vietnamese soldiers as heroic, omitting the communist ideological jargon that the government desired. Bao Ninh wrote straightforwardly and unflinchingly about the horrors of war, with all its death, destruction, and monotony. The Vietnamese government eventually lifted its ban and had the book published in Vietnamese, English, and many other languages. *The Sorrow of War* became the biggest seller in Vietnamese history. Bao Ninh has continued writing and has won numerous literary prizes.

After they took control of the south in April 1975, the North Vietnamese moved swiftly to consolidate their power. Saigon was renamed Ho Chi Minh City in honor of the North's late leader (Ho Chi Minh had died in 1969). In May 1976 the government announced Vietnam's reunification, with Hanoi serving as the capital. The new administration transformed the south into a socialist economy, established re-education camps to indoctrinate former partisans of the South Vietnamese government, and instituted an oppressive one-party communist regime.

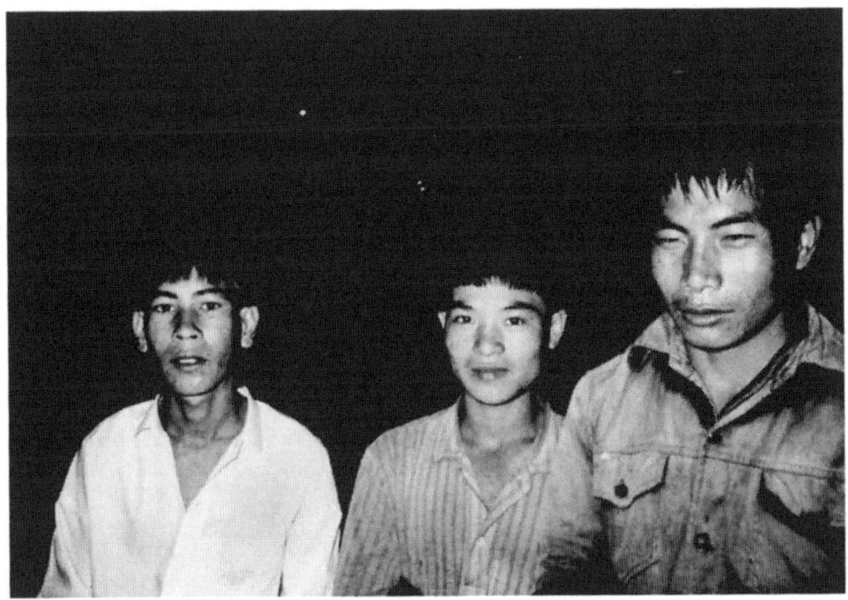

Figure 18. Amerasian Vietnamese
Some American soldiers fathered children by Vietnamese mothers. Most of these Amerasian children grew up with their mothers but later migrated to the United States.

The Vietnamese government sought to promote economic development, but instead the economy faltered and the people suffered hardships. Some of the problems stemmed from the nature of the communist regime, which lacked economic incentives for efficient production. But Vietnam also faced problems beyond the government's control. After all, the country had been devastated in the war, and in successive years it had suffered a series of natural disasters such as floods, droughts, and hurricanes. In addition, many of the nation's most talented citizens had fled the country in an exodus that especially included the highly educated, the entrepreneurs, and those with administrative experience. The country also suffered chronic food shortages followed by hyperinflation. By the late 1980s it was clear that Vietnam was falling ever further behind its neighbors.

In the years following reunification, the Vietnamese government sparred with Cambodia's Khmer Rouge government over territory and other issues. Vietnam also felt threatened by the friendship between the Khmer Rouge and Vietnam's northern neighbor, China. In December 1978, Vietnam invaded Cambodia, rid the nation of the genocidal Khmer Rouge government, and set up a new administration led by a pro-Vietnamese leader named Hun Sen. Vietnam's intervention angered China. The Chinese launched a military offensive meant to force Vietnam to withdraw from Cambodia, to "teach Vietnam a lesson," and to punish the country for its harsh treatment of overseas Chinese (for example, Vietnam had nationalized all the Chinese businesses). Chinese troops crossed into northern Vietnam in February 1979, but Vietnamese troops

Figure 19. Village memorial to Vietcong and North Vietnamese soldiers who died in the war

expelled the invaders and pushed them back to China, thereby "teaching China a lesson" that Vietnam was powerful. The Chinese invasion, together with that of the Vietnamese against Cambodia, belied the myth of communist solidarity in the region.

By the late 1980s the Vietnamese government realized that its economic policies were not working. In 1986, to turn around the faltering economy, the Vietnamese Communist Party (VCP) instituted a policy of *doi moi* (renovation) that allowed a free market system to develop with relatively little government interference. Farmers were allowed to sell their surplus on the open market, factories were privatized, and land was returned to the peasantry. Price controls were eliminated and the *dong* (the Vietnamese unit of currency) was allowed to float freely on international currency markets. Banks were established and a legal framework for business contracts was drawn up. The results of *doi moi* were astounding, as the nation moved to positive growth rates and Vietnam went from being a rice importer to a rice exporter. Foreign investors began taking an interest in the country. New trade relations with nations around the world led to an influx of new consumer products.

Figure 20. Modern Vietnam
Despite continuing restrictions, Vietnam is welcoming international investment to an unprecedented degree.

However, the liberalization did not extend to politics. Vietnam continues to be a highly centralized state in which only one party is allowed to lead. The Communist Party controls every facet of society, and its leadership remains contemptuous of Western-style democracy as inherently unstable and conflictual. Vietnam has an elected National Assembly, but it does not allow multiple political parties, and as a result the electorate has had only limited experience of competition for office. Since 1994 some assembly seats have actually been contested, but on those occasions both candidates were Communist Party members and the election was therefore not an occasion for contrasting political appeals. The state harshly circumscribes civil liberties to assure that there are no derogatory statements about the nation's leadership. Furthermore, the National Assembly does not really function as a representative institution, as it is primarily a rubber stamp for decisions made in the Communist Party politburo.

Still, the country has become more open in several important respects. More people are attending Buddhist temples, Chinese temples, and Christian churches than before, and newspapers occasionally print articles critical of particular government policies. However, the openness remains limited, and the Vietnamese government continues to control many aspects of the society and of public discussion. The result is a mismatch between the country's political and economic systems. It is not clear if the Vietnamese government can continue to combine a free-market economy with such a closed political system.

In 1997, the National Assembly (whose members had been selected at local party congresses) selected younger, more reform-minded leaders who were less concerned with Marxist ideology and more concerned about economic development. But the new leadership has brought little change. Many foreign investors, who had once been intrigued by the immense opportunities in Vietnam, began to become frustrated by the continuing corruption and administrative barriers that kept them from profiting from their investments.

Nevertheless, Vietnam has continued to move forward on the diplomatic front. Ever since the early 1990s, when the Soviet Union collapsed and communism ceased to be an influential world force, Vietnam has been working to mend fences with the Western capitalist world. In 1994 the United States lifted its trade embargo against Vietnam. In 1995, fully twenty years after the war had ended, the two countries reestablished diplomatic relations. In 1995, Vietnam also joined ASEAN (the Association of Southeast Asian Nations), an alliance that had initially been established precisely to oppose Vietnamese aggressive intentions in Southeast Asia. The irony was poignant for the Vietnamese, who were working out how a communist nation could become a major player in the capitalist world.

DISCUSSION QUESTIONS

1. Discuss the principal political events of each of Southeast Asia's eleven nations.

2. Why are some Southeast Asian nations rich and some poor?

3. Why are some Southeast Asian nations democratic and some autocratic?

SUGGESTED READINGS

For a detailed account of Southeast Asian history through 1986, see David J. Steinberg, ed., *In Search of Southeast Asia* (University of Hawai'i Press, Honolulu, 1987). Kevin Hewison has edited a book on contemporary politics in Thailand entitled *Political Change in Thailand: Democracy and Participation* (Routledge, New York, 1997). For an account of how personalism pervades the Philippines, see Alfred W. McCoy, ed., *An Anarchy of Families: State and Family in the Philippines* (University of Wisconsin, Center for Southeast Asian Studies, 1993). Michael Haas has edited a book, entitled *The Singapore Puzzle* (Praeger, Westport, 1999), which contains chapters that criticize the authoritarian nature of the Singaporean government. Robert I. Rotberg has also edited a book, this one entitled *Burma: Prospects for a Democratic Future* (The World Peace Foundation, Brookings Institution Press, Washington, D.C., 1998). Chapters include an analysis of Burma's political culture, its isolation from the world, the armed forces, and prospects for development and democracy. The twenty-fifth anniversary of the end of the war in Vietnam has been cause for many books on contemporary Vietnam. One of the most controversial is Michael Lind, *Vietnam: The Necessary War* (The Free Press, New York, 1999), a reinterpretation of America's military conflict. Lind sees the war as necessary because it was a part of the global conflict between the Soviet Union and the United States during the Cold War. For a fascinating account of Cambodia's despised Khmer Rouge leader, Pol Pot, see David P. Chandler, *Brother Number One: A Political Biography of Pol Pot* (Westview Press, Boulder, 1992).

7

LEADERS

Leaders interact with the values of their followers, and those values make possible many different styles of leadership. Contemporary Southeast Asia has featured leaders who are nationalistic (Sukarno of Indonesia), revolutionary (Pol Pot of Cambodia and Ho Chi Minh of Vietnam), conservative (Ngo Dinh Diem of Vietnam), populist (Prince Sihanouk of Cambodia), authoritarian-developmental (Suharto of Indonesia and Lee Kuan Yew of Singapore), and democratic (Aung San Suu Kyi of Burma and Corazon Aquino of the Philippines). These labels oversimplify even as they clarify, but they give some indication of the dramatic diversity of leadership the region has seen this century. Following are brief biographies of these leaders. The biographies have been written to provide yet another perspective on the nations of Southeast Asia.

Aung San Suu Kyi - Burma

In contemporary Burma, Aung San Suu Kyi (pronounced ahng sahn suu chee) was the first woman to be seriously considered for national leadership. Born in 1945, she is the daughter of Aung San, the nationalist leader who led Burma's struggle for independence from Great Britain and who died shortly before he was expected to become the nation's first president. Aung San Suu Kyi is an eloquent orator, has impeccable character, and has the courage to oppose the military government that has oppressed the Burmese people. Concerned by her effective leadership of the Burmese democratic movement, the Burmese military first imprisoned her and then kept her under house arrest for a decade.

Aung San Suu Kyi's ancestors were of the gentry class and were deeply imbued with Buddhist beliefs. Her father, Aung San, was the father of Burmese independence, the George Washington of his country. A fierce nationalist, Aung San had led pro-independence groups at Rangoon University, edited Burmese newspapers, traveled throughout the world to spread the word about the Burmese nationalist movement, and founded the "Thirty Comrades," a group of nationalist leaders who formed the backbone of the new Burma Independence Army. In the early years of World War II, Aung San ostensibly collaborated with the Japanese, but he actually was involved in secret resistance against his country's new oppressors. During the latter part of the war, he led a revolt against the Japanese and temporarily joined the Allied forces. By the end of World War II, Aung San had become the most popular Burmese leader and was ready to assume the top position of the new independent government. But on July 19, 1947, political opponents stormed a building where he was leading a meeting and assassinated him and eight other leaders of the independence movement.

Aung Sun had fathered three children, including a daughter named Aung San Suu Kyi. She was named Aung San after her father, Suu for her paternal grandmother, and Kyi after her mother Daw Khin Kyi. (Unlike many Burmese who change their names as they go through life, Aung San Suu Kyi appears to have had the same name since birth.) Aung San Suu Kyi's mother took up important government positions in the newly independent Burma led by prime minister U Nu. During this period Aung San Suu Kyi was brought up by relatives, who steeped her in Burmese literature and traditional culture. She attended private schools and was considered highly intelligent. In 1960, her mother was named Burma's ambassador to India, and Aung San Suu Kyi moved with her to New Delhi. There she became a devoted follower of the teachings of the late Mahatma Gandhi, from whose example she learned about nonviolence and civil disobedience. Meanwhile, back in Burma, General Ne Win took power in a 1962 *coup*. He placed Burma under a socialist and repressive regime, and he closed the country to Westerners. Aung San Suu Kyi stayed in India and did not engage in political activities in Burma.

After 1964, Aung San Suu Kyi studied at Oxford University in England. While she was in England, she met and fell in love with Michael Aris, a scholar of Tibet and Bhutan. In 1969 she moved to New York City, where she worked at the United Nations. While there, she brooded about her prospective marriage to Aris. In Burmese culture, an interracial marriage is tantamount to rejection of one's culture. In a letter that would later become famous, she prophetically wrote: "I only ask one thing, that should my people need me, you would help me to do my duty by them." Aris promised, and he did not renege when duty called on her almost two decades later. The two married in 1972, and soon thereafter Aung San Suu Kyi became the full-time mother of two sons. While she raised her children and supported her husband's work, she also retained her interest in Burma. She lived in Kyoto for one year to do research on her father. She and her family also took research trips to northern India.

In Burma, life under Ne Win was going from bad to worse. The Burmese suffered from chronic inflation, famine, a poor economic infrastructure, and low rates of development. Human rights were constantly violated. In 1988, in the midst of this atmosphere, Aung San Suu Kyi was telephoned by her family in Burma. They asked her to return to Rangoon to help take care of her mother, who had suffered a serious stroke. She went at once, arriving precisely at the time that student-led demonstrations were beginning against the oppressive Ne Win regime. The government replied ferociously to the protests, killing many students. Both dissident leaders and government officials went to Aung San Suu Kyi to ask her assistance with mediating the dispute. She believed that she had a responsibility to become involved. In August 1988 she formally gave her support to the democracy movement, proclaiming that her marriage to a foreigner and her life abroad had not lessened her love and devotion for her country. Her subsequent speeches reiterated the idea that the army and demonstrators needed to work together to find a solution, but her overall intent and effect was to give vitality to the democratic movement.

In late 1988 the Burmese government announced that it would hold multi-party elections. Soon afterwards, General Saw Maung suppressed public demonstrations and established the State Law and Order Restoration Council (SLORC), but the military leaders abided by the promise of elections, expecting they could dominate the electoral process. The opposition established the National League for Democracy (NLD), with Aung San Suu Kyi as general secretary. She launched a nation-wide speaking campaign and quickly became the most popular Burmese leader. The generals, frightened of her popularity, arrested NLD organizers and harassed Aung San Suu Kyi as she traveled. But she persisted in her campaign, and her courage made international headlines. On one memorable occasion, Aung San Suu Kyi walked calmly through a line of army troops who had their rifles aimed at her. Finally, in July 1989, SLORC placed her under house arrest and surrounded her compound with barbed wire and guards. She was separated from her family and from her fellow country men and women.

The SLORC set May 1990 as the date for the parliamentary elections, but it took steps to prevent an NLD victory. In early 1990 the SLORC formally disqualified Aung San Suu Kyi's candidacy for parliament, and in the months leading up to the election it controlled the media and the election officials. In a most extraordinary event, and despite the military's dominance, the NLD won 392 out of the 485 seats contested, more than 80 percent of the Assembly. SLORC's party won only ten seats. Burmese government officials were flabbergasted. They immediately announced that the election was null and void, and they said that its purpose had been not to elect a parliament, but rather to elect delegates to a constitutional convention. Members of the NLD were arrested. The government launched a campaign to dirty Aung San Suu Kyi's reputation, claiming that as the wife of a foreigner she threatened national unity.

Aung San Suu Kyi's house arrest dragged on for years, though on rare occasions Aung San Suu Kyi's husband and children were allowed to visit her. In 1991 her papers were collected by her husband and published in book form. She received the Nobel Peace Prize that same year. Meanwhile, the government remained oppressive, corruption flourished, and Burma continued to deteriorate economically. Aung San Suu Kyi was released from house arrest in 1995, but she still was not allowed to speak publicly or resume official leadership of the NLD. In 1999, the street of her home was still barricaded by the military and police, and it was almost impossible to meet with her. Her husband, Michael Aris, died of cancer in 1999, but Aung San Suu Kyi could not attend his funeral in England. From time to time she had been offered opportunities to leave the country, but she would have had to promise not to return, and she considered her proper place to be with her people. Most Burmese people continue to see her as their best hope for a democratic future.

Norodom Sihanouk - Cambodia

Norodom Sihanouk was a populist leader of Cambodia. Hand-picked for the throne by the French colonialists, he was originally expected to be a puppet monarch, but he became instead a fiery nationalist who eventually made common cause with the communists. Any assessment of Sihanouk is controversial, because he is both a great patriot and a self-absorbed naïf whom extremists, namely the Khmer Rouge (Cambodian Communists), duped to do their bidding. His lifelong goal was a free, neutral Cambodia, but his people paid a dreadful price for his inability to imagine how savage the Khmer Rouge would be during their reign of terror from 1975 to 1979.

Sihanouk is descended from a long line of royalty. When he became king in 1941, he was viewed by his people as a *devaraja*, a god-king responsible for Cambodia's stability and progress. Sihanouk was primarily responsible for persuading the French to grant Cambodian independence in 1953–54. Following this accomplishment, Sihanouk abdicated the throne and took the title of prince in order to enter electoral politics as a private citizen. He soon dominated every aspect of Cambodian politics, winning elections and referenda by percentages as high as 99 percent.

The 1950s were considered the "golden age" of Cambodian politics because there were no wars and the nation was led by a popular member of royalty. However, by the 1960s Sihanouk was finding it impossible to balance the country's many competing forces: peasants, urban intellectuals, bureaucrats, army officers, royalists, shopkeepers, and radical nationalists. During the Vietnam War he infuriated the Americans with his conciliatory policies toward Vietnam and China. For example, he allowed North Vietnam to base troops in Cambodia and to resupply the forces operating in South Vietnam along the Ho Chi Minh Trail that passed through Cambodian territory. By the end of the decade he had lost the support of the military and the bureaucrats, retaining only the support of the peasantry. Unfortunately for Sihanouk, the peasantry, although large in numbers, had very little clout in Cambodian policy making.

Figure 21. Prince Sihanouk

In 1970, a group of Cambodian military generals overthrew Sihanouk, and he was forced to live in exile, eventually settling in China. Just months after his ouster, American and South Vietnamese troops invaded Cambodia, thereby carrying the Vietnam War into another country. Cambodia's new military leaders also allowed the United States to bomb parts of Cambodia. This action helped unify the Cambodian rebels under Khmer Rouge leadership and spurred them to increased activity. By 1973, Sihanouk himself was proclaiming his support for the Khmer Rouge. The communist rebels were already implementing a harsh regime in the territories they controlled, but Sihanouk persistently discounted the reports of Khmer Rouge horrors. When in 1975 the Khmer Rouge took full control of the nation, Sihanouk lauded the victory and rejoiced at the defeat of "American imperialism." He continued to be a spokesperson for the Khmer Rouge after he was made a Khmer Rouge prisoner in 1975, even though many of his relatives were executed by the regime. Sihanouk eventually realized that he had sided with fanatics who were committing genocide against the Cambodian people, though he continued to make positive comments about the government in power. In December 1978 the Vietnamese invaded Cambodia, driving the Khmer Rouge off to the western mountains, where they continued to harass the Vietnamese-installed government. In the invasion's aftermath, Sihanouk seized the opportunity to return to exile in China.

From 1979 to 1997, Sihanouk had little to do with life in Cambodia. He remained in China and North Korea as life returned to normal for most of the Cambodians who had survived the grisly social experiments of Pol Pot and his Khmer Rouge. He continued observing from afar as the United Nations stepped into Cambodia to refurbish the government and prepare for elections. Sihanouk was named king again in 1993, thirty-eight years after he had stepped down from the throne to enter electoral politics as a prince. In that same year his son, Prince Norodom Ranarriddh, became co-prime minister along with Hun Sen, the man who had been made prime minister by the Vietnamese. However, Sihanouk himself remained distant from daily affairs. He was suffering from cancer, and he spent most of his days in China and North Korea, where treatment for his disease was said to be superior to that in Cambodia. He had to live with the knowledge that under his tutelage his once-peaceable country had turned tragic with unspeakable horrors from which it had not yet fully recovered.

Pol Pot - Cambodia

Most people have heard of great twentieth century tyrants such as Adolph Hitler and Joseph Stalin. Pol Pot can now be added to that infamous list. As leader of Cambodia's Khmer Rouge, Pol Pot was in power when his regime systematically executed and starved two million Cambodians, fully one of every four persons in the nation. There is no precedent for such a high casualty rate.

Pol Pot grew up in a prosperous rice-farming family. His given name was Saloth Sar. There is no evidence that he suffered any serious childhood traumas that might have led to the cruelty of the regime he would lead. Saloth Sar was given an elite education, and for a time he even lived in the royal palace. Few people can remember much about him, because he was "ordinary," "normal," and "nice." His socio-economic status was sufficiently high that he was chosen to study in Paris, France, where he became interested in Marxism and learned how to perform heavy manual labor.

When he returned to Cambodia in the early 1950s, Saloth Sar joined the Indochinese Communist Party. Even at this early date, he was anti-Vietnamese because of Vietnam's invasions of Cambodian territory in the nineteenth century and earlier. Saloth Sar taught at a private *lycée* (a prep school for university) and at a private college. But his personal security was endangered when Prince Sihanouk launched a strong anti-communist pogrom against "enemies within." Pol Pot was soon forced to live underground. Little is known about his life during the 1960s, a period when communist insurgency was growing throughout Cambodia.

During the 1970s, Pol Pot (still known as Saloth Sar) dominated the Cambodian communist rebels, insisting on strict discipline among his followers. He avoided the limelight, shunned publicity and encouraged secrecy. When the Khmer Rouge took over Phnom Penh in 1975, most people had never heard of him. There was no cult of personality, nor were there statues or pictures of Pol Pot. The country was run by the *angka,* whose name meant "the organization," and no one was sure who was in charge of the new government.

As soon as the Khmer Rouge had captured Phnom Penh, Cambodia's capital city, Pol Pot implemented a drastic plan to evacuate the city's entire population. He then instituted throughout the country a brutal administration that led to the deaths of all Cambodians who had any involvement in previous governments. Cambodia became a "killing field." Families were split apart, Buddhism ended, schools closed, and money abolished. Citizens were taught to inform on each other, so that no one could trust anyone else. All professionals and other educated people were executed in order to bring Cambodia back to the Year Zero, with everyone being "equal peasants." And the killing did not stop there. Pol Pot trusted no one except for his closest comrades. The revolution began to turn on itself when thousands of Khmer Rouge cadres were arrested and tortured to death.

The horror of the Khmer Rouge killing fields ended when the Vietnamese invaded in December 1978 and forced the Khmer Rouge to the western mountains of Cambodia. Pol Pot went into hiding, but he continued to be the organization's leader. He headed a government-in-exile that consisted of three separate armed groups that opposed the Vietnamese installed administration: the Khmer Rouge, the anti-communist Khmer People's National Liberation Front, and the Sihanoukists who supported Prince Sihanouk. These three disparate groups cooperated solely out of opportunism. Despite the Khmer Rouge's record as the worst violator of human rights in history (by this time its excesses were well known), both the United States and the United Nations recognized Pol Pot's government-in-exile as the "legitimate" government of Cambodia. Khmer Rouge resistance continued through the 1980s and most of the 1990s, though the organization cooperated briefly when the United Nations arranged elections for a new government in the early 1990s.

In the late 1990s Pol Pot lost control of the remains of his organization. In 1997, he was captured by his own Khmer Rouge followers, put on trial, and placed under house arrest. He died on April 15, 1998, still claiming that he had no guilty conscience. His picture showed a person who looked like a bland grandfather, but in reality he was responsible for the deaths of millions. Cambodians breathed a sigh of relief at his demise because they no longer had to fear that he could return to power.

There are several possible explanations for the terrible things that Pol Pot did. For example, he had an ideological commitment to creating a "perfect society," which he thought would return Cambodia to the eminence it had enjoyed in the days of Angkor. Some have suggested that the United States' unmerciful bombing of Cambodia in the 1970s caused the Khmer Rouge to become more extreme. Others have suggested that Pol Pot felt Prince Sihanouk's support for his movement legitimated his actions. Finally, it has been suggested that Pol Pot's extreme views and practices were rooted in Cambodian culture, which has long taught that those who disagree with the government are tantamount to enemies. While any or all of these factors may have been at work, it is still not really known why such a "nice" person as Pol Pot would have imposed such a bloody reign of terror over an entire country.

Sukarno – Indonesia

Sukarno was the father of modern Indonesia. As the country's leader he sought independence and autonomy from powerful competing forces both at home and abroad. Charismatic, energetic, and visionary, he was the unquestioned leader of Indonesia's independence movement and served as the country's first president from 1949 to 1965. Sukarno brought both poverty and pride to his countrymen. But he eventually lost power because he was a poor administrator and lost the support of his own army. Though he died over thirty years ago (in 1970), Sukarno remains a preeminent presence for many Indonesians.

Sukarno was born on the island of Java in 1901, at a time when the Dutch were putting the finishing touches on their Netherlands East Indies Empire. Sukarno was early imbued with the values of nationalism. He founded and led the Partai Nasional Indonesia (PNI), the leading nationalist party. Soon he became famous throughout the archipelago for his fiery and courageous speeches against the Dutch colonialists. Flamboyant, brilliant, dynamic, reckless, undisciplined, and charismatic, he was viewed as the spokesperson for the Indonesian farmers and the poor. He was twice arrested by the authorities, eventually being exiled to a remote part of the colony. These arrests turned Sukarno into a martyr and increased his fame.

In 1942 the Japanese conquered Indonesia, imprisoned the Dutch, and brought Sukarno back from exile, returning him to center stage. They hoped that Sukarno would collaborate with them due to their mutual interest in keeping the Dutch from dominating the islands again. Sukarno did indeed collaborate, considering that an uprising against the Japanese would be futile. After the war's end in 1945, Sukarno immediately declared independence. But the Dutch desired to recover their empire, and a terrible war ensued until the Dutch recognized Indonesia's independence on December 27, 1949.

Independent Indonesia entered a period of instability with Sukarno as president. Political crises occurred often, with frequent cabinet shuffles and military mutinies. Sukarno used his prodigious speaking abilities to calm the waters. He was one of the century's great orators, often using Javanese mythology to relate to his followers. He also publicly argued with leaders of the world's major powers as a means of proving his courage and devotion to his country. In the early 1960s he even threatened to crush newly independent Malaysia, a nation he viewed as still under British control, and he mounted an armed demonstration that convinced the Dutch to turn western New Guinea over to Indonesia.

After a failed period of multi-party democracy in the early 1950s, Sukarno concluded that Western-style "50 percent plus 1 democracy" did not suit Indonesia. He therefore announced a policy of "guided democracy," based on indigenous principles from village life, that promoted a more authoritarian and centralized style of rule with Sukarno as the central authority. Sukarno continued to rail against the West, extolling the virtues of the newly independent nations. Soon, the Indonesian political system was solely Sukarno, who controlled every aspect of life. The economy of Indonesia was in chaos, with shockingly high levels of inflation and unemployment, a deteriorating infrastructure, and corruption everywhere.

Sukarno made himself the "balancer" between the Indonesian Communist Party (PKI) and the army, bending sometimes toward the former and sometimes toward the latter, while always assuring that neither would become powerful enough to threaten his supreme position. However, in the early 1960s Sukarno's policies became increasingly close to those of the PKI, then the second-largest communist party in the world. He aligned himself closely with China, withdrew from the United Nations, and became a strong critic of the United States. Sukarno's left-leaning politics outraged the army. When his health deteriorated in 1964, his adversaries began plotting to overthrow him.

On the night of September 29, 1965, a dissident unit of soldiers staged a *coup* in which they kidnapped and killed several generals. The *coup* leaders were defeated in a counterattack led by General Suharto, who had not been included among the kidnap victims. To this day the identity of the *coup* perpetrators is a subject of debate, and Sukarno's personal role in the action is unclear. But President Sukarno was said to be behind the *coup*, and he was placed under house arrest while General Suharto gradually took over the president's duties. Sukarno was left with nothing when he died on June 21, 1970.

Figure 22. Sukarno

Suharto – Indonesia

Suharto dominated Indonesian politics from 1968 to 1998. He was an army general who transformed Indonesia's dying economic system into a moderately productive capitalist economy. It is difficult to imagine a person more different from Sukarno. Whereas Sukarno was charismatic but administratively undisciplined, Suharto lacked personal charm but was an effective administrator. Suharto undid many of Sukarno's policies, bringing order to the country's internal politics, smoothing its international relations, and implementing a "New Order" regime that (at least until the Asian financial crisis of 1997) was considered a model of economic development. However, Suharto was also authoritarian and was surrounded by corrupt cronies, some of them members of his own family. These failings have hurt his reputation among many Indonesians.

Suharto was born in Java in 1921. Little is known of his childhood, because he did not come from a prominent family. He became a competent army officer and had a devoted arranged marriage that produced six children. He became a brigadier general in 1960 and led the military operation that resulted in western New Guinea becoming part of Indonesia. In 1965, Suharto was commanding the elite force known as Kostrad when a group of dissident officers staged the *coup* that led to Sukarno's overthrow. Suharto was the only important general not slated for assassination. He quickly took command of the government's forces and suppressed the rebellion. Despite this decisive action, there has been speculation that Suharto himself knew in advance about the *coup* attempt, because he had ties with the *coup* leaders and had consulted with them prior to the putsch. Whatever the case, the *coup* and its suppression effectively put Suharto in power. The United States immediately announced its support for the anticommunist Suharto, and Indonesians carried out a pogrom in which they slaughtered indiscriminately both PKI members and the indigenous Chinese.

Few persons knew much about Suharto when he came into power. His military career had not been especially noteworthy. He was known as "The Smiling General," a private family man, and a *halus* person, a Javanese characteristic akin to "refinement." Suharto always appeared composed and refined, unemotional and secretive. Yet he was the ultimate administrator: colorless, pragmatic, and concerned with the daily issues of development and the bureaucracy. Unlike his predecessor, Suharto's issues as leader were not those of independence and autonomy from the world. Rather, he worked to reintegrate Indonesia into the world capitalist system, surrounding himself with technocrats and foreign specialists. Suharto ended Sukarno's confrontation against Malaysia, broke ties with China, and aligned Indonesia with the West.

Though he was the country's *de facto* leader, Suharto did not immediately have the title of president. Between 1965 and 1968 he maneuvered deftly to ease Sukarno out of power and to consolidate his own authority, moving slowly so that pro-Sukarno citizens would not protest. Suharto finally became president in 1967–68. On six subsequent occasions the National Assembly re-elected him president, always by a unanimous vote.

Suharto implemented an authoritarian style of rule, but he was not a totalitarian leader in the mode of Pol Pot. Although he arrested opponents and ignored human rights abuses by his supporters, he did not use terror on a wide scale. He believed in a strong state without a meaningful opposition, and he ruled according to the Javanese principles of obedience to superiors and respect for those in power. The heart of Suharto's administration was The New Order, an arrangement in which administrators, technocrats, and military officers ran Indonesia.

This authoritarian system featured close ties among Suharto, his favorite generals, his family members, his close Chinese-Indonesian business friends, and a few foreigners. His main concerns were political stability and economic growth.

In many respects it is difficult not to argue that Suharto's rule was immensely successful. He stabilized the currency, ended inflation, achieved self-sufficiency in rice production, strengthened the infrastructure (especially the transportation sector), built schools, promoted family planning, and brought Indonesia's literacy rate to over 90 percent. At the same time, he ended any semblance of liberal democracy, allowed the military free reign throughout the nation, and systematized corruption among his family members. He was also responsible for the violent invasion of East Timor that sparked decades of demonstrations against the Indonesian government's occupation of that territory. (Since 1975 more than 100,000 East Timorese have died from Indonesian military action there.)

Suharto became vulnerable when the Asian currency crisis hit Indonesia in late 1997. The crisis made it clear that corruption prevailed among the country's top leaders, especially on the part of Suharto's own wife, children, and other family members. The Suharto family controlled many sectors of the economy, forming an economic dynasty with no equal. Business executives avoided bidding against the Suharto children for fear of retaliation. Suharto was also allowing his cronies to engage in questionable financial pursuits, many of which turned out to be disastrous for the Indonesian economy.

When the crisis hit, the Indonesian economy deteriorated rapidly. Many Javanese suggested that the *wahyu*, the gift of power, had left Suharto and was seeking a home elsewhere. Newspapers suddenly dared to publish articles criticizing the government. Protests arose throughout the archipelago. Although the Assembly had unanimously elected Suharto president, he now became a target of assemblymen's wrath. On May 21, 1998, Suharto resigned as president, asking forgiveness for "any mistakes and shortcomings" on his part. He was succeeded by his hand-picked vice president, B. J. Habibie, who instituted reforms and organized elections that were held in June 1999. The newly elected Consultative Assembly chose Abdurrahman Wahid as president and the popular opposition leader Megawati Sukarnoputri as vice president. After his resignation, Suharto lived in solitude and ill-health.

Megawati Sukarnoputri - Indonesia

When Megawati Sukarnoputri became Indonesia's fifth president, she took on a position once held by her father, President Sukarno, who is known as the father of Indonesian independence. It is difficult to imagine two more different persons than father and daughter. Sukarno (he used only one name) was charismatic, flamboyant, and messianic. Sukarnoputri (referred to as Megawati by Indonesians) is shy, quiet, and a person of few words who once described herself as a simple housewife. What the two leaders share is widespread backing by the Indonesian citizenry and a strong sense of nationalist pride for their country, especially during the times of trouble that both have faced as the nation's leaders. Megawati has deliberately sought to invoke her father's memory, constantly referring to him and his leadership

When Megawati came to power in July 2001, the nation's economy was askew, separatist violence threatened to tear the country asunder, and the increasingly notorious Islamic terrorists who would soon shatter Indonesia's fragile stability with a bomb attack on the island of Bali. She was the leader of the Indonesian Democractic Party of Struggle (PDI-P), which in the 1999 elections had won 34 percent, the largest plurality of any party. In the aftermath of these, the first democratic elections in more than forty years, Abdurrahman Wahid was chosen president by the legislature despite his party having won just 12 percent of the vote. Megawati's gender and her decision not to campaign vigorously for the post worked against her at that time. Nevertheless, she became Vice President under President Abdurrahman Wahid. When the Indonesian legislature ousted him in 2001, she was named president for the rest of his term, serving until the next scheduled elections in 2004.

Megawati has married three times and has three children. Her first husband was killed in a plane crash. Her second marriage, to an Egyptian diplomat, was annulled two weeks after their elopement. Her third husband, Taufik Kiemas, is a controversial, wealthy businessman who owns a group of gas stations. She did not enter politics until the mid-1990s but she quickly rose to prominence after troops, under orders from President Suharto, attacked her party's headquarters. Enigmatic and with limited education she has kept to herself, which is both a strength and a weakness. In Indonesia, keeping silent is considered a virtue, a sign of being *halus* (refined). On the other hand, her lack of involvement in day-to-day issues is viewed by some critics as a sign of shallowness and an indication that she will be a puppet of the military. Known as "Mother Mega" throughout the archipelago, she is popular especially among the poorer classes, who believe she will restore Indonesia's lost pride and glory, as they believe it had flourished under her father.

Megawati faces separatist struggles and a weak economy. Many of the business leaders that prospered under President Suharto are still dominant today. Moreover, the terrorist strike against the United States in 2001, shortly after her inauguration, inflamed elements of the Muslim majority in Indonesia, thereby undermining her authority. Her intentions are unknown because she rarely gives speeches. In the aftermath of the bombing in Bali she warned Indonesians that their nation is now home to international terrorists, reversing her previous view that terrorism did not exist in Indonesia.

Balancing these pressures is Megawati's popularity and the country's relative political stability. It helps that it may also have been wise of her to let the presidency pass to Wahid in 1999, for by 2001 she came into office in a bloodless transition. Those Indonesians who had opposed her because she is a woman in a male-dominated society had had time to adjust. Megawati's position was also strengthened when the economy of Indonesia stabilized after its long period of transition and decline following the end of the Suharto government. Since becoming President of Indonesia, she has met with U.S. President George W. Bush and though she continues to say little in public, overall she has attempted to find a balance between her desire to keep Indonesia stable and to press for changes needed to bring Indonesia into the modern world. She has also taken steps to improve Indonesia's human rights record, acknowledging that mistakes were made by police and soldiers in the province of Aceh, where the government was fighting rebels of the Free Aceh Movement.

Megawati Sukarnoputri is president of the world's most populous Islamic nation. She is an international figure and role-model for Muslims and non-Muslims alike. It is striking that a person who has so famously kept to herself is now so much in the spotlight.

Corazon Cojuangco Aquino – Philippines

On February 7, 1986, a "simple housewife" became president of the Philippines and an instant international icon for peace and democracy. Like other women leaders of Southeast Asia (for example, Aung San Suu Kyi of Burma and Megawati Sukarnoputri of Indonesia), Corazon Aquino initially became famous because of her relationship to a famous man. Aquino's husband was Benigno (Ninoy) Aquino, a charismatic politician and the leading democratic opponent of dictator Ferdinand Marcos. In 1983 Benigno Aquino was assassinated by Marcos's henchmen as he stepped from an airplane at Manila's international airport (subsequently named the Benigno Aquino International Airport). This tragic event gave Corazon Aquino the status of martyred widow and made her subsequent career a symbol of hope for Filipinos embarrassed and disgusted by Marcos.

Aquino was born into a rich Chinese landowning family in the province of Tarlac in central Luzon island. Her immediate relatives included leading politicians, senators, and congressmen. She studied in the United States at a private Catholic school in New York. She was a devout Catholic, and in her days as president she often substituted prayer for negotiation; her followers would call her "Saint Cory." She married Senator Benigno Aquino, a member of another of the nation's major families. Senator Aquino was a flamboyant figure, and everyone expected him to become president. Cory was bright and capable, but she was not politically ambitious, and she was happy to be a helpmate to her husband. Even after his death, she entered politics as a substitute for her husband rather than as a person seeking power for herself.

Senator Aquino's death galvanized public discontent against Marcos. People looked to Corazon to lead the opposition. She lacked experience and was reluctant to lead, but these qualities enhanced her image as a sincere, honest, and incorruptible person who was the very antithesis of Marcos. In late 1985 the beleaguered president called "snap" elections for February 1986, certain that he could control the results and win a renewed mandate for continuing his rule. Aquino soon announced that she would run against Marcos for president.

Since she had experienced politics only second-hand as Senator Aquino's wife, Corazon Aquino's candidacy for the presidency was viewed by many as farfetched. She was thought to be mismatched against the man who had dominated Philippine life for almost three decades. Knowing she could not compete with Marcos's money and organization, she proclaimed a "people's campaign" and began to give speeches that criticized Marcos's corruption and stressed her own sincerity and honesty. Her speeches were often alliterative. She spoke about how Marcos and his misguided minions prostituted professionalism in the military and converted the Supreme Court into a compliant cabal of callous collaborators. She accused the president of cowardice and challenged him "to stand up, like a woman," and answer her charges.

At first, Aquino's speeches were poorly attended because the media did not dare to announce her schedule. However, news of her campaign spread among the people and thousands began showing up. When someone reminded her that Marcos might have her assassinated, she replied that it would not matter because she would be with her late husband Ninoy (Senator Aquino) all the sooner. These words from a person who had suffered under Marcos resonated with the millions of Filipinos who themselves had despaired under his rule.

For his part, Marcos ran a campaign focused on his experience as contrasted with Cory's "naiveté." He stressed the need for "strong" male leadership rather than "weak" female leadership, and in one speech he said that a woman's place was in the bedroom rather than in the political arena. His wife, Imelda, suggested that Filipinos would not vote for Aquino because Aquino did not wear enough makeup. She also said that the people wanted a beautiful woman, such as Imelda, to be the first lady of the land.

The voting was marred by fraud carried out by Marcos and his supporters. When Philippine government officials announced that

Marcos had "won" the elections, Aquino launched a "People's Power" civil disobedience campaign. Soon, Defense Minister Juan Ponce Enrile and Lieutenant General Fidel Ramos defected from Marcos and supported Aquino's ascension to the presidency. The United States government had long supported the anti-communist Marcos, but at the last moment it urged Marcos to leave the Philippines. He fled to exile in Hawai'i. Students, Catholic leaders, shop owners, and farmers had all come together to force Marcos out of office.

As President, Aquino brought pride back to the Filipinos. Her courage, her tenacity, and her unsurpassed ability to energize and inspire her followers had overwhelmed the Marcos juggernaut and catapulted her into a position where she had an opportunity to revolutionize Philippine society. She restored democracy, rejuvenated governmental institutions that Marcos had been made impotent, released political prisoners, opened the press and media, and ousted corrupt officials. For her accomplishments, Time Magazine named her 1986 Person of the Year. The economy also improved. Inflation was brought under control, and the economic growth rate went from a minus figure to a plus figure of more than 6 percent per year.

Despite Aquino's monumental achievement of restoring democracy, her presidency did not achieve its full potential. She undercut the practice of "crony capitalism," a system in which decisions were made on the basis of personal contacts rather than qualifications, but she did not fundamentally change the feudalistic economic system. The nation continued to be characterized by oligarchic rule, economic and social inequality, desperate poverty, and the politics of personalism. Aquino put forth no far-reaching agrarian land reform plan despite the overwhelming desire among the people for just such a plan. Herself a member of one of the wealthiest landowning families in the Philippines, she felt that she could not overthrow the traditional order, as her family would have construed such act as disloyalty.

Aquino's popularity began to ebb during her presidency. No fewer than six *coup* attempts were made against her by dissident elements of the military. Electrical brownouts devastated Manila. Traffic jams and crime increased. In 1990 a horrible earthquake devastated northern Luzon, and it was followed by a typhoon that swept over the islands and claimed some four hundred lives. Even more devastating was the 1991 eruption of Mount Pinatubo, which killed over five hundred persons and caused hundreds of thousands to lose their homes and livelihoods. A few months later a tropical storm caused eight thousand deaths and ruined countless farms. These events were considered omens, and they hurt Aquino's relations with the people. However, she continued to have a great deal of popular influence. She chose not to run for a second term (doing so would have raised serious constitutional issues because presidents were restricted to one term), but her *protégé*, Fidel Ramos, was elected her successor. After she stepped down from office, she continued to enjoy prestige as the nation's premier stateswoman.

Lee Kuan Yew – Singapore

Few world leaders are held in higher esteem than Lee Kuan Yew, formerly Prime Minister and now Senior Minister of Singapore. Lee is one of a small number of long-serving national executives who has been able to finish his tenure with his reputation unsullied and even heightened. When Lee Kuan Yew became prime minister in 1959, Singapore was economically primitive, politically chaotic, and socially unstable. With virtually no natural resources except for human capital, the city-state was viewed by most of the world as a corrupt, mafia-ridden, soon-to-be-communist backwater. By 1990, when Lee voluntarily retired as prime minister, Singapore had become one of the world's wealthiest nations and had developed a reputation for free enterprise, incorruptibility, and stability. Much of that remarkable growth was due solely to Lee.

Lee was born in Singapore and grew up in a middle-class Chinese family. He was brilliant, outspoken, and pushy. His middle-class life was shaken when the Japanese invaded Singapore. He was shocked by the ease with which the Japanese dominated Singapore, and he vowed that his home would never again be put into such a situation. There are gaps in information about Lee's role during World War II, though some speculate that he collaborated with the Japanese in service of what he deemed to be Singapore's best long-term interests. How he attained his country's leadership is also not clear. After the war he studied law in Britain, graduating from Cambridge University with highest honors. In 1950 he married Geok Choo at a lavish wedding. He pursued a law career in Singapore and was introduced to politicians and community leaders. He became involved in socialist politics, although it is not clear if he did so for opportunistic or ideological reasons. He was a principal founder of the People's Action Party (PAP), which began as a pragmatically oriented socialist party. He won a seat in parliament in the 1955 elections, and he was the PAP's leader when it won the 1959 elections, thereby making him prime minister.

Lee's fame grew as he established firm control of the PAP. At first, the PAP's victory made the foreign business community nervous, because the PAP was suspected of having communist connections. Indeed the party had some radical left-wing members and had worked closely with communist-oriented groups. However, Lee himself was not a communist, and he favored a moderate socialist system that would meet the people's needs while remaining sensitive to the needs of capitalist investors. A brilliant tactician, he undercut prospective communist influence both in the PAP and in the country. By meeting the people's needs while always working to keep himself in power, Lee was able to guide the government to a moderate position with himself in firm control.

Lee's most momentous decision in the early years of independence was to join Malaya, Sabah, and Sarawak in the Federation of Malaysia. Concern for Singapore's survival was a major impetus for the merger. Malaya's ruler, Tunku Abdul Rahman, feared that Singapore might become communist if it stood alone. (Singapore's leaders shared this concern.) In addition, Singapore's leaders felt that Malaya's agricultural resources were necessary for their city's economic stability and growth. Despite these mutual advantages, the federation lasted only two years before Singapore was ousted by the Tunku, who was suspicious of Lee's desire for more Chinese influence in Malaysian politics. Lee was initially devastated by the ouster, but he rallied to the tasks before him as the leader of a reluctantly independent country. Singapore immediately began a program to industrialize and to join the world capitalist system. British air and sea bases were overhauled and turned into trade zones and repair facilities. Trade unions were circumscribed in order to achieve a strike-free economy. Economic growth rates increased dramatically, and within two decades Singapore had achieved the status of a highly developed nation. Singapore's literacy rates also rose, improving from 52 percent in 1965 to 90 percent just twenty years later.

Lee Kuan Yew was integrally involved in every aspect of the policies that turned Singapore into an economic "Asian Tiger." It is not possible to conceive of Singapore's growth without Lee's involvement. Exploiting the nation's strategic location at a crossroads of commercial shipping, he converted it into a major trade center. He pushed for advanced infrastructure that has made Singapore a sophisticated technological center, and he oversaw Singapore's transformation into an international banking center. He attracted foreign investment by demanding that the island offer tax breaks and conveniences to overseas investors. At the same time, he saw to the citizens' welfare. He was responsible for making Singapore the nation with the highest percentage of citizens owning their own home. He advanced a modern health care and educational system, and he insisted that all housing programs include recreational facilities and related amenities. He also saw to the city's beautification. Today, no city of the world is landscaped as extensively as Singapore.

These accomplishments were carried out under a parliamentary system based on the British model. But Lee dominated every aspect of the system. Only one party, the PAP, prevailed in the elections, and Lee brooked no opposition on matters of public policy. He was the quintessential Confucianist leader—highly authoritarian, impeccably incorruptible, wise, and taciturn. By combining Western-style democratic institutions with a political system dominated by a single party, Lee was able to maintain a strong hold over the country's politics while also winning support and legitimacy from the people.

In the late 1980s, shortly before he stepped down as prime minister, Lee's consummate political skill lost some of its edge as he tipped even further toward authoritarianism and away from open and pragmatic policies. He jailed dissidents and restricted newspapers critical of his administration, ostensibly to assure the continuation of stable politics. He was one of the leading proponents of "Asian values," arguing that in the Chinese tradition there was no concept of a loyal opposition. Lee believed that as long as he was meeting the needs of the people and ruling wisely, he had the "mandate of heaven" and was therefore the legitimate ruler. When he resigned as prime minister in 1990 he chose his *protégé* Goh Chok Tong as his successor. Lee then became Senior Minister, making him still the most important person in Singapore. Lee's son, Brigadier General Lee Hsien Loong, became Deputy Prime Minister and appeared to be patiently awaiting his turn to become prime minister. For many Singaporeans, Lee Kuan Yew was and is the state. His strength came from charisma, intelligence, political skill, and the ability to fashion an effective state. But his drive for stability also sometimes featured repression.

King Bhumibol Adulyadej – Thailand

Thailand is a constitutional monarchy. The head of state is King Bhumibol Adulyadej, who has reigned since 1946. King Bhumibol's half-century reign is the longest in the Kingdom's history and also the longest of any currently-reigning monarch in the world. In 1999, he celebrated the completion of his sixth twelve-year Buddhist cycle (seventy-two years old). Revered by virtually all of Thailand's citizens, King Bhumibol is given more effusive and sincere deference than perhaps any living person in the world. He works on behalf of the poor and ethnic minorities, and he supports projects to alleviate the nation's problems. He is also an inventor, musician, sailor, car racer, painter, photographer, scholar, and humanitarian. For much of King Bhumibol's reign, the military led the government. No single general stands out as especially influential, but in ensemble they epitomized anti-communist, corrupt, elitist, yet sometimes-effective leadership that built on Thailand's record as the only nation of Southeast Asia never to be colonized. In recent years, partly with the king's encouragement, Thailand has also taken steps toward true democracy.

King Bhumibol is not a descendant of the Sukhothai and Ayuthaya kings who so ably established the Thai state and saw it through from the thirteenth to the eighteenth centuries. Instead, he is the ninth king of the Chakri Dynasty, which took the throne in the late eighteenth century. After the fall of Ayuthaya in 1767, a young general called Taksin, a man of Chinese heritage, reunified the country and established the capital at Thonburi. When he apparently went crazy, another general, by the name of Chakri, was named king in 1782. The new king, who later became known as Rama I (King Bhumibol is known as Rama IX), moved the capital across the river to a small fishing town called Bangkok, which quickly became the country's leading city and today continues to be the nation's capital. Today, the most stunning tourist destinations in Bangkok are the Grand Palace and the related temple complexes built by the early Chakri kings. Royal Bangkok is a spectacular, even out-of-place area in a city characterized by poverty, pollution, and modern high-rises. The city's royal landmarks border on the gaudy, being covered with millions of pieces of glass and gold leaf, but they also reflect the Thai people's reverence toward their king.

Figure 23. King Bhumibol Adulyadej
Virtually every home in Thailand has a calendar bearing a picture of His Majesty.

The first seven kings of the Chakri dynasty ruled as absolute monarchs. Though they did not claim ties of heredity to the earlier Thai monarchs, they were like them in many ways. Like the Sukhothai kings, the Chakris were paternalistic and tried to meet the needs of the ordinary people. They also carried on the traditions of the Ayuthaya kings, traditions ultimately derived from the famous Angkor civilization, that emphasized absolutism, noblesse oblige, and authoritarian rule. The early Chakri kings also carried on the Ayuthaya tradition of organizing society hierarchically in a system so tightly structured that every Thai citizen knew his or her exact place. Everyone was assigned a *sakdi na*, a numerical figure that in theory indicated how much land each citizen had been assigned to control but in fact indicated the person's royally assigned social rank. Yet, these absolutist kings also oversaw the implementation of modernizing reforms while keeping the country free from European colonial rule. By the early twentieth century the *sakdi na* system had been abolished, and by the middle of the twentieth century the absolute monarchy had also passed away. Yet, in a more limited sense, the Chakri kings continued to combine the paternalistic Sukhothai characteristics with the absolutist Ayuthaya ways, and in the end this unique dynasty produced the most venerated king in modern history—King Bhumibol Adulyadej.

In 1932, fourteen years before King Bhumibol ascended the throne, the system of absolute kingship was overthrown by a group of republican military and civilian officials, most of whom had been socialized into the values of republican democracy while studying in European nations. The new power holders set up a constitutional monarchy in which the king retained ceremonial duties while leaving daily governmental chores to the new leaders. Despite its reduced power, the Thai kingship managed to keep its regal stature in the minds of the people. Throughout the period of the constitutional monarchy, no non-royal Thai leader has come close to rivaling the level of veneration that is given to the kings. Moreover, Thai law protects the monarchy by placing the king above criticism: *lèse majesté* laws forbid any person to express antimonarchist sentiments or make other statements that sully the dignity of the institution.

King Bhumibol has the distinction of being the only world monarch who was born in the United States. He was born in 1927 in Cambridge, Massachusetts, where his father, Prince Mahidol, was studying to become a medical doctor. King Bhumibol is the grandson of the illustrious King Chulalongkorn, also known as Rama V (reigned 1868–1910), who was responsible for many of the reforms and much of the diplomacy that kept Thailand free from Western imperialism. Chulalongkorn himself was the son of King Mongkut (Rama IV), the celebrated king who was featured in the musical *The King and I*. Chulalongkorn had seventy-seven children by ninety-two wives. Two of his sons became kings Rama VI and Rama VII. Neither king had male children (by law the monarch had to be a male who was not married to a foreigner), so when Rama VII abdicated in 1935 the throne passed to the line of Prince Mahidol, who was a half-brother of Rama VI and VII. Mahidol had already died, so the throne passed to Mahidol's oldest son, Prince Ananda Mahidol, who became Rama VIII. In a still unresolved mystery, Rama VIII died of a gunshot wound on June 9, 1946, and his younger brother, Bhumibol Adulyadej, became Rama IX. Any discussion of Ananda Mahidol's death is forbidden in Thailand. The most likely explanation for the death is suicide, although such an act is inconceivable to the predominantly Buddhist Thai. Ananda was apparently in love with a European woman, but as king he was forbidden by law to takc a European as wife. Unfortunately, Thai officials used the death as a pretext to prosecute two "left-wing" servants and then overthrow the civilian government in order to place back in power the right-wing military leader, former prime minister Phibun Songkram, who had allied with Japan in World War II.

King Bhumibol Adulyadej had spent most of his childhood studying in private schools in Switzerland, and he came to the throne with talents in music, the arts, and the humanities. He is beloved by his subjects, because throughout his 50 years on the throne he has worked assiduously for the common people. He has invented ways to improve the standard of living of the people, and he has always comported himself in a gentlemanly and diplomatic manner. He has given out thousands of graduate degrees to college students. He has met with high officials from around the world. He performs Buddhist ceremonies. He is universally respected as the symbol of unity of the Thai people. Today, he and his wife Queen Sirikit live in Chitlada Palace in Bangkok (different from the Grand Palace visited by many tourists). They have four children, all of whom are fully grown. The king has one glass eye as a result of a car accident; consequently, he wears dark glasses.

The heir apparent is Prince Vajiralongkorn, the king's only son, who was born in 1952. In contrast to his beloved father, the prince is controversial, as many Thai believe he does not have the right values to be king. The prince is viewed as a playboy, and he has been known to mistreat those around him. Second in line is his younger sister, Princess Sirindhorn, who is much favored by the people. There has never been a female monarch in Thai history, but the law has been changed to allow it. Princess Sirindhorn has studied to the Ph.D. level, receiving all her college degrees from prestigious universities in Bangkok. Like her father, she has developed interests in the arts and humanities.

King Bhumibol is theoretically above politics, but on numerous occasions he has actively intervened to assure the stability of the polity and to rid the country of its worst leaders. He supported the students in their 1973 pro-democracy revolt against military dictators, and in both 1981 and 1985 he supported the government of Prime Minister Prem Tinsulanond when military *coups* attempted to overthrow that administration. The king's most important intervention occurred during the 1992 crisis, when pro-democracy demonstrators called on General Suchinda to step down as prime minister. The military's violent response brought the country to the brink of civil war. King Bhumibol admonished the nation's competing leaders to settle the conflict peacefully, and he demanded Suchinda's resignation. The king subsequently vetoed the new prime minister proposed by the parties who had supported Suchinda, instead bringing back the respected civilian, Anand Panyarachun, to serve as a caretaker prime minister until new elections could be held. The king was universally praised for his involvement in this affair.

To the Thai people, King Bhumibol is the embodiment of Thai Buddhism and the Thai nation. He is aware of Thailand's absolutist past and also of its new, more pragmatic, more Western approach. His genius has been to bridge effectively the gap between the two legacies. As a result, his influence has continued to increase. Today Thai political leaders know that if they engage in extreme measures, the king may intervene. If he does, the Thai people are sure to support the monarch. Therefore, modern Thai politics have been increasingly characterized by moderate actions, as political leaders want to ensure that the king need not get involved.

Thaksin Shinawatra - Thailand

Thailand's 23rd Prime Minister, is Police Lieutenant Colonel Thaksin Shinawatra who took office on February 9, 2001. Thaksin reflects the new breed of leadership in Thailand: educated, business-oriented, civilian, and authoritarian, yet following the legalities of democracy. Having graduated from the Police Cadet Academy in 1973, Thaksin earned a Masters Degree and Ph.D. in Criminal Justice from Eastern Kentucky University and Sam Houston State University respectively. He was also an active businessman who succeeded in the telecommunications business becoming Thailand's wealthiest person.

He entered government service in 1994 as foreign minister, then as deputy prime minister in several administrations. In 1998 he became founder and leader of the Thai Rak Thai (Thais Love Thais) political party.

Thaksin's wealth came both from his affluent family in Chiang Mai Province and from his successes as chairman of the Shinawatra Computer and Communications Group (later expanded and renamed Shin Corporation). Thaksin won contracts with the Thai Police Department and other major organizations for computer software, and soon had a monopoly on communications technology throughout the Kingdom. His company evolved into the cellular phone business and he launched communications satellites.

When his Thai Rak Thai Party won the January 2001 elections, Thaksin was just fifty-one years old and leader of a party that won a huge mandate receiving 340 seats in the 500 member parliament. Despite having an already commanding majority of the seats, Thaksin heightened his position by forging a coalition with two other political parties. Despite the clear majority, Thaksin's position as the nation's leader was initially in jeopardy. Prior to the election, the country's anti-graft agency, the National Counter Corruption Commission, indicted Thaksin for having failed to disclose his assets fully in 1997, when he was serving as a minister in a previous administration. Moreover, he was alleged to have "hidden" assets by transferring them to his maids and family, all of whom instantly became, at least on paper, among the richest people in Thailand. However, the Constitutional Court, by an eight-to-seven vote, eventually acquitted him. Despite protests that the Court had been bought off, Thaksin never looked back and immediately launched policies based on his political campaign. If he had been found guilty, he would have been banned from politics for five years.

Thaksin's campaign stressed four major issues. First, he promised inexpensive health care for all Thais, and this promise became the basis for his "30-*baht*" health care plan which provided the citizenry with health services for under one dollar. Second, he promised a debt moratorium for farmers. Third, he promised to allocate about one million *baht* (U.S. $23,000) for development purposes for each of the country's 70,000 villages. Fourth, he promised to establish a Thai Asset Management Corporation (TAMC) designed to keep Thailand from falling into another recession like the one that hit the nation in 1997. The TAMC was established to take over non-performing loans from banks in order to free the banks to make new and supposedly legitimate loans to prospective entrepreneurs. The success or lack of success of these four promises is debatable. Thaksin's supporters point to his continued wide popularity among Thais, especially those in rural areas. In addition, in Thaksin's years as Prime Minister, Thailand has boasted the highest growth rates in Southeast Asia. His critics point to the high cost of his programs, the great opportunity for corruption in each of the four, and suggest that his "populist" policies will founder when the bills are to be paid.

Thaksin's record on democracy is equally debatable. He has stated that his first priority is improving the livelihood of his people, and that democracy was a means to that end. Hence, he has engaged in behavior that is generally considered contrary to democratic ideals, stating that he admires Prime Minister Mahathir of Malaysia (who stepped down as leader on October 31, 2003) who was famous for his authoritarian manner and policies. Thaksin has silenced much of the Thai press, harassed opponents, and carried out a crackdown on drugs in ways that violated judicial standards. His critics deem him arrogant and self-serving, to which Thaksin responds by noting that it is more important to be respected than liked.

Prime Minister Thaksin has enjoyed widespread popularity at home and has taken steps to become a major leader in Southeast Asia. He has joined President Bush in counter-terrorism efforts and has become a spokesperson for Southeast Asian trade and security concerns. Thailand's dramatic move from recession to rapid economic growth assures Thaksin of continued influence in Southeast Asia. He exemplifies the notion that economic concerns are now in command in Southeast Asia.

Ho Chi Minh - Vietnam

Perhaps the most famous leader of Southeast Asia is Ho Chi Minh, the revolutionary Vietnamese communist and patriot who died in 1969. Ho merged Marxism with Vietnamese nationalism. He become famous as the leader who was responsible for winning Vietnamese independence and for dealing the Americans their first defeat in war as the communist nationalist movement he had founded worked to unite the country under its leadership.

Ho Chi Minh was a man of mystery. Many aspects of his life are unknown, including his birth date, his real name, and whether he was married. He used more than one hundred aliases during his life, but while he was leader of Vietnam he settled on Ho Chi Minh (He Who Enlightens). Ho's nationalism emerged during the period of French colonialism. He believed the French had destroyed important Vietnamese institutions and traditions, including Confucianism. The Vietnamese were being treated as second-class citizens in their own country. Village autonomy had been ended and the rich were being given land to harvest so they would become even richer. Ho reportedly taught for a year, but he decided not to pursue a career that could serve the interests of French colonial rule. So he left for self-imposed exile overseas, where he stayed for thirty years (1911 to 1941). Ho lived in France, England, Russia, and China, learning socialist and communist ideology as he traveled. He believed that communism was the only ideology committed to anti-colonialism, and he was awed by Lenin's success in carrying out a successful revolution against the Tsars of Russia. He became the acknowledged leader of expatriate Vietnamese Marxists, for which honor he served various stints in jail.

Following his return to Vietnam in 1941, Ho stayed underground, organizing anti-French and anti-Japanese groups and making contact with American officials who indicated their support for his proposed plan of Vietnamese independence. On September 2, 1945, Ho proclaimed the independence of the Democratic Republic of Vietnam, doing so with words borrowed from the American Declaration of Independence. However, the Allies betrayed Vietnam and supported the return of the French. The result was the first Indochina War (1946–54), a war that devastated Vietnam but ended with the French agreeing to a settlement following the famous battle of Dien Bien Phu. Surprisingly, Ho did not insist on immediate independence for the entire nation. Instead, he accepted a temporary partition of Vietnam at the seventeenth parallel, with communist forces regrouping north of the line and anticommunist forces moving to the south. The demarcation line soon became a state boundary separating North and South Vietnam, with Ho the leader of the North, and Ngo Dinh Diem ruling the South.

Figure 24. Ho Chi Minh

Even as ruler of the North, Ho Chi Minh lived simply, like the peasants. The Vietnamese affectionately called him "Uncle Ho," a term of respect that symbolized his close rapport with the common people. In the early years of his administration, he oversaw a disastrous land reform program that ended in famine. The people did not blame Ho for the catastrophe, even though he was the country's leader. Instead, they criticized lower level functionaries. A few years after defeating the French, Ho led his people through the opening years of the Second Indochina War, this time fighting against the Americans who had intervened in Vietnam to fill the gap left by the defeated French. Ho decided to support the insurgent southerners led by the National Liberation Front (also known as the Vietcong) who had risen against Diem's oppressive government.

Ho Chi Minh died of a heart attack in 1969. The Russians built a gaudy mausoleum for his body despite his publicly stated wish to have his ashes scattered throughout the nation. Ho did not live to see the reunification of his country nor did he see the harsh administration that the North would implement in the South. To this day he is considered the father of his country. He is as close to being perceived a saint as is any modern Vietnamese leader.

Ngo Dinh Diem - Vietnam

Ngo Dinh Diem was the conservative Vietnamese nationalist who founded the short-lived Republic of Vietnam (also known as South Vietnam). A Catholic in a Buddhist country, and a status-oriented strongman in a time of popular revolution, Diem never developed rapport with his people. Unlike Ho, who lived like the peasants, Diem wore Western sharkskin suits, surrounded himself with limousines, lived in opulent palaces, and allowed himself to be viewed as a lackey of American officials. He was an improbable man in an impossible situation. His confidence, self-assuredness, discipline, and adherence to personal principles were the tools that initially made him strong, but these very virtues eventually became the vices that destroyed him. The opposite of Ho Chi Minh in both dress and personal style, Diem would never be known as "Uncle Diem."

Diem was born into a prominent Catholic family in 1901. He received a law degree and entered the imperial bureaucracy as a mandarin (scholar-official), rising quickly due to his intelligence. He held a high-level ministerial position in the administration of Bao Dai, Vietnam's last emperor, who retained an administrative role under the French. Diem eventually resigned his position, because he considered the emperor to be no more than a French puppet. Diem despaired for Vietnam's future, because he hated both the French and the communists, and the future seemed to lie in a choice between the two.

After leaving the Vietnamese bureaucracy, Diem traveled the United States on lecture tours. Americans were receptive to his anti-communist message, and he became a hero to important American politicians and media moguls. When Diem returned to Vietnam in 1954, Emperor Bao Dai asked him to form a government in South Vietnam. Diem agreed, contingent upon being given full powers. Thus was Diem appointed by a repudiated emperor to serve as leader of a nonexistent nation. The next year Diem sponsored a referendum that deposed the emperor. Diem was now undisputed leader of his new Republic of Vietnam.

Diem won the support of the Catholic minority, the wealthy landowners, and the members of the new urban middle class who thrived on the new influx of money and consumer products from the United States. He also had the support of officials in the United States Embassy. As his presidency progressed he became viewed more and more as a lackey of the Americans. Indeed, almost all of South Vietnam's budget was funded by the United States. By 1956, the United States was spending about $270 million a year to shore up Diem.

But Diem was unknown to the Vietnamese peasants and workers who formed the bulk of the southern population, and his aristocratic and imperious style did not bring him closer to these people. His self-assured strong-man style of rule eventually undermined his legitimacy even among many of the people who had initially supported him. His isolation, his excessive reliance on members of his own family (some of whom were corrupt), his intolerance of democratic opposition, his oppression, and the rising Vietcong insurgency all worked to undermine his position. By 1963 Diem had lost the "mandate of heaven," the traditional notion that those in power have the right to rule as long as they do so in the best interests of the people. Diem's fall was precipitated by his harsh treatment of Buddhist monks who opposed his regime. American support for him was undermined by newspaper articles that featured pictures of monks committing public self-immolation (suicide by burning). In the end, President Kennedy approved a plan to have the Vietnamese military take power by means of a *coup d'etat* headed by leading South Vietnamese generals. The military captured Diem and his brother (who was a close advisor) and murdered them both. Kennedy was shocked by the deaths but was himself assassinated three weeks later. Following Diem's death, a series of military governments attempted to govern South Vietnam, but the war escalated and in April 1975 the communists took full control. Though Diem was an intelligent man who had created a state out of almost nothing, he is not remembered fondly. Today there are no statues or monuments in Diem's honor anywhere in Vietnam.

DISCUSSION QUESTIONS

1. What similarities do you find among the modern leaders of Southeast Asia? Do you find patterns that would help explain why these people became national leaders?

2. Which of the contemporary leaders of Southeast Asia do you find particularly heroic? Why?

SUGGESTED READINGS

The newest book on Asian leadership is Ross Marlay and Clark Neher, *Patriots and Tyrants: Ten Asian Leaders* (Rowman and Littlefield Publishers, Boulder, 1999). The book includes essays on Ho Chi Minh, Ngo Dinh Diem, Pol Pot, Sihanouk, Suharto, and Sukarno. Benedict Anderson has written an insightful book on nationalism and revolutionary leadership titled *Imagined Communities: Reflections on the Origin and Spread of Nationalism* (Verso, London, 1986).

8

CONCLUSION

Southeast Asia – Problems and Prospects

There may be no more diverse and fascinating area of the world than Southeast Asia. The nations' histories are replete with great leaders and traditions, and their cultures draw on influences from around the world. Their contemporary situations are full of both promise and woes. There is fantastic wealth, as in Singapore, Brunei, and Malaysia, but also poverty, as in Laos, Cambodia, and Burma. The region's governments include not only democracy but also authoritarian communism and military dictatorship. Southeast Asia is undergoing remarkable change as the eleven nations move from somnolence and underdevelopment to vibrancy and modernity.

The Southeast Asian nations' cultural richness, ethnic and religious variations, and divergent histories make region-wide generalizations difficult. Each nation must find its own balance between the competing desires for growth and stability, authority and freedom, nationalism and interdependence, and modernization and cultural integrity. These balances are difficult to achieve, but in comparison to earlier periods Southeast Asia is now a region relatively free of crisis. The earlier historical flash points are no longer volatile. The struggles for independence from colonialism are over, the charismatic leaders have disappeared, and wars no longer plague the region. The area also shows economic vitality (notwithstanding the recent currency crisis) and is not threatened by any major powers or communist ideology. Except for Burma, all of the Southeast Asian nations have joined the international capitalist world.

Yet problems remain. The September 11, 2001 attack on the United States affected Southeast Asia in myriad ways. About 210 million Muslims live in Southeast Asia, mostly in Indonesia, and a large number of these Islamic adherents view the anti-terrorist policies of the United States as anti-Islamic. Never in modern history had the United States been held in such low repute among Southeast Asian Muslims as during America's 2003 war with Iraq.

The 2003 war came at a time when popular devotion to Islam was a rising force in Southeast Asia. Especially in Indonesia, there is an increased devoutness expressed in the more prevalent use of Islamic dress and in the rise of Islamic organizations. Local Muslims are increasingly connected to international currents through information from television, newspapers, and the internet. Known as "Islamization," the increased devoutness can be seen in greater concern with theology, more displays of piety, concern with dietary restrictions, support for Sharia law, and the increased use of head coverings by women. At the same time, many moderate Muslims have become concerned by the growing support of enforcing Islamic values on society. They also worry that militant Islam is breeding more societal violence, as in the horrific bombing in Bali, in October 2002, that killed more than two hundred persons, the great majority foreign. In recent years, some provinces in Indonesia had adopted Sharia, or strict interpretations of Islamic law, in ways that are thought to be counter to the interests of many Indonesians.

Recent years have also seen a rising political separatism in areas populated by Islamic ethnic groups, and many of these movements have become linked to radical Islam. It is not clear if this increased interest in Islamic separatism is a product of deteriorating economic and social conditions, the general spread of Islamic fundamentalism, a desire to emulate the Taliban, opposition to the American war in Iraq, or more specific local issues. Southeast Asia has long had separatist Islamic based movements, for example in southern Thailand, in Aceh province in Indonesia, and in the southern islands of the Philippines. But the movements have taken an increasingly radical turn as radical Islamic groups in the region have gained easier access to funding. In addition, Southeast Asian borders are easily penetrable and immigration controls relatively lax, thereby making the area a sanctuary for potential terrorists. It is not clear how much al-Qaeda, the terrorist organization led by Osama bin Laden, has penetrated Southeast Asia. However, al-Qaeda has been alleged to be active in the Philippines and Indonesia, with secondary activities in Singapore and Malaysia. In addition, Singapore's Internal Security Department arrested in January 2002 several alleged terrorists who were associated with the radical Islamic group Jemaah Islamiah (JI), which is based in Indonesia and believed to have been supported by al-Qaeda as the organizational center for the bombings in Bali.

The United States has assiduously worked to build an anti-terrorist response among the leaders of Southeast Asia's nations. The main arguments used by U.S. diplomats are that 1) Southeast Asia's vibrant tourist economy will be in jeopardy if the region is deemed unstable by prospective visitors; 2) Western investors will pull out their aid and investments if terrorism exists in Southeast Asia; and 3) Indonesia, the Philippines, and Malaysia, in particular, are in jeopardy of disintegrating at the hands of radical terrorists.

The majority of Southeast Asia's inhabitants appear to agree that terrorism jeopardizes the continued stability of their nations. On the other hand, many view the United States as heavy-handed in its anti-terrorist policies. In addition, America's strong support for Israel in the Middle East is viewed negatively by the bulk of Southeast Asia's Muslim inhabitants, who almost universally abhor Israel's role in the Middle East. Moreover, rapid economic development, especially in urban Southeast Asia, has led many to despise the new westernized secular morality of the cities, which is viewed as decadent and counter to the mores of Islam. This latter belief has fed into the hands of radical terrorists who claim to desire a traditional Islamic society rather than a secularized Western society.

In the months after September 11, 2001 American foreign policy throughout the world made counter-terrorism its number one priority. However, the policy varied from country to country. The United States has made counter-terrorism a primary issue in its dealings with some Southeast Asian countries while in its dealings with others terrorism has taken a backseat to other priorities. The next few paragraphs detail the range of issues currently highlighted in America's foreign policy relations with the various Southeast Asian countries, with special attention to the relationship of the terrorism issue.

Brunei Darussalam's population is overwhelmingly Muslim, and the country is ruled by a sultan who has absolute power and who is the head of Islam in the country. The government maintains extensive authority over the practicing Muslim community, and does not allow religious groups to form who are considered a threat to the ruler's position. Consequently, the United States has not been concerned about Islamic terrorist activity in this country.

Terrorist concerns have also not been significant in U.S. relations with Burma even though an estimated 4 percent of the population is Muslim and even though that minority has suffered discrimination from the present military rulers. In addition, Burma's border with Bangladesh is porous and there is much movement of Muslims between the two nations. Other issues have taken priority, particularly America's discomfort with Burma's continued poor record on democracy and human rights. In the years since September 2001, very little has changed in Burma that promises improved relations with the United States. The Burmese government has refused to begin a dialogue with the oppositionist National League for Democracy. Its leader, Aung San Suu Kyi, was rearrested, and returned to house arrest after some months of "freedom" during which she had undergone gynecological surgery. Meanwhile, one of the three ruling generals, Secretary One Khin Nyint, has been appointed Prime Minister, though it is not clear if his new position is a demotion or promotion. Human rights abuses have continued and there is virtually no meaningful freedom of speech, press, assembly, or travel.

In Cambodia as well as in Burma, counter-terrorism has been secondary to the goals of promoting a peaceful and non-corrupt democratic government. In the July 27, 2003 National Assembly elections, Hun Sen's party won a plurality, and he was slated to continue as Prime Minister, a position he has held since 1979. Cambodia was beset by violence in January 2003 but not as a result of terrorism. Anti-Thai riots broke out after a Thai movie star allegedly stated that the magnificent Angkor civilization belonged to Thailand, not Cambodia. In reaction, some Cambodians destroyed Thai businesses and even assaulted the Thai embassy in Phnom Penh. The Cambodian government, especially Hun Sen, was criticized internationally for its slow response to the riots and for using the violence as a pretext for suppressing the political opposition and the media. Some months later, Cambodian businessmen (primarily casino owners who realized their profits would be lost if the Thai-Cambodian border was closed) paid the Thais compensation for the destruction, and relations between the two nations returned to normal.

The United States has long supported an international tribunal to bring to justice senior members of the Khmer Rouge who were believed to be responsible for the genocide that occurred between 1975 and 1979. Though Cambodia has long resisted direct international involvement in this matter, by 2003, the Cambodian government had agreed that a tribunal could indeed have jurisdiction in accordance with international standards. However, little progress has been made in setting up the tribunal, while more and more former Khmer Rouge leaders die of natural causes. Hun Sen's own participation in the Khmer Rouge was suspected as a motive for the contrived delays in the establishment of a tribunal.

East Timor's post-September 2001 status as an independent nation has kept it from being viewed as an important part of the American foreign policy of counter-terrorism. Instead, the focus has been on Indonesia which is still in the process of moving from the authoritarianism of Sukarno and Suharto to a pluralist democracy led, at present, by President Megawati Sukarnoputri. The transition to democracy is normally a time of experimenting with the promotion of human rights and the rule of law, neither of which has played a major role in Indonesia's past. In Indonesia's case terrorism, separatism, and communal religious violence have undermined the democratic experiment at precisely the time stability is needed. Suharto's fall from power in 1998 opened the door to extremist political forces that had previously been controlled.

The challenge these groups pose is a difficult one for Indonesia's government. Megawati Sukarnoputri ascended to the presidency in July

2001 when her successor, Abdurrahman Wahid, was forced out of office. Whereas her predecessor was both a political and religious leader, President Sukarnoputri's secular leadership may have enabled Islamic forces to raise questions about her position as head of a predominantly Muslim nation. For her part, the president had to find a balance between satisfying the rising fundamentalism of her constituents and opposing the threat posed by radical groups such as Jemaah Islamiah and Laskar Jihad. The United States placed pressure on the president to crack down on such groups. The bombing in Bali in 2002 provided Megawati with the rationale she needed to make arrests of radical leaders. Widespread reports asserted that the horror in Bali came from orders by al-Qaeda forces but the blame remains questionable. Nevertheless, Indonesia became the center for the war on terrorism in Southeast Asia, a fact that exacerbated the already unstable political and economic situation there. Thus far, Indonesia's government has sided with America's anti-terrorism campaign and has conducted a thorough crackdown against terrorist groups. The bombing in Bali acted as an especially important event leading to stronger anti-terrorist policies in Indonesia.

The potential risks from Indonesia's failure to consolidate its democracy are frightening. The aforementioned radical group known as Jemaah Islamiah (JI), headquartered in Indonesia, aims to establish an autonomous Islamic state that includes present-day Indonesia, the southern Philippines, Malaysia, and Brunei. JI lost much of its leadership when some 30 persons were arrested following the Bali bombing. In addition, in 2003 an alleged leader of JI, Riduan Isamuddin, also known as Hambali, was arrested by Thai and U.S. authorities in Ayuthaya, Thailand. Howeiver, JI is not the only active terrorist group. A second terrorist organization in Indonesia, known as Laskar Jihad (LJ), was established in 2000 to fight against Christian inhabitants of the Malukus Islands in Indonesia. LJ was believed to receive aid from Indonesian military officers, but as with so many terrorist groups, detailed information is impossible to know. LJ's goals are similar to those of al-Qaeda though no direct connection between the organizations has been established

America's stance toward Indonesia's counter-terrorism policies has been ambiguous because of continuing concerns about the political role of the country's military. The military had long governed Indonesia in virtually all major respects, and it is feared by the many Indonesians who suffered under its leadership. The American congress has banned direct support to the Indonesian military, due to its continued poor human rights record. However, the Indonesian military has recently been stepping back from politics. Not only did the Indonesian military not intervene in the 1999 elections but in 2001 it also stayed out of events that led to President Wahid's impeachment and his eventual succession by President Megawati Sukarnoputri. In addition, the military has accepted a major reduction in appointed parliamentary seats, which will result in it having no parliamentary representation after 2004. Nevertheless, the United States remains concerned about the military's record and is trying to balance its desire to promote continued improvement in Indonesian human rights with its struggle against terrorism.

American policy in Laos has continued to emphasize American soldiers Missing-in-Action despite the fact that the war in Vietnam and Laos ended some 30 years ago. In addition, American foreign policy has focused on the slow move toward democratic government and the somewhat faster transition to an open market economy. In the human rights arena, the U.S. has alleged that the Lao government has used violent methods to "stabilize" its ethnic minorities. Terrorism has not been a primary focus of U.S. policy in Laos. Thus far, counter-terrorism cooperation has focused on keeping Laos from becoming a target or base for terrorist activities.

In Malaysia the terrorist attack on the United States did not appreciably change relations between the two countries. Since September 11, 2001 Malaysia has arrested large numbers of suspected terrorists and Mahathir has approved joint Malaysian-American anti-terrorist programs. Nevertheless, Mahathir's decision to retire on October 31, 2003 (he is the longest-serving democratically elected prime minister in the world) was greeted with sighs of relief by many American officials, who viewed Mahathir as an articulate spokesperson for anti-Americanism. In early 2003 he had criticized America's war in Iraq, and in a speech to Muslim world leaders in 2003, Mahathir made anti-Semitic remarks that concerned many of his critics. The policies of his successor, Abdullah Ahmad Badawi, are difficult to predict. However, it is thought that his qualifications as a Muslim scholar may help him as he takes charge of this predominantly Muslim country.

The Philippines is viewed as a "frontline" state in the struggle against international terrorism. The most famous group in the Philippines believed to be connected with al-Qaeda is known as Abu Sayyaf (Father of the Sword), which apparently began during the war between Russia and Afghanistan in the 1980s. Since 2000, the Abu Sayyaf has committed numerous terrorist acts in the Philippines including kidnappings, bombings, and the production of general mayhem, for the purpose of establishing an Islamic state separate from the Philippines. Meanwhile, the Philippines has continued to confront major insurgency and terrorism carried out by the New People's Army, the military wing of the Communist People's Party. The Moro Islamic Liberation Front (MILF) also has attacked infrastructure and civilians in the southern islands. Philippine president Gloria Arroyo has vowed to end Abu Sayyaf's role and to work with the United States to counter terrorism by this and other groups.

Singapore's government has strongly supported the American war in Iraq and has publicly stated its disdain for Saddam Hussein, despite having a sizable Muslim minority of about 15 percent. Singapore has arrested numerous terrorist suspects, including members of the Jemaah Islamiyah network headquartered in Indonesia. Singapore has also allowed American ships access to its military facilities, and the two nations regularly participate in combined military exercises.

Similarly, U.S. relations with Thailand are strong despite differences of opinion about some issues. Thailand has supported the United States in its wars in Korea, Vietnam, Afghanistan, and Iraq. Two-way trade between the two nations comes to about $20 billion each year, and the U.S. is the second largest foreign investor in Thailand (behind Japan). Joint efforts to fight drugs have gone on for many years. At the same time, the U.S. has voiced concern about Thai Prime Minister Thaksin's 2003 war on drugs which produced an estimated 1,500 extra-judicial deaths. In addition, the Thaksin government has periodically spoken about Thailand's need for more autonomy from the major powers, and the two nations have disagreed openly about the best way to deal with the oppressive military regime in Burma. Thailand has favored a policy of "constructive engagement" with Burma, while the U.S. has favored harsh sanctions designed to hurt the country's economy and bring down the military regime.

In recent years Thailand has faced terrorist attacks on military bases in its four southern provinces, which have a Muslim majority. Prime Minister Thaksin has decided to be part of the broad counter-terrorism coalition and has received praise from U.S. President Bush for Thailand's counterterrorism role in international affairs. The Thai government has arrested Thai Muslims suspected of planning terrorist attacks on embassies in Bangkok, and in 2003 arrested Jemaah Islamiah leader Hambali in the up-country city of Ayuthaya. There is some evidence, but not definitive, that al-Qaeda members have helped train Thai terrorists. However, grievances of Thailand's Muslims are long-standing, and include economic neglect, suppression of Muslim culture, and disdain by corrupt Thai officials.

In contrast to its foreign policy in much of Southeast Asia, where terrorism has been the major focus, America's relations with Vietnam have not specifically emphasized counter-terrorism since September 11, 2001. However, diplomatic relations have been troubled. On the one hand, bilateral economic relations have never been more dynamic, with particular emphasis on trade and economic development. The Bilateral Trade Agreement (BTA) has become the centerpiece of the two nations' relations. Nevertheless, the United States continues to be concerned about Vietnam's human rights record owing to periodic reports of discrimination against Buddhist leaders, political oppositionists, and ethnic minorities. Moreover, American corporations have found it difficult to invest in Vietnam because of its oppressive bureaucracy. Vietnam resists American complaints about these issues, because its leaders still view the United States as a colonialist power intent on making Vietnam a bourgeois-capitalist replica of itself.

Southeast Asia cannot seem to move smoothly toward democratic rule. The region's tendency to authoritarianism has roots both in local traditions and in the colonial experience. The influence of Hindu-derived traditions in Burma, Thailand, Cambodia, and Laos; of Confucianism in Vietnam and Singapore; and of absolute monarchy in most of the pre-colonial states all helped lay the foundation for centralized, hierarchical rule. Later, colonial rule strengthened the elite groups who had the most to gain by collaborating with the European colonialists. Neither in the colonial nor in the contemporary period have the bureaucrats or the general masses possessed the shared cultural values, attitudes, and beliefs that are most conducive to flourishing democratic rule, values that include trust, faith in the views of the masses, belief in civil liberties, and individualism. The dominant values tend instead to emphasize dependence, nonparticipation, deference to authority, and preference for dictatorship in times of crisis. Democracy is still considered a luxury, even in nations that enjoy strong free-enterprise economies, successful family planning, internal stability, freedom from outside intervention, and highly educated leaders.

The region also continues to be home to simmering conflicts. In Indonesia tensions have appeared among ethnic groups and between the Muslim and Christian communities. In the Philippines the desire for land reform has yet to be addressed. In the South China Sea, tension simmers over the Spratly Islands, which are claimed by as many as five different countries. Yet overall the level of tension is much lower than in the 1960s and 70s, when war raged in Vietnam, strong insurgencies threatened in Burma and the Philippines, and ethnic violence rocked Malaysia and Indonesia.

Spratly Islands

Situated in the South China Sea, the Spratly Islands are claimed by five different nations. Although almost no one lives on the islands—they are uninhabitable—there is some evidence that oil reserves exist among the atolls. That possibility has raised tensions among the claimants: the People's Republic of China, Taiwan, Vietnam, the Philippines, and Malaysia. Periodic skirmishes have taken place and there has been no progress toward a solution to the competing claims.

The region's relations with the major world powers have also changed. At one time Southeast Asia's politics and economics were inextricably tied to the policies of the great powers; Japan, the United States, China, and the former Soviet Union were particularly influential. Today, the Southeast Asian nations are far more self-reliant and self-determining. Each individual country's prospects rests more and more on that nation's internal capacity to meet the needs of its people by fostering a higher standard of living. At the same time, the countries are increasingly cooperating through such organizations as the Association of Southeast Asian Nations (ASEAN).

One of the great ironies of America's relations with Southeast Asia is the aftermath of the Vietnam War. Some American leaders had argued that the unification of Vietnam under a communist regime would mean the loss of the entire region to communism. That has not happened. On the contrary, the present era in Southeast Asia gives the impression that the Americans' aims during the war in Vietnam have been achieved, as several of the nations have become more democratic, and as almost all of the nations—including Vietnam—have joined international economic networks and are promoting capitalist-style economic development.

ASEAN

The Association of Southeast Asian Nations (ASEAN) was established in 1967 by the foreign ministers of the five leading anti-communist nations of Southeast Asia: Thailand, Malaysia, Indonesia, Singapore, and the Philippines. ASEAN expanded in 1984 when Brunei joined. By 1999, every nation of Southeast Asia had joined, including the communist nations of Vietnam and Laos and the authoritarian regimes of Burma and Cambodia.

ASEAN's original purpose was to deter Vietnam and China from making advances against the non-communist countries and to devise a policy of free trade among the member states. Today the organization continues working to lower trade and travel barriers among the member nations. ASEAN's members have never attempted to establish a political union with common governmental policies.

Southeast Asians in America

Over three million people from Southeast Asia have made their home in the United States. The nation responsible for the largest number of immigrants is the Philippines, which has contributed almost two-thirds of the total. This disproportionate flow of immigrants no doubt stems from the Philippines' historical connections with the United States. Filipino immigrants had a relatively privileged status in the United

States because of the colonial relationship and because of the close cooperation between the two nations in World War II. In addition, it has been relatively easy for Filipino-Americans to be accepted in American society. They were generally able to speak English due to the widespread use of English in Philippine schools, and their Catholic-Christian religion fit with the dominant American religions. Filipinos made their new home primarily in Hawai'i and California, perhaps because of favorable weather conditions, although Filipino immigrants are found today in every part of the United States. Los Angeles is sometimes referred to as the "second largest Filipino city in the world, after Manila."

Southeast Asian immigrants came to the United States for a variety of reasons. The usual motivation was economic: The immigrants sought opportunities to practice their professions and to receive a decent wage. For example, thousands of dentists, nurses, and doctors have arrived in the past thirty years. In the 1960s, the average salary of a medical doctor in Manila was about $1,000 per year, whereas the same doctor could receive fifty times that amount in the United States. Similar salary gaps existed in virtually every profession. The large number of immigrant professionals constitutes a "brain drain" from Southeast Asia, as many of the most educated citizens have left their home countries for the better opportunities available in the United States. Many of the immigrants sent money home to help their families. For example, Filipino-Americans sent huge remittances to their relatives back in the Philippines.

Since the end of the Vietnam War in 1975, over one million Southeast Asian refugees have come to the United States from Vietnam, Cambodia, and Laos. Between 1975 and 1985 more than 700,000 Southeast Asians were admitted to the United States, most of them from these war-torn countries. Rarely a week goes by without news reports about this highly diverse new immigrant population. Some of the new immigrants are high achievers: Newspapers regularly herald news of class valedictorians, disproportionately Vietnamese-Americans who come from a culture that traditionally values education. Such articles are countered by news of the high incidence of welfare among the Hmong people from Laos, and of child brides among the same group. (Hmong men have taken brides as young as 12 years old, a practice presenting a classic confrontation between Hmong culture and American law.)

Immigrants from Vietnam, Laos, and Cambodia have been viewed as "refugees," a somewhat vague term referring to people forced to leave their native country out of fear of persecution or because of economic need. The political refugees who claim fear of persecution have a more privileged status than the economic refugees who claim financial distress. But in many cases it is impossible to distinguish between the two because both motives may be cited by the same people. For example, many of the Vietnamese who arrived in the United States after 1975 cited terrible economic conditions and fear of being sent to "reeducation" centers. Many of these refugees, known as boat people, had risked their lives on flimsy water craft as they desperately attempted to escape their homeland's oppression and to provide their children with a chance of a decent life. Tens of thousands of boat people drowned or were robbed and raped by pirates in the seas around Vietnam.

Once they had arrived in the United States, the refugees had to decide if their goal was acculturation, integration, assimilation, or separatism (retaining their cultural and linguistic identity). There has been no clear pattern, because the new immigrants reflected a great diversity of occupations, social classes, degrees of social cohesion, and levels of education. The American government's initial policy was to scatter the refugees throughout the country so they would be forced to assimilate. The dispersion did not work, and eventually many relocated to centers that had large refugee populations. The most famous of these centers is in Westminster, California, which is known as Little Saigon because of its majority Vietnamese population.

Boat People

One of the great tragedies of the Vietnam War and the communist victory was the decision by one and a half million Vietnamese to leave the country under the most desperate of situations. Sailing on rickety boats through the South China Sea, these refugees faced pirates, high seas, starvation, and a harsh welcome from countries that did not want them. A large majority of the boat people were Chinese Vietnamese, an entrepreneurial group that had much to lose under a communist government. All told, about one million Vietnamese refugees settled in the United States. By 1994, Vietnam had liberalized its economic policies, and there were no new boat people. Many of the people still in camps were sent back to Vietnam at this time.

The diverse communities of Southeast Asian immigrants have greatly strengthened American society with their new ideas, entrepreneurial pursuits, and productivity. At the same time, most Southeast Asians have yet to catch up economically with the majority white American population. There also remain serious and sensitive differences in cultural experiences. One purpose of this text has been to break down some of those cultural barriers by providing students with knowledge about the new American citizens and their original societies.

Toward the Future

Southeast Asia still has many problems. The most salient are the widening gap between the rich and the poor, the incursion of modernization, the growing AIDS crisis, terrorism, the deterioration of the environment, and corruption. But the traditional capacity of the Southeast Asian nations to cope with change suggests optimism. . . . Southeast Asia is at the crossroads.

DISCUSSION QUESTIONS

1. Why has democracy had difficulty flourishing in Southeast Asia?

2. What political-economic role should the United States play in Southeast Asia?

3. How has the United States been affected by the arrival of Southeast Asian refugees who have become American citizens?

4. Are you optimistic or pessimistic about Southeast Asia's future? Why?

SUGGESTED READINGS

There are many excellent books offering a better understanding of Southeast Asian Americans. Some of them are focused on specific national groups. To learn more about Filipino-Americans, see Barbara M. Posadas, *The Filipino Americans* (Greenwood Publishing Group, Westport, 1999) and Yen Le Espiritu, *Filipino American Lives* (Temple University Press, Philadelphia, 1995). For more on Cambodian-Americans, see Nancy Smith-Hefner, *Khmer American* (University of California Press, Berkeley, 1999); May Ebihara, Carol Mortland, and Judy Ledgerwood, *Cambodian Culture Since 1975* (Cornell University Press, Ithaca, 1994); and Joan Criddle, *Bamboo and Butterflies: From Refugee to Citizen* (East-West Publishing, Dixon, California, 1992). For more on Vietnamese-Americans, see Paul Rutledge, *The Vietnamese Experience in America* (Indiana University Press, Bloomington, 1992); James Freeman, *Hearts of Sorrow: Vietnamese-American Lives* (Stanford University Press, Stanford, 1989); and Nazli Kibria, *Family Tightrope: The Changing Lives of Vietnamese Americans* (Princeton University Press, Princeton, 1993). Also important are Sucheng Chan, ed., *Hmong Means Free: Life in Laos and America* (Temple University Press, Philadelphia, 1994); John Tenhula, *Voices from Southeast Asia* (Holmes and Meier, New York, 1991); and Jeremy Hein, *From Vietnam, Laos, and Cambodia: A Refugee Experience in the United States* (Twayne, Boston, 1995). For an understanding of gender roles in this immigrant population, see Penny Van Esterik, ed., *Women of Southeast Asia* (Center for Southeast Asian Studies, Northern Illinois University, 1996).

Index